German Socialist
Philosophy

The German Library: Volume 40
Volkmar Sander, General Editor

GERMAN SOCIALIST PHILOSOPHY

Ludwig Feuerbach
Karl Marx
Friedrich Engels

Edited by Wolfgang Schirmacher

CONTINUUM · NEW YORK

1997
The Continuum Publishing Company
370 Lexington Avenue
New York, NY 10017

The German Library
is published in cooperation with Deutsches Haus,
New York University.
This volume has been supported by Inter Nationes,
and by a grant from Daimler-Benz-Fonds.

Printed in the United States of America

Library of Congress Cataloging-in-Publication Data

Feuerbach, Ludwig, 1804–1872.
  German socialist philosophy / Ludwig Feuerbach, Karl Marx,
Friedrich Engels ; edited by Wolfgang Schirmacher.
      p.   cm. — (The German Library ; 40)
  Includes bibliographical references.
  ISBN 0-8264-0748-X (hardcover : alk. paper). — ISBN 0-8264-0749-8
(pbk. : alk. paper)
  1. Socialism—Germany—History—19th century—Sources.
2. Philosophy, German—19th century—Sources. I. Marx, Karl,
1818–1883. II. Engels, Friedrich, 1820–1895. III. Schirmacher,
Wolfgang. IV. Title. V. Series.
HX273.F48   1997
335′.00943—dc20   96-26124
                                                              CIP

Acknowledgments will be found on page 287,
which constitutes an extension of the copyright page.

Contents

vi · *Contents*

Contents · vii

Introduction

Feuerbach, Marx, and Engels: The Realization of Philosophy

Ludwig Feuerbach has stood in the shadow of Karl Marx and Friedrich Engels for the past one hundred fifty years. In the communist part of the world, Marx and Engels were firmly instated as the greatest theorists of mankind whose sacred teachings were beyond criticism, whereas Feuerbach appeared merely as a footnote acknowledging his influence on the early intellectual biographies of these two giants. Non–Marxist philosophers considered Feuerbach a renegade Hegelian notable for his fierce attack on Christianity, a respected critic in company with David-Friedrich Strauß and Sören Kierkegaard. But this long-accepted view changed profoundly with the sudden bankruptcy of the socialist states at the end of the 1980s, when Marx and Engels lost their status as founding fathers of a new political religion and were brought back down to earth, as German socialist philosophers. As Left Hegelians who turned from idealism to materialism and shared the goal of the realization of philosophy, Feuerbach, Marx, and Engels can be seen as belonging to the same philosophical movement. All pursued their education within the intellectual climate of Hegel's idealistic attempt to redeem metaphysics and its unifying spiritual world view; however, their materialistic turn to a more realistic understanding of humanity and the functioning of society was a response to an altered individual as well as social consciousness of a new generation. The anthropological turning in philosophy originated with Feuerbach, the shift which, as Engels reports in *Feuerbach and the End of Classical German Philosophy* (1888), liberated Marx and himself from Hegelian Idealism. In 1844, Marx described his philosophical hero as "the only one with a seriously critical relationship" to Hegel's philosophy. Feuerbach's major work *The Essence of Christianity* (1841) placed materialism first and confirmed nature as being the foundation of all science. Notoriously underestimated, Feuerbach's impact on modern thought nearly rivals that of Marx and Engels if one disregards their political exploitation. Together with Arthur Schopenhauer, who disliked his "brutal" affirmation of the world, Feuerbach has influenced Kierkegaard, Friedrich Nietzsche, Sigmund Freud, and Max Scheler as well as Nikolai Berdjajew, Martin Buber, and Erich Fromm. Blending Feuerbach with Schopenhauer, Richard Wagner praised Feuerbach's anthropological materialism as a fruitful effort "to dissolve philosophy into humanity." According to Feuerbach, it is the duty of philosophy "to utter honestly what humankind has in mind at a certain period."

Two texts in particular, *The Holy Family* and *The German Ideology* (both 1845), reveal the common ground Marx and Engels shared with Feuerbach; but theirs was an aspiration toward scientific, not utopian socialism, and they criticized Feuerbach's "universal orgy of reconciliation." His all-too-abstract morality is "designed to suit all times, all people, all conditions," whereas Marx and Engels attempt to determine precisely the historical conditions of an application of philosophy. The Revolution of 1848 appeared to sweep Feuerbach aside; he had not "grasped the significance of revolutionary, of practical–critical activity," an anticipatory analysis made by Marx in his *Theses on Feuerbach* in 1845. The eleventh thesis later became famous: "Philosophers have merely interpreted the world in various ways; the point is to change it." But Marx and Engels had reasons more political than philosophical for distancing themselves from Feuerbach, the academic outsider and loner treated unfairly by those theorists—such as Marx—who label his fearless criticism a "sensuous contemplation" as opposed to "practical, human–sensuous activity." Feuerbach's basic intention is less economical than ethical, and he is unerringly committed to his single most important insight: "The secret of theology is anthropology." He does not perceive human beings as solipsistic individuals, as Max Stirner asserts in *The Ego and His Own* (1845), but rather as conscious members of our species who understand themselves as finite beings and bound to the social sphere. Only as a species are we humans infinite beings. In light of this, Feuerbach may well provide the missing dimension of anthropology to Marxism, an omission Jean-Paul Sartre deplored in his *Critique of Dialectical Reason* (1960). Feuerbach's humanism is firmly rooted in our senses without being reduced to naturalism, and his philosophy of the future is grounded in an acceptance of the other, be it a "thou" (Martin Buber) or a social "me" (George Herbert Mead).

Feuerbach's Sensual Anthropology and the Essence of Religion

"You are what you eat" is a well-known, provocative statement of Feuerbach's that mocks the idealistic notion of man as Homo sapiens and points to the naturalistic foundation of our existence. "The deepest secrets of nature can be found in the simplest natural things," the philosopher maintains. Feuerbach proves to be a true student of Hegel's dialectics when he emphasizes the mutual dependency of man and nature, and claims nature has attained its goal in the human species. Far from being irrational, Feuerbach's struggle is a striving for an authentic understanding of the human condition with its interaction between self and species. Immanuel Kant had dared us to think for ourselves: *sape audere;* but Feuerbach dares us to be ourselves and reclaim the essence of humanity alienated by religion. Feuerbach exposed the essence of humankind—"emancipatory sensuality" (Alfred Schmidt) painted over by religion with the face of God inserted in place of humankind's. Thus, in Feuerbach's view, the perception of authentic humanity beyond religious ideology reveals a perfect being with the power of reason, a prevailing will, and a brave heart unshakable in its affirmation of life.

Ludwig Feuerbach was born in 1804 in Landshut, Bavaria, and his father, Paul Johann Anselm Feuerbach, was a respected law professor of wide repute. In accordance with his parents' wishes, Feuerbach began studies in theology at the University of Heidelberg in 1823, but then the theologian Carl Daub, a follower of Hegel, introduced him to German Idealism. Feuerbach transferred to the University of Berlin in 1824 and attended all of Hegel's lectures, with the exception of Aesthetics, and even heard him read on Logic twice. His first doubts concerned the transition from Logic to Nature: How does the Hegelian Spirit manifest itself in a systematic way in the alien sphere of nature, without being decisionistic? The student Feuerbach was not at all persuaded that Hegel's absolute Idea could descend from theological heaven. In his *Preliminary Theses on the Reform of Philosophy* (1842) Feuerbach called it "a nebulous decision" that something as absolute as Hegel's Idea should even bother with nature or history. By praising Hegel as "the most accomplished philosophical artist," Feuerbach rejected Hegel's absolute philosophy in favor of empirical and concrete perception. He was especially opposed to the hierarchy of manifestations of the Absolute, and instead endorsed a coexistence of all beings modeled after the "tolerance of space." Philosophy must begin not with itself but with reality; this was Feuerbach's guiding precept, and he stressed, in opposition to Hegel, that fundamental principles could be found only in the "natural grounds and causes of things."

Feuerbach received his Ph.D. in 1828 at the University of Erlangen, where he became a lecturer in philosophy, remaining until 1832. In *Thoughts on Death and Immortality,* published anonymously in 1830, he criticized the Christian denial of death as is evident in the doctrine of a personal immortality. "You are able to die because you are a free, thinking, conscious being," wrote Feuerbach and reaffirmed—as did Existentialism one hundred years later—the importance of mortality for our understanding of humanity. Feuerbach turned to history in search of forerunners who shared his conviction that "philosophy is the science of reality in its truth and totality," and in 1833 he published *A History of Modern Philosophy from Bacon to Spinoza.* With great self-confidence, Feuerbach challenged his former idol in a widely read article "Toward a Critique of Hegel's Philosophy" (1839), which so impressed "avant-garde Feuerbachians" (Louis Althusser) such as Marx and Engels that in the aftermath of Feuerbach's attack they considered "Hegel's system exploded." Feuerbach's anthropology, incorporating nature in physiological terms, shows us who we really are: perceives human beings a natural beings, in all situations, and especially in such existential, trying situations as death and sexuality. For the first time, a teaching on the human condition holds the unabashed promise of the *Principles of the Philosophy of the Future* (1843): we exist "in order to think, love, and will."

"Illusion only is sacred, truth profane." All of Feuerbach's writings deal in some way with religion and theology, but his stance is one of an antitheologian and atheist who reveals the face of humans in the teachings about God. According to Feuerbach, religion is not an absurdity, nor pure illusion, as our conception of God reflects the being of man. "God is man's self-awareness"; this is Feuerbach's central thesis and he strives to change "the friends of God into friends of man," the love of God into the love of our fellow man. The philosopher of religion within German socialist philosophy, as Engels phased it, revived the tradition of the German mystics Angelus Silesius, Meister Eckhart, and Sebastian Franck among others, who contended that God cannot exist without us and is "the essence of human feeling" (Franck). "The task of the modern era was the realization and humanization of God—the transformation and dissolution of theology into anthropology." This challenge to traditional religion was offered in Feuerbach's epoch-making book *The Essence of Christianity*. At the time, only a scholar without affiliation to a university would dare transform man into God; Feuerbach had resigned his professorship in 1838 and lived as a financially independent philosophical writer in Bruckberg near Ansbach.

"Truth, reality, and sensuousness are one and the same thing," declared Feuerbach, and theologians of every confession detested the philosopher who made man the measure of God: *Homo homini Deus est*. Even liberal theologians such as Karl Barth, who agreed with Feuerbach's analysis of anthropomorphism in religion, called his theory "a platitude," and Arthur Schopenhauer, who accused Feuerbach of overlooking the ascetic core of Christianity, noted sarcastically in his personal copy of *The Essence of Christianity*: "Here he was drunk." But Feuerbach unapologetically denied the "fantastic projection" of theology in order to reaffirm the real human essence, "a free and self-reliant citizen of the earth." In 1848 and early 1849, the philosopher everyone loved to hate held a series of well-attended public lectures in Heidelberg's Town Hall on "The Essence of Religion," this notoriety coming at a time when Feuerbach began making plans to emigrate to the United States. But they never materialized and Feuerbach remained in Germany. After 1848, his influence diminished rapidly and he was nearly forgotten when the socialist workers' movement chose Marx and Engels, and their "scientific socialism," over Feuerbach's passionate humanism. Barth may ultimately have a point when he suggests that Feuerbach had underestimated death and evil in his attempt to glorify the human species. The philosopher of a better future for humanity failed in his own pursuit of happiness and in 1877 he died in poverty at the age of sixty-eight.

Marx: From Human Praxis to a Just Society

Karl Marx is arguably the most influential of the socialist philosophers, but the end of communism as a state ideology has made his future stature uncertain. Althusser's appeal "to read Marx" was good advice in the 1970s and helped lead to the rediscovery of Marx as a powerful and original thinker of modern alienation, and the dynamics of social life. There is still no better advice today. A fearless and polemic theorist, Marx established the connection between the analysis of society in economic terms and political morality, and addressed the actual driving forces of history. He unblinkingly faced the not-so-pleasant material character of volatile human nature and explored the economic conditions in a strictly scientific spirit. He discussed the activities of individuals organized into a society—which the ancient Greeks called *praxis*—in terms of labor within the context of industrial production and dared to make for these conditions authentic praxis the touchstone of philosophical truth.

Marx's political thought followed a high-spirited path chosen early in life, as his *Reflections of a Young Man on the Choice of a Profession* reveal: "The chief guide which must direct us in the choice of a profession is the welfare of mankind and our own perfection." In his youth, the philosopher longed to join the fabled German "idealists who have the audacity to want to turn men into human beings." His humanism was formed by the Enlightenment and the French Revolution alike, and endorsed a realistic view of mankind. His acclaimed *Economic and Philosophical Manuscripts,* written in 1844 but not discovered until 1932, shows Marx under the influence of the Young Hegelians; besides Feuerbach, his heroes were Moses Heβ, Arnold Ruge, and Bruno Bauer, former Hegel students turned his critics. In his formative years, Marx had been an advocate of a mundane humanism, but even then his critical theory showed all signs of becoming "a material force as soon as it has gripped the masses." Modern estrangement from our true essence is the main issue of this humanism which owes a great deal to Feuerbach, but Marx is not satisfied with "self-clarification" or with abolition of Christianity. He pushes for a political revolution anticipated by German radical theory: "Can Germany attain a revolution which will raise it not only to the official level of the modern nations but to the height of humanity which will be the near future of these nations?"

Karl Marx was born in Trier in 1818. Both parents descended from a long line of rabbis. His father was an esteemed attorney who, together with his family, was baptized in the Protestant faith in 1824. Marx studied national economy, philosophy, and history in Bonn and Berlin, and was introduced to German Idealism by Hegel's heirs who were divided into a leftist and a conservative faction after their mentor died of cholera in 1831. Marx became a political journalist, and at the age of twenty-four was editor of the *Rheinische Zeitung,* a liberal weekly that was suppressed in 1843, leading to his first, temporary, exile from Germany. Brief sojourns followed in Paris and Brussels where he worked for the Communist League, and in collaboration with Friedrich Engels wrote the infamous *Communist Manifesto* (1848). Taking advantage of the revolutionary spirit then prevailing in Germany, Marx revived his newspaper in Cologne. But it was a short-lived euphoria, and Marx was permanently expelled from the country in 1849; he settled in London until his death in 1883. He spent his days studying in the library of the British Museum, always hard pressed for money, and he also free-lanced as correspondent for the *New York Tribune.* In 1864, he helped found the *First International,* an initial attempt to bring about international solidarity among the workers, and in 1867 the first volume of *Capital* appeared; the following two volumes were edited and published posthumously by Engels. It was a life spent mostly in exile, under difficult circumstances, devoted to establishing "scientific socialism" that clearly distinguished itself from the utopian socialism of the past. In the age of science, Marx claimed to have discovered the crucial laws of historic–economic development, analogous to the discovery of natural laws, enabling humankind to take advantage of inevitable changes in course, such as the turn from capitalism to communism. The scientific knowledge of the dialectics of history made transparent the economic foundations of society, and Marx's intention was to provide the scientific tools for a successful socialist revolution that would finally put an end to the inhumane "exploitation of man by man."

During his lifetime, Marx was seldom really studied by the European labor leaders who quoted him; they more often simply borrowed his thoughts to further their own agendas, and the philosopher's political influence in the socialist movement was, in fact, marginal. Just the opposite effect, however, could be observed among intellectuals and scholars who were excited by Marx's materialistic reading of Hegel and intrigued by a dialectical methodology, developed through analysis of alienation as well as of surplus value, which allowed for antagonistic complexity in society. Marx's famous claim to have found Hegel upside down to turn him rightside up is an implicit acknowledgment of the great part Hegel's conception of history, with its fruitful conflicts of interests, plays in Marxism. Dialectics in both the Hegelian and Marxian systems admits of oppositions as the driving forces of human life and regards labor as a liberating activity, a means of overcoming the given conditions of nature. Unlike Hegel, Marx introduced a humanistic fervor into the study of history by judging harshly, and not without partiality, in asking who is ethically right or wrong within a certain epoch. The conditions of the working class in the industrial society, especially, led Marx to his indictment of a basic injustice: "that the profit, the comfort, the luxury of one man is paid for by the loss, the misery, the denial of another." But Marx's ethical socialism was different from other social critiques of his time in its understanding of the human condition not in general terms but rather in specific reference to a defined type of society, a particular historical epoch, and status of the productive forces. Religion and morality should not be viewed independently from our real existence or the historical context, maintained Marx and Engels in their *German Ideology,* and their most trenchant criticism of alienation was directed toward the deplorable condition that "man's own deed becomes an alien power opposed to him, which enslaves him instead of being controlled by him."

Though Marx's theory failed to live up to its promise that a scientific analysis of the social structure and economic foundation would allow for dependable prognoses of future trends, this in no way diminishes the validity of his pinpointing and interpreting major forces the importance of which for society was formerly underestimated. Productive forces such as technology, climate, geography, and skills determine, in Marx's view, the specific mode of production that in turn necessarily shapes the development of a society; and it was his conviction that the capitalistic society with its emphasis on private property would lead to a class struggle climaxing in a proletarian revolution. The revolution of 1848, though swiftly crushed and silenced, appeared to confirm Marx's educated guess in the *Communist Manifesto* that "in place of the old bourgeois society, with its classes and class antagonisms, we shall have an association, in which the free development of each is the condition for the free development of all." Misguided by the belief in rapid and inevitable progress—shared by most people of his century—Marx did not appreciate the slower pace of reform. This impatient prophet of a better tomorrow did not foresee to what extent capitalism could be reformed by laws protecting the poor and powerless, nor that the middle class between capitalists and proletarians, thought to be soon eliminated, would display such surprising staying power. But Marx's emancipatory philosophy, which defined and analyzed the political economy of capitalism and fostered hope in the proletariat class the world over, will be remembered not for its unrealized predictions, but rather for its eminent effort to change our understanding of how theory and practice are interdependent. After Marx, theorists can never again so blatantly dare to disregard the economic and political facets of humanity, and are bound to view injustice as a question of material circumstances as well. Marx urges us never to forget that "in the social production which men carry on they enter into definite relations which are indispensible and independent of their will." In the face of indignant opposition from theologians, moralists, and idealistic social reformers, Marx remained steadfast: there will never be love, peace, and freedom in the world as long as these have no equivalents in the sphere of production. *Metanoia,* the personal call for fundamental change, remains futile in a society blighted by inequality and there can be no possibility for a good life before the realization of philosophy has been attained: and this means only when humanistic goals have become everyday practice.

Engels's Down-to-Earth Philosophy

We think that we make our history ourselves but to a great extent we are ignorant of the determining conditions and forces at sway, economics decisive among them. Without his friend and closest collaborator Friedrich Engels, Marx could not have survived financially, and his theory would lack its famous knack for bringing economy to life through illustrative details of its everyday operations. Ironically, Engels was a capitalist as well as a leader of the international workers' movement, and his down-to-earth approach provided the "meat" to the theoretical "bones" of Marxism. Without a formal education, Engels nevertheless proved a brilliant student of history, combining it with political economy. The ugly face of early capitalism was revealed in Engels's *Conditions of the Working Class in England* (1845), a classic on the fate of the workers in an industrial society. England was the first country to experience an industrial revolution, and Engels noted the political apathy of the industrial workers with disappointment. For this eminent practical genius, German socialist philosophy was certainly inspired by Hegel's system as well as Feuerbach's anthropology but, more importantly, was produced by the class antagonism existing in modern society between wage workers and capitalists, the possessors and the nonpossessors. Engels's Historical Materialism described the laws of societal action and defined science and technology as vehicles of progress. The goal of this practical philosopher was "a leap of mankind from the realm of necessity to the realm of freedom," which for Engels was not a utopian dream but a promise of scientific socialism.

Friedrich Engels was born in Barmen in 1820. His father was a wealthy cotton manufacturer. In 1837, Engels was compelled to leave grammar school and work in his father's office. A year's service in the Guards Artillery of the Prussian Army (1841–42) led to a lifelong interest in military affairs and strategic theory. In Berlin, Engels became associated with the Young Hegelians, a circle of defenders of the heritage of Hegelian Idealism, and contributed to the *Rheinische Zeitung* in Cologne, when Marx was its editor. A first meeting with Marx in 1842 proved fateful for both. Engels moved to Manchester to work as a clerk for Ermen and Engels, but occasionally joined Marx in Paris and Brussels. In 1845, he and Marx wrote *The Holy Family* and *The German Ideology*, outlining the concept of a materialism breaking with his Hegelian past: "Nature exists independent from all philosophy, and nothing exists except nature and human beings." Engels's handwriting is obvious in the *Communist Manifesto*, excerpted only briefly in this volume. (A portion of the text is included in volume 41 of The German Library.) The *Manifesto* was intended to bolster the Communist League that Engels had helped to establish in 1847, but remained virtually unknown for some time until it was perceived worldwide as the ultimate declaration of communism.

In 1850, Engels settled in England permanently and, having become a partner in 1846, stayed with his firm in Manchester for twenty years in order to be able to support his friend financially. At Marx's request, Engels wrote *Anti–Dühring* (1878), a first comprehensive account of Marxism that clarifies the difference between Eugen Dühring's "bumptious pseudoscience," quite influential in the socialist movement at the time, and Marx's economic philosophy. Engels's help in researching *Capital* was invaluable to Marx; and to counter socialist phraseology, which was rarely based on solid knowledge, Engels reviewed the rich material of human history for *The Origin of the Family, Private Property, and State* (1884), a principal work of Historical Materialism. After Marx's death in 1883, Engels became his prophet to an even greater extent, editing the second volume of *Capital* in 1885 and the third volume in 1894. Highly regarded in the workers' movement but, like Marx, never wielding real political clout, Engels influenced the 1891 Erfurt Program of the German Socialists and in 1893 was named Honorary President of the International Socialist Congress in Zurich. When the philosopher—who had often sacrificed his own literary work to enable Marx to write—died in London in 1895, his main treatise, *Dialectics of Nature*, was unfinished. Posthumously published in 1927, Engels's bold attempt to establish dialectical principles in natural history and to overcome the impression that Marxism could be valid only for a political philosophy stimulated the desire for new directions in the philosophy of nature as well as showing us his keen eye for the pattern of ecological destruction caused by heedless advancement; but it also initiated the ill-fated search for a "socialist science of nature" in the 1930s.

Marx and Engels, who had lived in England for so many years, were discouraged by the failure of the English proletariat to attack their capitalist oppressors. With sinking expectations, they still hoped to witness the collapse of capitalism. Yet, despite the gruesome conditions of the wage workers, English capitalism survived all crises. At the end of his very productive life, Engels returned to the theoretical sources of German socialist philosophy and wrote *Feuerbach and the End of Classical German Philosophy* (1888) in which Marx's "Theses on Feuerbach" were also published for the first time. This treatise, rarely mentioned during the sixty years of state socialism in the Eastern bloc, today reveals the rightful place of Marx and Engels within the history of philosophy. They will be remembered as the two most politically influential philosophers of all time who achieved for decades a status usually reserved for founders of religion. The enormous scope of scholarship these two thinkers engendered is certainly not easily matched, but has to be taken with a grain of salt and cannot escape the question: What survives of Marx and Engels? What is of lasting value in their thought? They remain two of the greatest philosophers of the nineteenth century who owe their theoretical challenge to Kant and Hegel, and their evidence to the Industrial Revolution. Together with Feuerbach, they define the individual's place in nature and in society as central, and refused to abdicate the personal responsibility we alone bear for our lives. By incorporating the forces of economy, science, and technology, and by stressing the importance of methodically controlled research in philosophy, Feuerbach, Marx, and Engels became the founders of applied philosophy, once perceived as purely political philosophy but which can be found today in such diverse enterprises as the philosophy of technology, deep ecology, bioethics, media philosophy, philosophy of the body, and philosophy for children. Philosophy is never an end in itself, but always a critique of existing conditions. In this sense, the sole task of philosophical work is to make itself superfluous through a fundamental change in our societal praxis, the workings and humanity of which no longer have need of criticism. When life has become worth living, philosophy disappears. This is at the core of the German socialist philosophy and its claim to the future.

Erich Hahn of Berlin, a leading philosopher of the former German Democratic Republic and often enough in the past my resourceful Marxist opponent during international philosophy congresses, gave generously of his time in suggesting those texts by Marx and Engels with staying power. I would gratefully like to acknowledge his advice, which was to the point and extremely helpful. I also wish to thank my trusted American translator Virginia Cutrufelli, who, as always, became a collaborator by asking questions and encouraging clarifications.

W. S.
Translated by Virginia Cutrufelli

LUDWIG FEUERBACH

The Essence of Christianity

The Essential Nature of Man

Religion has its basis in the essential difference between man and
the brute—the brutes have no religion. It is true that the old un-
critical writers on natural history attributed to the elephant, among
other laudable qualities, the virtue of religiousness; but the religion
of elephants belongs to the realm of fable. Cuvier, one of the greatest authorities on the animal kingdom, assigns, on the strength of
his personal observations, no higher grade of intelligence to the
elephant than to the dog.

But what is this essential difference between man and the brute?
The most simple, general, and also the most popular answer to this
question is—consciousness—but consciousness in the strict sense;
for the consciousness implied in the feeling of self as an individual,
in discrimination by the senses, in the perception and even judgment of outward things according to definite sensible signs, cannot
be denied to the brutes. Consciousness in the strictest sense is present only in a being to whom his species, his essential nature, is an
object of thought. The brute is indeed conscious of himself as an
individual—and he has accordingly the feeling of self as the common centre of successive sensations—but not as a species: hence,
he is without that consciousness which in its nature, as in its name,
is akin to science. Where there is this higher consciousness there is
a capability of science. Science is the cognisance of species. In practical life we have to do with individuals; in science, with species.
But only a being to whom his own species, his own nature, is an
object of thought, can make the essential nature of other things or
beings an object of thought.

Hence the brute has only a simple, man a twofold life: in the brute, the inner life is one with the outer; man has both an inner and an outer life. The inner life of man is the life which has relation to his species, to his general, as distinguished from his individual, nature. Man thinks—that is, he converses with himself. The brute can exercise no function which has relation to its species without another individual external to itself; but man can perform the functions of thought and speech, which strictly imply such a relation, apart from another individual. Man is himself at once I and thou; he can put himself in the place of another, for this reason, that to him his species, his essential nature, and not merely his individuality, is an object of thought.

Religion being identical with the distinctive characteristic of man, is then identical with self-consciousness—with the consciousness which man has of his nature. But religion, expressed generally, is consciousness of the infinite; thus it is and can be nothing else than the consciousness which man has of his own—not finite and limited, but infinite nature. A really finite being has not even the faintest adumbration, still less consciousness, of an infinite being, for the limit of the nature is also the limit of the consciousness. The consciousness of the caterpillar, whose life is confined to a particular species of plant, does not extend itself beyond this narrow domain. It does, indeed, discriminate between this plant and other plants, but more it knows not. A consciousness so limited, but on account of that very limitation so infallible, we do not call consciousness, but instinct. Consciousness, in the strict or proper sense, is identical with consciousness of the infinite; a limited consciousness is no consciousness; consciousness is essentially infinite in its nature. The consciousness of the infinite is nothing else than the consciousness of the infinity of the consciousness; or, in the consciousness of the infinite, the conscious subject has for his object the infinity of his own nature.

What, then, *is* the nature of man, of which he is conscious, or what constitutes the specific distinction, the proper humanity of man?* Reason, Will, Affection. To a complete man belong the

---

*The obtuse Materialist says: "Man is distinguished from the brute *only* by consciousness—he is an animal with consciousness superadded"; not reflecting, that in a being which awakes to consciousness, there takes place a qualitative change, a differentiation of the entire nature. For the rest, our words are by no means intended to depreciate the nature of the lower animals. This is not the place to enter further into that question.

power of thought, the power of will, the power of affection. The power of thought is the light of the intellect, the power of will is energy of character, the power of affection is love. Reason, love, force of will, are perfections—the perfections of the human being—nay, more, they are absolute perfections of being. To will, to love, to think, are the highest powers, are the absolute nature of man as man, and the basis of his existence. Man exists to think, to love, to will. Now that which is the end, the ultimate aim, is also the true basis and principle of a being. But what is the end of reason? Reason. Of love? Love. Of will? Freedom of the will. We think for the sake of thinking; love for the sake of loving; will for the sake of willing—i.e., that we may be free. True existence is thinking, loving, willing existence. That alone is true, perfect, divine, which exists for its own sake. But such is love, such is reason, such is will. The divine trinity in man, above the individual man, is the unity of reason, love, will. Reason, Will, Love, are not powers which man possesses, for he is nothing without them, he is what he is only by them; they are the constituent elements of his nature, which he neither has nor makes, the animating, determining, governing powers—divine, absolute powers—to which he can oppose no resistance.*

How can the feeling man resist feeling, the loving one love, the rational one reason? Who has not experienced the overwhelming power of melody? And what else is the power of melody but the power of feeling? Music is the language of feeling; melody is audible feeling—feeling communicating itself. Who has not experienced the power of love, or at least heard of it? Which is the stronger—love or the individual man? Is it man that possesses love, or is it not much rather love that possesses man? When love impels a man to suffer death even joyfully for the beloved one, is this death-conquering power his own individual power, or is it not rather the power of love? And who that ever truly thought has not experienced that quiet, subtle power—the power of thought? When thou sinkest into deep reflection, forgetting thyself and what is around thee, dost thou govern reason, or is it not reason which governs and absorbs thee? Scientific enthusiasm—is it not the most glorious triumph of intellect over thee? The desire of knowledge—is it not a simply irresistible, and all-conquering power? And when thou suppressest a passion, renouncest a habit, in short, achievest a vic-

---

* "Toute opinion est assez forte pour se faire exposer au prix de la vie."—Montaigne

tory over thyself, is this victorious power thy own personal power, or is it not rather the energy of will, the force of morality, which seizes the mastery of thee, and fills thee with indignation against thyself and thy individual weaknesses?

Man is nothing without an object. The great models of humanity, such men as reveal to us what man is capable of, have attested the truth of this proposition by their lives. They had only one dominant passion—the realization of the aim which was the essential object of their activity. But the object to which a subject essentially, necessarily relates, is nothing else than this subject's own, but objective, nature. If it be an object common to several individuals of the same species, but under various conditions, it is still, at least as to the form under which it presents itself to each of them according to their respective modifications, their own, but objective, nature.

Thus the Sun is the common object of the planets, but it is an object to Mercury, to Venus, to Saturn, to Uranus, under other conditions than to the Earth. Each planet has its own sun. The Sun which lights and warms Uranus has no physical (only an astronomical, scientific) existence for the Earth; and not only does the Sun appear different, but it really is *another* sun on Uranus than on the Earth. The relation of the Sun to the Earth is therefore at the same time a relation of the Earth to itself, or to its own nature, for the measure of the size and of the intensity of light which the Sun possesses as the object of the Earth is the measure of the distance which determines the peculiar nature of the Earth. Hence each planet has in its sun the mirror of its own nature.

In the object which he contemplates, therefore, man becomes acquainted with himself; consciousness of the objective is the self-consciousness of man. We know the man by the object, by his conception of what is external to himself; in it his nature becomes evident; this object is his manifested nature, his true objective *ego*. And this is true not merely of spiritual, but also of sensuous objects. Even the objects which are the most remote from man, *because* they are objects to him, and to the extent to which they are so, are revelations of human nature. Even the moon, the sun, the stars, call to man *Gnothi seauton*. That he sees them, and so sees them, is an evidence of his own nature. The animal is sensible only of the beam which immediately affects life; while man perceives the ray, to him physically indifferent, of the remotest star. Man alone has purely intellectual, disinterested joys and passions; the eye of man alone keeps theoretic festivals. The eye which looks into the starry heavens, which gazes at that light, alike useless and harmless, having nothing in common with the earth and its necessities—this eye sees in that light its own nature, its own origin. The eye is heavenly in its nature. Hence man elevates himself above the earth only with the eye; hence theory begins with the contemplation of the heavens. The first philosophers were astronomers. It is the heavens that admonish man of his destination, and remind him that he is destined not merely to action, but also to contemplation.

The *absolute* to man is his own nature. The power of the object over him is therefore the power of his own nature. Thus the power of the object of feeling is the power of feeling itself; the power of the object of the intellect is the power of the intellect itself; the power of the object of the will is the power of the will itself. The man who is affected by musical sounds is governed by feeling; by the feeling, that is, which finds its corresponding element in musical sounds. But it is not melody as such, it is only melody pregnant with meaning and emotion, which has power over feeling. Feeling is only acted on by that which conveys feelings, i.e., by itself, its own nature. Thus also the will; thus, and infinitely more, the intellect. Whatever kind of object, therefore, we are at any time conscious of, we are always at the same time conscious of our own nature; we can affirm nothing without affirming ourselves. And since to will, to feel, to think, are perfections, essences, realities, it is impossible that intellect, feeling, and will should feel or perceive themselves as limited, finite powers, i.e., as worthless, as nothing. For finiteness and nothingness are identical; finiteness is only a euphemism for nothingness. Finiteness is the metaphysical, the theoretical—nothingness the pathological, practical expression. What is finite to the understanding is nothing to the heart. But it is impossible that we should be conscious of will, feeling, and intellect, as finite powers, because every perfect existence, every original power and essence, is the immediate verification and affirmation of itself. It is impossible to love, will, or think, without perceiving these activities to be perfections—impossible to feel that one is a loving, willing, thinking being, without experiencing an infinite joy therein. Consciousness consists in a being becoming objective to itself; hence it is nothing apart, nothing distinct from the being which is conscious of itself. How could it otherwise become conscious of itself? It is therefore impossible to be conscious of a perfection as an imperfection, impossible to feel feeling limited, to think thought limited.

Consciousness is self-verification, self-affirmation, self-love, joy in one's own perfection. Consciousness is the characteristic mark of a perfect nature; it exists only in a self-sufficing, complete being. Even human vanity attests this truth. A man looks in the glass; he has complacency in his appearance. This complacency is a necessary, involuntary consequence of the completeness, the beauty of his form. A beautiful form is satisfied in itself; it has necessarily joy in itself—in self-contemplation. This complacency becomes vanity only when a man piques himself on his form as being his individual form, not when he admires it as a specimen of human beauty in general. It is fitting that he should admire it thus: he can conceive no form more beautiful, more sublime than the human.* Assuredly every being loves itself, its existence—and fitly so. To exist is a good. *Quidquid essentia dignum est, scientia dignum est.* Everything that exists has value, is a being of distinction—at least this is true of the species: hence it asserts, maintains itself. But the highest form of self-assertion, the form which is itself a superiority, a perfection, a bliss, a good, is consciousness.

Every limitation of the reason, or in general of the nature of man, rests on a delusion, an error. It is true that the human being, as an individual, can and must—herein consists his distinction from the brute—feel and recognise himself to be limited; but he can become conscious of his limits, his finiteness, only because the perfection, the infinitude of his species, is perceived by him, whether as an object of feeling, of conscience, or of the thinking consciousness. If he makes his own limitations the limitations of the species, this arises from the mistake that he identifies himself immediately with the species—a mistake which is intimately connected with the individual's love of ease, sloth, vanity, and egoism. For a limitation which I know to be merely mine humiliates, shames, and perturbs me. Hence to free myself from this feeling of shame, from this state of dissatisfaction, I convert the limits of my individuality into the limits of human nature in general. What is incomprehensible to me is incomprehensible to others; why should I trouble myself further?

---

*Homini homine nihil pulchrius. (Cic. De Nat. D. l. i.) And this is no sign of limitation, for he regards other beings as beautiful besides himself; he delights in the beautiful forms of animals, in the beautiful forms of plants, in the beauty of nature in general. But only the absolute, the perfect form, can delight without envy in the forms of other beings.

It is no fault of mine; my understanding is not to blame, but the understanding of the race. But it is a ludicrous and even culpable error to define as finite and limited what constitutes the essence of man, the nature of the species, which is the absolute nature of the individual. Every being is sufficient to itself. No being can deny itself, i.e., its own nature; no being is a limited one to itself. Rather, every being is in and by itself infinite—has its God, its highest conceivable being, in itself. Every limit of a being is cognisable only by another being out of and above him. The life of the ephemera is extraordinarily short in comparison with that of longer-lived creatures; but nevertheless, for the ephemera this short life is as long as a life of years to others. The leaf on which the caterpillar lives is for it a world, an infinite space.

That which makes a being what it is, is its talent, its power, its wealth, its adornment. How can it possibly hold its existence non-existence, its wealth poverty, its talent incapacity? If the plants had eyes, taste, and judgment, each plant would declare its own flower the most beautiful; for its comprehension, its taste, would reach no farther than its natural power of production. What the productive power of its nature has brought forth as the highest, that must also its taste, its judgment, recognise and affirm as the highest. What the nature affirms, the understanding, the taste, the judgment, cannot deny; otherwise the understanding, the judgment, would no longer be the understanding and judgment of this particular being, but of some other. The measure of the nature is also the measure of the understanding. If the nature is limited, so also is the feeling, so also is the understanding. But to a limited being its limited understanding is not felt to be a limitation; on the contrary, it is perfectly happy and contented with this understanding; it regards it, praises and values it, as a glorious, divine power; and the limited understanding, on its part, values the limited nature whose understanding it is. Each is exactly adapted to the other; how should they be at issue with each other? A being's understanding is its sphere of vision. As far as thou seest, so far extends thy nature; and conversely. The eye of the brute reaches no farther than its needs, and its nature no farther than its needs. And so far as thy nature reaches, so far reaches thy unlimited self-consciousness, so far art thou God. The discrepancy between the understanding and the nature, between the power of conception and the power of production in the human consciousness, on the one hand, is merely of individual significance and has not a universal application; and, on the other hand, it is only apparent. He who, having written a bad poem, knows it to be bad, is in his intelligence, and therefore in his nature, not so limited as he who, having written a bad poem, admires it and thinks it good.

It follows that if thou thinkest the infinite, thou perceivest and affirmest the infinitude of the power of thought; if thou feelest the infinite, thou feelest and affirmest the infinitude of the power of feeling. The object of the intellect is intellect objective to itself; the object of feeling is feeling objective to itself. If thou hast no sensibility, no feeling for music, how perceivest in the finest music nothing more than in the wind that whistles by thy ear, or than in the brook which rushes past thy feet. What, then, is it which acts on thee when thou art affected by melody? What dost thou perceive in it? What else than the voice of thy own heart? Feeling speaks only to feeling; feeling is comprehensible only by feeling, that is, by itself—for this reason, that the object of feeling is nothing else than feeling. Music is a monologue of emotion. But the dialogue of philosophy also is in truth only a monologue of the intellect; thought speaks only to thought. The splendours of the crystal charm the sense, but the intellect is interested only in the laws of crystallisation. The intellectual only is the object of the intellect.*

All therefore which, in the point of view of metaphysical, transcendental speculation and religion, has the significance only of the secondary, the subjective, the medium, the organ—has in truth the significance of the primary, of the essence, of the object itself. If, for example, feeling is the essential organ of religion, the nature of God is nothing else than an expression of the nature of feeling. The true but latent sense of the phrase, "Feeling is the organ of the divine," is, feeling is the noblest, the most excellent, i.e., the divine, in man. How couldst thou perceive the divine by feeling, if feeling were not itself divine in its nature? The divine assuredly is known only by means of the divine—God is known only by himself. The divine nature which is discerned by feeling is in truth nothing else than feeling enraptured, in ecstasy with itself—feeling intoxicated with joy, blissful in its own plenitude.

It is already clear from this that where feeling is held to be the organ of the infinite, the subjective essence of religion,—the external data of religion lose their objective value. And thus, since feel-

---

*"The understanding is percipient only of understanding, and what proceeds thence."—Reimarus (Wahrh. der Natürl. Religion, iv. Abth. § 8).

ing has been held the cardinal principle in religion, the doctrines of Christianity, formerly so sacred, have lost their importance. If, from this point of view, some value is still conceded to Christian ideas, it is a value springing entirely from the relation they bear to feeling; if another object would excite the same emotions, it would be just as welcome. But the object of religious feeling is become a matter of indifference, only because when one feeling has been pronounced to be the subjective essence of religion, it in fact is also the objective essence of religion, though it may not be declared, at least directly, to be such. I say directly; for indirectly this is certainly admitted, when it is declared that feeling, as such, is religious, and thus the distinction between specifically religious and irreligious, or at least non-religious, feelings is abolished—a necessary consequence of the point of view in which feeling only is regarded as the organ of the divine. For on what other ground than that of its essence, its nature, dost thou hold feeling to be the organ of the infinite, the divine being? And is not the nature of feeling in general also the nature of every special feeling, be its object what it may? What, then, makes this feeling religious? A given object? Not at all; for this object is itself a religious one only when it is not an object of the cold understanding or memory, but of feeling. What then? The nature of feeling—a nature of which every special feeling, without distinction of objects, partakes. Thus, feeling is pronounced to be religious, simply because it is feeling; the ground of its religiousness is its own nature—lies in itself. But is not feeling thereby declared to be itself the absolute, the divine? If feeling in itself is good, religious, i.e., holy, divine, has not feeling its God in itself?

But if, notwithstanding, thou wilt posit an object of feeling, but at the same time seekest to express thy feeling truly, without introducing by thy reflection any foreign element, what remains to thee but to distinguish between thy individual feeling and the general nature of feeling;—to separate the universal in feeling from the disturbing, adulterating influences with which feeling is bound up in thee, under thy individual conditions? Hence what thou canst alone contemplate, declare to be the infinite, and define as its essence, is merely the nature of feeling. Thou hast thus no other definition of God than this: God is pure, unlimited, free Feeling. Every other God, whom thou supposest, is a God thrust upon thy feeling from without. Feeling is atheistic in the sense of the orthodox belief, which attaches religion to an external object; it denies an objective God—it is itself God. In this point of view only the negation of feeling is the negation of God. Thou art simply too cowardly or too narrow to confess in words what thy feeling tacitly affirms. Fettered by outward considerations, still in bondage to vulgar empiricism, incapable of comprehending the spiritual grandeur of feeling, thou art terrified before the religious atheism of thy heart. By this fear thou destroyest the unity of thy feeling with itself, in imagining to thyself an objective being distinct from thy feeling, and thus necessarily sinking back into the old questions and doubts—is there a God or not?—questions and doubts which vanish, nay, are impossible, where feeling is defined as the essence of religion. Feeling is thy own inward power, but at the same time a power distinct from thee, and independent of thee; it is in thee, above thee; it is itself that which constitutes the objective in thee—thy own being which impresses thee as another being; in short, thy God. How wilt thou, then, distinguish from this objective being within thee another objective being? how wilt thou get beyond thy feeling?

But feeling has here been adduced only as an example. It is the same with every other power, faculty, potentiality, reality, activity—the name is indifferent—which is defined as the essential organ of any object. Whatever is a subjective expression of a nature is simultaneously also its objective expression. Man cannot get beyond his true nature. He may indeed by means of the imagination conceive individuals of another so-called higher kind, but he can never get loose from his species, his nature; the conditions of being, the positive final predicates which he gives to these other individuals, are always determinations or qualities drawn from his own nature—qualities in which he in truth only images and projects himself. There may certainly be thinking beings besides men on the other planets of our solar system. But by the supposition of such beings we do not change our standing point—we extend our conceptions *quantitatively* not *qualitatively*. For as surely as on the other planets there are the same laws of motion, so surely are there the same laws of perception and thought as here. In fact, we people the other planets, not that we may place there different beings from ourselves, but *more* beings of our own or of a similar nature.

The Essence of Religion Considered Generally

What we have hitherto been maintaining generally, even with regard to sensational impressions, of the relation between subject and object, applies especially to the relation between the subject and the religious object.

In the perceptions of the senses consciousness of the object is distinguishable from consciousness of self; but in religion, consciousness of the object and self-consciousness coincide. The object of the senses is out of man, the religious object is within him, and therefore as little forsakes him as his self-consciousness or his conscience; it is the intimate, the closest object. "God," says Augustine, for example, "is nearer, more related to us, and therefore more easily known by us, than sensible, corporeal things." The object of the senses is in itself indifferent—independent of the disposition or of the judgment; but the object of religion is a selected object; the most excellent, the first, the supreme being; it essentially presupposes a critical judgment, a discrimination between the divine and the non-divine, between that which is worthy of adoration and that which is not worthy. And here may be applied, without any limitation, the proposition: the object of any subject is nothing else than the subject's own nature taken objectively. Such as are a man's thoughts and dispositions, such is his God; so much worth as a man has, so much and no more has his God. Consciousness of God is self-consciousness, knowledge of God is self-knowledge. By his God thou knowest the man, and by the man his God; the two are identical. Whatever is God to a man, that is his heart and soul; and conversely, God is the manifested inward nature, the expressed self of a man,—religion the solemn unveiling of a man's hidden treasures, the revelation of his intimate thoughts, the open confession of his love-secrets.

But when religion—consciousness of God—is designated as the self-consciousness of man, this is not to be understood as affirming that the religious man is directly aware of this identity; for, on the contrary, ignorance of it is fundamental to the peculiar nature of religion. To preclude this misconception, it is better to say, religion is man's earliest and also indirect form of self-knowledge. Hence, religion everywhere precedes philosophy, as in the history of the race, so also in that of the individual. Man first of all sees his nature as if *out of* himself, before he finds it in himself. His own nature is in the first instance contemplated by him as that of another being. Religion is the childlike condition of humanity; but the child sees his nature—man—out of himself; in childhood a man is an object to himself, under the form of another man. Hence the historical progress of religion consists in this: that what by an earlier religion was regarded as objective, is now recognised as subjective; that is, what was formerly contemplated and worshiped as God is now perceived to be something *human*. What was at first religion becomes at a later period idolatry; man is seen to have adored his own nature. Man has given objectivity to himself, but has not recognised the object as his own nature: a later religion takes this forward step; every advance in religion is therefore a deeper self-knowledge. But every particular religion, while it pronounces its predecessors idolatrous, excepts itself—and necessarily so, otherwise it would no longer be religion—from the fate, the common nature of all religions: it imputes only to other religions what is the fault, if fault it be, of religion in general. Because it has a different object, a different tenor, because it has transcended the ideas of preceding religions, it erroneously supposes itself exalted above the necessary eternal laws which constitute the essence of religion—it fancies its object, its ideas, to be superhuman. But the essence of religion, thus hidden from the religious, is evident to the thinker, by whom religion is viewed objectively, which it cannot be by its votaries. And it is our task to show that the antithesis of divine and human is altogether illusory, that it is nothing else than the antithesis between the human nature in general and the human individual; that, consequently, the object and contents of the Christian religion are altogether human.

Religion, at least the Christian, is the relation of man to himself, or more correctly to his own nature (i.e., his subjective nature); but a relation to it, viewed as a nature apart from his own. The divine being is nothing else than the human being, or, rather, the human nature purified, freed from the limits of the individual man, made objective—i.e., contemplated and revered as another, a distinct being. All the attributes of the divine nature are, therefore, attributes of the human nature.

In relation to the attributes, the predicates, of the Divine Being, this is admitted without hesitation, but by no means in relation to the subject of these predicates. The negation of the subject is held to be irreligion, nay, atheism; though not so the negation of the predicates. But that which has no predicates or qualities, has no effect upon me; that which has no effect upon me has no existence for me. To deny all the qualities of a being is equivalent to denying the being himself. A being without qualities is one which cannot become an object to the mind, and such a being is virtually nonexistent. Where man deprives God of all qualities, God is no longer anything more to him than a negative being. To the truly religious man, God is not a being without qualities, because to him he is a positive, real being. The theory that God cannot be defined, and consequently cannot be known by man, is therefore the offspring of recent times, a product of modern unbelief.

As reason is and can be pronounced finite only where man regards sensual enjoyment, or religious emotion, or aesthetic contemplation, or moral sentiment, as the absolute, the true; so the proposition that God is unknowable or undefinable, can only be enunciated and become fixed as a dogma, where this object has no longer any interest for the intellect; where the real, the positive, alone has any hold on man, where the real alone has for him the significance of the essential, of the absolute, divine object, but where at the same time, in contradiction with this purely worldly tendency, there yet exist some old remains of religiousness. On the ground that God is unknowable, man excuses himself to what is yet remaining of his religious conscience for his forgetfulness of God, his absorption in the world: he denies God practically by his conduct,—the world has possession of all his thoughts and inclinations,—but he does not deny him theoretically, he does not attack his existence; he lets that rest. But this existence does not affect or incommode him; it is a merely negative existence, an existence without existence, a self-contradictory existence,—a state of being which, as to its effects, is not distinguishable from nonbeing. The denial of determinate, positive predicates concerning the divine nature is nothing else than a denial of religion, with, however, an appearance of religion in its favor, so that it is not recognized as a denial; it is simply a subtle, disguised atheism. The alleged religious horror of limiting God by positive predicates is only the irreligious wish to know nothing more of God, to banish God from the mind. Dread of limitation is dread of existence. All real existence, i.e., all existence which is truly such, is qualitative, determinative existence. He who earnestly believes in the Divine existence is not shocked at the attributing even of gross sensuous qualities to God. He who dreads an existence that may give offence, who shrinks from the grossness of a positive predicate, may as well renounce existence altogether. A God who is injured by determinate qualities has not the courage and the strength to exist. Qualities are the fire, the vital breath, the oxygen, the salt of existence. An existence in general, an existence without qualities, is an insipidity, an absurdity. But there can be no more in God than is supplied by religion. Only where man loses his taste for religion, and thus religion itself becomes insipid, does the existence of God become an insipid existence—an existence without qualities.

There is, however, a still milder way of denying the divine predicates than the direct one just described. It is admitted that the predicates of the divine nature are finite, and, more particularly, human qualities, but their rejection is rejected; they are even taken under protection, because it is necessary to man to have a definite conception of God, and since he is man he can form no other than a human conception of him. In relation to God, it is said, these predicates are certainly without any objective validity; but to me, if he is to exist for me, he cannot appear otherwise than as he does appear to me, namely, as a being with attributes analogous to the human. But this distinction between what God is in himself, and what he is for me destroys the peace of religion, and is besides in itself an unfounded and untenable distinction. I cannot know whether God is something else in himself or for himself than he is for me; what he is to me is to me all that he is. For me, there lies in these predicates under which he exists for me, what he is in himself, his very nature; he is for me what he can alone ever be for me. The religious man finds perfect satisfaction in that which God is in relation to himself; of any other relation he knows nothing, for God is to him what he can alone be to man. In the distinction above stated, man takes a point of view above himself, i.e., above his nature, the absolute measure of his being; but this transcendentalism is only an illusion; for I can make the distinction between the object as it is in itself, and the object as it is for me, only where an object can really appear otherwise to me, not where it appears to me such as the absolute measure of my nature determines it to appear—such as it must appear to me. It is true that I may have a merely subjective conception, i.e., one which does not arise out of the general constitution of my species; but if my conception is determined by the constitution of my species, the distinction between what an object is in itself, and what it is for me ceases; for this conception is itself an absolute one. The measure of the species is the absolute measure, law, and criterion of man. And, indeed, religion has the conviction that its conceptions, its predicates of God, are such as every man ought to have, and must have, if he would have the true ones—that they are the conceptions necessary to human nature; nay, further, that they are objectively true, representing God as he is. To every religion the gods of *other* religions are only notions concerning God, but its own conception of God is to it God himself, the true God—God such as he is in himself. Religion is satisfied only with a complete Deity, a God without reservation; it will not have a mere phantasm of God; it demands God himself. Religion gives up its own existence when it gives up the nature of God; it is no longer a truth when it renounces the possession of the true God. Skepticism is the arch-enemy of religion; but the distinction between object and conception—between God as he is in himself, and God as he is for me—is a skeptical distinction, and therefore an irreligious one.

That which is to man the self-existent, the highest being, to which he can conceive nothing higher—that is to him the Divine Being. How then should he inquire concerning this being, what he is in himself? If God were an object to the bird, he would be a winged being: the bird knows nothing higher, nothing more blissful, than the winged condition. How ludicrous would it be if this bird pronounced: To me God appears as a bird, but what he is in himself I know not. To the bird the highest nature is the bird-nature; take from him the conception of this, and you take from him the conception of the highest being. How, then, could he ask whether God in himself were winged? To ask whether God is in himself what he is for me, is to ask whether God is God, is to lift oneself above one's God, to rise up against him.

Wherever, therefore, this idea, that the religious predicates are only anthropomorphisms, has taken possession of a man, there has doubt, has unbelief, obtained the mastery of faith. And it is only the inconsequence of faint-heartedness and intellectual imbecility which does not proceed from this idea to the formal negation of the predicates, and from thence to the negation of the subject to which they relate. If thou doubtest the objective truth of the predicates, thou must also doubt the objective truth of the subject whose predicates they are. If thy predicates are anthropomorphisms, the subject of them is an anthropomorphism too. If love, goodness, personality, etc. are human attributes, so also is the subject which thou presupposest, the existence of God, the belief that there is a God, an anthropomorphism—a presupposition purely human. Whence knowest thou that the belief in a God at all is not a limitation of man's mode of conception? Higher beings—and thou supposest such—are perhaps so blessed in themselves, so at unity with themselves that they are not hung in suspense between themselves and a yet higher being. To know God and not oneself to be God, to know blessedness and not oneself to enjoy it, is a state of disunity, of unhappiness. Higher beings know nothing of this unhappiness; they have no conception of that which they are not.

Thou believest in love as a divine attribute because thou myself lovest; thou believest that God is a wise, benevolent being because thou knowest nothing better in thyself than benevolence and wisdom; and thou believest that God exists, that therefore he is a subject—whatever exists is a subject, whether it be defined as substance, person, essence, or otherwise—because thou thyself existest, art myself a subject. Thou knowest no higher human good than to love, than to be good and wise; and even so thou knowest no higher happiness than to exist, to be a subject; for the consciousness of all reality, of all bliss, is for thee bound up in the consciousness of being a subject, of existing. God is an existence, a subject to thee, for the same reason that he is to thee a wise, a blessed, a personal being. The distinction between the divine predicates and the divine subject is only this, that to thee the subject, the existence, does not appear an anthropomorphism, because the conception of it is necessarily involved in thy own existence as a subject, whereas the predicates do appear anthropomorphisms, because their necessity—the necessity that God should be conscious, wise, good, etc.—is not an immediate necessity, identical with the being of man, but is evolved by his self-consciousness, by the activity of his thought. I am a subject, I exist, whether I be wise or unwise, good or bad. To exist is to man the first datum; it constitutes the very idea of the subject; it is presupposed by the predicates. Hence man relinquishes the predicates, but the existence of God is to him a settled, absolutely certain, objective truth. But, nevertheless, this distinction is merely an apparent one. The necessity of the subject lies only in the necessity of the predicate. Thou art a subject only insofar as thou art a human subject; the certainty and reality of thy existence lie only in the certainty and reality of thy human attributes. What the subject is lies only in the predicate; the predicate is the *truth* of the subject—the subject only the personified, existing predicate, the predicate conceived as existing. Subject and predicate are distinguished only as existence and essence. The negation of the predicates is therefore the negation of the subject. What remains of the human subject when abstracted from the human attributes? Even in the language of common life the divine predicates—Providence, Omniscience, Omnipotence—are put for the divine subject.

The certainty of the existence of God, of which it has been said that it is as certain, nay, more certain to man than his own existence, depends only on the certainty of the qualities of God—it is in itself no immediate certainty. To the Christian the existence of the Christian God only is a certainty; to the heathen that of the heathen God only. The heathen did not doubt the existence of Jupiter, because he took no offence at the nature of Jupiter, because he could conceive of God under no other qualities, because to him these qualities were a certainty, a divine reality. The reality of the predicate is the sole guarantee of existence.

Whatever man conceives to be true, he immediately conceives to be real (that is, to have an objective existence), because, originally, only the real is true to him—true in opposition to what is merely conceived, dreamed, imagined. The idea of being, of existence, is the original idea of truth; or, originally, man makes truth dependent on existence, subsequently, existence dependent on truth. Now God is the nature of man regarded as absolute truth,— the truth of man; but God, or, what is the same thing, religion, is as various as are the conditions under which man conceives this his nature, regards it as the highest being. These conditions, then, under which man conceives God, are to him the truth, and for that reason they are also the highest existence, or rather they are existence itself; for only the emphatic, the highest existence, is existence, and deserves this name. Therefore, God is an existent, real being, on the very same ground that he is a particular, definite being; for the qualities of God are nothing else than the essential qualities of man himself, and a particular man is what he is, has his existence, his reality, only in his particular conditions. Take away from the Greek the quality of being Greek, and you take away his existence. On this ground it is true that for a definite positive religion—that is, relatively—the certainty of the existence of God is *immediate;* for just as involuntarily, as necessarily, as the Greek was a Greek, so necessarily were his gods Greek beings, so necessarily were they real, existent beings. Religion is that conception of the nature of the world and of man which is essential to, i.e., identical with, a man's nature. But man does not stand above this his necessary conception; on the contrary, it stands above him; it animates, determines, governs him. The necessity of a proof, of a middle term to unite qualities with existence, the possibility of a doubt, is abolished. Only that which is apart from my own being is capable of being doubted by me. How then can I doubt of God, who is my being? To doubt of God is to doubt of myself. Only when God is thought of abstractly, when his predicates are the result of philosophic abstraction, arises the distinction or separation between subject and predicate, existence and nature—arises the fiction that the existence or the subject is something else than the predicate, something immediate, indubitable, in distinction from the predicate, which is held to be doubtful. But this is only a fiction. A God who has abstract predicates has also an abstract existence. Existence, being, varies with varying qualities.

The identity of the subject and predicate is clearly evidenced by the progressive development of religion, which is identical with the progressive development of human culture. So long as man is in a mere state of nature, so long is his god a mere nature-god—a personification of some natural force. Where man inhabits houses, he also encloses his gods in temples. The temple is only a manifestation of the value which man attaches to beautiful buildings. Temples in honor of religion are in truth temples in honor of architecture. With the emerging of man from a state of savagery and wildness to one of culture, with the distinction between what is fitting for man and what is not fitting, arises simultaneously the distinction between that which is fitting and that which is not fitting for God. God is the idea of majesty, of the highest dignity: the religious sentiment is the sentiment of supreme fitness. The later more cultured artists of Greece were the first to embody in the statues of the gods the ideas of dignity, of spiritual grandeur, of imperturbable repose and serenity. But why were these qualities in their view attributes, predicates of God? Because they were in themselves regarded by the Greeks as divinities. Why did those artists exclude all disgusting and low passions? Because they perceived them to be unbecoming, unworthy, unhuman, and consequently ungodlike. The Homeric gods eat and drink;—that implies eating and drinking is a divine pleasure. Physical strength is an attribute of the Homeric gods: Zeus is the strongest of the gods. Why? Because physical strength, in and by itself, was regarded as something glorious, divine. To the ancient Germans the highest virtues were those of the warrior; therefore their supreme god was the god of war, Odin—war, "the original or oldest law." Not the attribute of the divinity, but the divineness or deity of the attribute, is the first true Divine Being. Thus what theology and philosophy have held to be God, the Absolute, the Infinite, is not God; but that which they have held not to be God is God: namely, the attribute, the quality, whatever has reality. Hence he alone is the true atheist to whom the predicates of the Divine Being,—for example, love, wisdom, justice,—are nothing; not he to whom merely the subject of these predicates is nothing. And in no wise is the negation of the subject necessarily also a negation of the predicates considered in themselves. These have an intrinsic, independent reality; they force their recognition upon man by their very nature; they are self-evident truths to him; they prove, they attest themselves. It does not follow that goodness, justice, wisdom, are chimeras because the existence of God is a chimera, nor truths because this is a truth. The idea of God is dependent on the idea of justice, of benevolence; a God who is not benevolent, not just, not wise, is no God; but the converse does not hold. The fact is not that a quality is divine because God has it, but that God has it because it is in itself divine: because without it God would be a defective being. Justice, wisdom, in general every quality which constitutes the divinity of God, is determined and known by itself independently, but the idea of God is determined by the qualities which have thus been previously judged to be worthy of the divine nature; only in the case in which I identify God and justice, in which I think of God immediately as the reality of the idea of justice, is the idea of God self-determined. But if God as subject is the determined, while the quality, the predicate, is the determining, then in truth the rank of the godhead is due not to the subject, but to the predicate.

Not until several, and those contradictory, attributes are united in one being, and this being is conceived as personal—the personality being thus brought into especial prominence—not until then is the origin of religion lost sight of, is it forgotten that what the activity of the reflective power has converted into a predicate distinguishable or separable from the subject, was originally the true subject. Thus the Greeks and Romans deified accidents as substances; virtues, states of mind, passions, as independent beings. Man, especially the religious man, is to himself the measure of all things, of all reality. Whatever strongly impresses a man, whatever produces an unusual effect on his mind, if it be only a peculiar, inexplicable sound or note, he personifies as a divine being. Religion embraces all the objects of the world: everything existing has been an object of religious reverence; in the nature and consciousness of religion there is nothing else than what lies in the nature of man and in his consciousness of himself and of the world. Religion has no material exclusively its own. In some even the passions of fear and terror had their temples. The Christians also made mental phenomena into independent beings, their own feelings into qualities of things, the passions which governed them into power that governed the world, in short, predicates of their own nature, whether recognised as such or not, into independent subjective existences. Devils, cobolds, witches, ghosts, angels, were sacred truths as long as the religious spirit held undivided sway over mankind.

In order to banish from the mind the identity of the divine and human predicates, and the consequent identity of the divine and human nature, recourse is had to the idea that God, as the absolute, real Being, has an infinity of various predicates, of which we here know only a part, and those such as are analogous to our own; while the rest, by virtue of which God must thus have quite a different nature from the human or that which is analogous to the human, we shall only know in the future—that is, after death. But an infinite plentitude or multitude of predicates which are really different, so different that the one does not immediately involve the other, is realized only in an infinite plentitude or multitude of different beings or individuals. Thus the human nature presents an infinite abundance of different predicates, and for that very reason it presents an infinite abundance of different individuals. Each new man is a new predicate, a new phasis of humanity. As many as are the men, so many are the powers, the properties of humanity. It is true that there are the same elements in every individual, but under such various conditions and modifications that they appear new and peculiar. The mystery of the inexhaustible fulness of the divine predicates is therefore nothing else than the mystery of human nature considered as an infinitely varied, infinitely modifiable, but, consequently, phenomenal being. Only in the realm of the senses, only in space and time, does there exist a being of really infinite qualities or predicates. Where there are really different predicates there are different times. One man is a distinguished musician, a distinguished author, a distinguished physician; but he cannot compose music, write books, and perform cures in the same moment of time. Time, and not the Hegelian dialectic, is the medium of uniting opposites, contradictories, in one and the same subject. But distinguished and detached from the nature of man, and combined with the idea of God, the infinite fulness of various predicates is a conception without reality, a mere phantasy, a conception derived from the sensible world, but without the essential conditions, without the truth of sensible existence, a conception which stands in direct contradiction with the Divine Being considered as a spiritual, i.e., an abstract, simple, single being; for the predicates of God are precisely of this character, that one involves all the others, because there is no real difference between them. If, therefore, in the present predicates I have not the future, in the present God not the future God, then the future God is not the present, but they are two distinct beings.* But this distinction is in contradiction with the unity and simplicity of the theological God. Why is a given predicate a predicate of God? Because it is divine in its nature, i.e., because it expresses no limitation, no defect. Why are other predicates applied to him? Because, however various in themselves, they agree in this, that they all alike express perfection, unlimitedness. Hence I can conceive innumerable predicates of God, because they must all agree with the abstract idea of the Godhead, and must have in common that which constitutes every single predicate a divine attribute. Thus it is in the system of Spinoza. He speaks of an infinite number of attributes of the divine substance, but he specifies none except Thought and Extension. Why? Because it is a matter of indifference to know them; nay, because they are in themselves indifferent, superfluous; for with all these innumerable predicates, I yet always mean to say the same thing as when I speak of Thought and Extension. Why is Thought as attribute of substance? Because, according to Spinoza, it is capable of being conceived by itself, because it expresses something indivisible, perfect, infinite. Why Extension or Matter? For the same reason. Thus, substance can have an indefinite number of predicates, because it is not their specific definition, their difference, but their identity, their equivalence, which makes them attributes of substance. Or rather, substance has innumerable predicates only because (how strange!) it has properly no predicate; that is, no definite, real predicate. The indefinite unity which is the product of thought, completes itself by the indefinite multiplicity which is the product of the imagination. Because the predicate is not *multum*, it is *multa*. In truth, the positive predicates are Thought and

---

*For religious faith there is no other distinction between the present and future God than that the former is an object of faith, of conception, of imagination, while the latter is to be an object of immediate, that is, personal, sensible perception. In this life and in the next he is the same God; but in the one he is incomprehensible, in the other comprehensible.

Extension. In these two infinitely more is said than in the nameless innumerable predicates; for they express something definite—in them I have something. But substance is too indifferent, too apathetic to be *something;* that is, to have qualities and passions; that it may not be something, it is rather nothing.

Now, when it is shown that what the subject is lies entirely in the attributes of the subject; that is, that the predicate is the true subject; it is also proved that if the divine predicates are attributes of the human nature, the subject of those predicates is also of the human nature. But the divine predicates are partly general, partly personal. The general predicates are the metaphysical, but these serve only as external points of support to religion; they are not the characteristic definitions of religion. It is the personal predicates alone which constitute the essence of religion—in which the Divine Being is the object of religion. Such are, for example, that God is a Person, that he is the moral Lawgiver, the Father of mankind, the Holy One, the Just, the Good, the Merciful. It is, however, at once clear, or it will at least be clear in the sequel, with regard to these and other definitions, that, especially as applied to a personality, they are purely human definitions, and that consequently man in religion—in his relation to God—is in relation to his own nature; for to the religious sentiment these predicates are not mere conceptions, mere images, which man forms of God, to be distinguished from that which God is in himself, but truths, facts, realities. Religion knows nothing of anthropomorphisms; to it they are not anthropomorphisms. It is the very essence of religion, that to it these definitions express the nature of God. They are pronounced to be images only by the understanding, which reflects on religion, and which while defending them yet before its own tribunal denies them. But to the religious sentiment God is a real Father, real Love and Mercy; for to it he is a real, living, personal being, and therefore his attributes are also living and personal. Nay, the definitions which are the most sufficing to the religious sentiment are precisely those which give the most offence to the understanding, and which in the process of reflection on religion it denies. Religion is essentially emotion; hence, objectively also, emotion is to it necessarily of a divine nature. Even anger appears to it an emotion not unworthy of God, provided only there be a religious motive at the foundation of this anger.

But here it is also essential to observe, and this phenomenon is an extremely remarkable one, characterizing the very core of religion, that in proportion as the divine subject is in reality human, the greater is the apparent difference between God and man; that is, the more, by reflection on religion, by theology, is the identity of the divine and human denied, and the human, considered as such, is depreciated.* The reason of this is, that as what is positive in the conception of the divine being can only be human, the conception of man, as an object of consciousness, can only be negative. To enrich God, man must become poor; that God may be all, man must be nothing. But he desires to be nothing in himself, because what he takes from himself is not lost to him, since it is preserved in God. Man has his being in God; why then should he have it in himself? Where is the necessity of positing the same thing twice, of having it twice? What man withdraws from himself, what he renounces in himself, he only enjoys in an incomparably higher and fuller measure in God.

The monks made a vow of chastity to God; they mortified the sexual passion in themselves, but therefore they had in heaven, in the Virgin Mary, the image of woman—an image of love. They could the more easily dispense with real woman in proportion as an ideal woman was an object of love to them. The greater the importance they attached to the denial of sensuality, the greater the importance of the heavenly virgin for them: she was to them in the place of Christ, in the stead of God. The more the sensual tendencies are renounced, the more sensual is the God to whom they are sacrificed. For whatever is made an offering to God has an especial value attached to it; in it God is supposed to have special pleasure. That which is the highest in the estimation of man is naturally the highest in the estimation of his God; what pleases man pleases God also. The Hebrews did not offer to Jehovah unclean, ill-conditioned animals; on the contrary, those which they most highly prized, which they themselves ate, were also the food of God. (*Cibus Die*, Lev. iii.2). Wherever, therefore, the denial of the sensual delights is made a special offering, a sacrifice well-pleasing to God, there the highest value is attached to the senses, and the sensuality which has been renounced is unconsciously re-

---

*Inter creatorem et creaturam non potest tanta similitudo notari, quin inter eos major sit dissimilitudo notanda.—Later. Conc. Can. 2. (Summa Omn. Conc. Carranza. Antw. 1559. p. 326) The last distinction between man and God, between the finite and infinite nature, to which the religious speculative imagination soars, is the distinction between Something and Nothing, Ens and Non-Ens; for only in Nothing is all community with other beings abolished.

stored, in the fact that God takes the place of the material delights which have been renounced. The nun weds herself to God; she has a heavenly bridegroom, the monk a heavenly bride. But the heavenly virgin is only a sensible presentation of a general truth, having relation to the essence of religion. Man denies as to himself only what he attributes to God. Religion abstracts from man, from the world; but it can only abstract from the limitations, from the phenomena; in short, from the negative, not from the essence, the positive, of the world and humanity: hence, in the very abstraction and negation it must recover that from which it abstracts, or believes itself to abstract. And thus, in reality, whatever religion consciously denies—always supposing that what is denied by it is something essential, true, and consequently incapable of being ultimately denied—it unconsciously restores in God. Thus, in religion man denies his reason; of himself he knows nothing of God, his thoughts are only worldly, earthly; he can only believe what God reveals to him. But on this account the thoughts of God are human, earthly thoughts: like man, he has plans in his mind, he accommodates himself to circumstances and grades of intelligence, like a tutor with his pupils; he calculates closely the effect of his gifts and revelations; he observes man in all his doings; he knows all things, even the most earthly, the commonest, the most trivial. In brief, man in relation to God denies his own knowledge, his own thoughts that he may place them in God. Man gives up his personality; but in return, God, the Almighty, infinite, unlimited being, is a person; he denies human dignity, the human *ego;* but in turn God is to him a selfish, egoistical being, who in all things seeks only himself, his own honour, his own ends; he represents God as simply seeking the satisfaction of his own selfishness, while yet he frowns on that of every other being; his God is the very luxury of egoism.* Religion further denies goodness as a quality of human nature; man is wicked, corrupt, incapable of good; but, on the other hand, God is only good—the Good Being. Man's nature demands as an object goodness, personified as God; but is it not hereby declared that goodness is an essential tendency of man? If my heart is wicked, my understanding perverted, how can I per-

---

*Gloriam suam plus amat Deus quam omnes creaturas. "God can only love himself, can only think of himself, can only work for himself. In creating man, God seeks his own ends, his own glory," etc.—Vide P. Bayle, Ein Beitrag zur Geschichte der Philos. u. Menschh., pp. 104–7.

ceive and feel the holy to be holy, the good to be good? Could I perceive the beauty of a fine picture if my mind were aesthetically an absolute piece of perversion? Though I may not be a painter, though I may not have the power of producing what is beautiful myself, I must yet have aesthetic feeling, aesthetic comprehension, since I perceive the beauty that is presented to me externally. Either goodness does not exist at all for man, or, if it does exist, therein is revealed to the individual man the holiness and goodness of human nature. That which is absolutely opposed to my nature, to which I am united by no bond, no sympathy, is not even conceivable or perceptible by me. The holy is in opposition to me only as regards the modifications of my personality, but as regards my fundamental future it is in unity with me. The holy is a reproach to my sinfulness; in it I recognize myself as a sinner; but in my doing, while I blame myself, I acknowledge what I am not, but ought to be, and what, for that very reason, I, according to my destination, can be; for an "ought," which has no corresponding capability, does not affect me, is a ludicrous chimera without any true relation to my mental constitution. But when I acknowledge goodness as my destination, as my law, I acknowledge it, whether consciously or unconsciously, as my own nature. Another nature than my own, one different in quality, cannot touch me. I can perceive sin as sin, only when I perceive it to be a contradiction of myself with myself—that is, of my personality with my fundamental nature. As a contradiction of the absolute, considered as another being, the feeling of sin is inexplicable, unmeaning.

The distinction between Augustinianism and Pelagianism consists only in this, that the former expresses after the manner of religion what the latter expresses after the manner of Rationalism. Both say the same thing, both indicate the goodness of man; but Pelagianism does it perfectly, in a rationalistic and moral form; Augustinianism indirectly, in a mystical, that is, a religious form.* For that which is given to man's God is in truth given to man

---

*Pelagianism denies God, religion—isti tantam tribuunt potestatem voluntati, ut pietati auferant orationem. (Augustin de Nat. Et Grat. Cont. Pelagium, c. 58.) It has only the Creator, i.e., Nature, as a basis, not the Saviour, the true God of the religious sentiment—in a word, it denies God; but, as a consequence of this, it elevates man into a God, since it makes him a being not needing God, self-sufficing, independent. (See on this subject Luther against Erasmus and Augustine, l. c. c. 33.) Augustinianism denies man; but, as a consequence of this, it reduces God to the level of man, even to the ignominy of the cross, for the sake of man. The former

himself; what a man declares concerning God, he in truth declares concerning himself. Augustinianism would be a truth, and a truth opposed to Pelagianism, only if man had the devil for his God, and, with the consciousness that he was the devil, honored, reverenced, and worshiped him as the highest being. But so long as man adores a good being as his God, so long does he contemplate in God the goodness of his own nature.

As with the doctrine of the radical corruption of human nature, so is it with the identical doctrine, that man can do nothing good, i.e., in truth, nothing of himself—by his own strength. For the denial of human strength and spontaneous moral activity to be true, the moral activity of God must also be denied; and we must say, with the Oriental nihilist or pantheist: the Divine being is absolutely without will or action, indifferent, knowing nothing of the discrimination between evil and good. But he who defines God as an active being, and not only so, but as morally active and morally critical—as a being who loves, works, and rewards good, punishes, rejects, and condemns evil—he who thus defines God only in appearance denies human activity, in fact, making it the highest, the most real activity. He who makes God act humanly, declares human activity to be divine; he says: A god who is not active, and not morally or humanly active, is no god; and thus he makes the idea of the Godhead dependent on the idea of activity, that is, of human activity, for a higher he knows not.

Man—this is the mystery of religion—projects his being into objectivity,* and then again makes himself an object to this projected image of himself thus converted into a subject; he thinks of himself as an object to himself, but as the object of an object, of another being than himself. Thus here. Man is an object to God. That man is good or evil is not indifferent to God; no! He has a lively, profound interest in man's being good; he wills that man should be good, happy—for without goodness there is no happi-

___

puts man in the place of God, the latter puts God in the place of man; both lead to the same result—the distinction is only apparent, a pious illusion. Augustinianism is only an inverted Pelagianism; what to the latter is a subject, is to the former an object.

*The religious, the original mode in which man becomes objective to himself, is (as is clearly enough explained in this work) to be distinguished from the mode in which this occurs in reflection and speculation; the latter is voluntary, the former involuntary, necessary—as necessary as art, as speech. With the progress of time, it is true, theology coincides with religion.

ness. Thus the religious man virtually retracts the nothingness of
human activity, by making his dispositions and actions an object
to God, by making man the end of God—for that which is an
object to the mind is an end in action; by making the divine activity
a means of human salvation. God acts, that man may be good and
happy. Thus man, while he is apparently humiliated to the lowest
degree, is in truth exalted to the highest. Thus, in and through
God, man has in view himself alone. It is true that man places the
aim of his action in God, but God has no other aim of action than
the moral and eternal salvation of man: thus man has in fact no
other aim than himself. The divine activity is not distinct from
the human.

How could the divine activity work on me as its object, nay,
work in me, if it were essentially different from me; how could it
have a human aim, the aim of ameliorating and blessing man, if it
were not itself human? Does not the purpose determine the nature
of the act? When man makes his moral improvement an aim to
himself, he has divine resolutions, divine projects; but also, when
God seeks the salvation of man, he has human ends and a human
mode of activity corresponding to these ends. Thus in God man
has only his own activity as an object. But for the very reason that
he regards his own activity as objective, goodness only as an object,
he necessarily receives the impulse, the motive not from himself,
but from this object. He contemplates his nature as external to
himself, and this nature as goodness; thus it is self-evident, it is
mere tautology to say that the impulse to good comes only from
thence where he places the good.

God is the highest subjectivity of man abstracted from himself;
hence man can do nothing of himself, all goodness comes from
God. The more subjective God is, the more completely does man
divest himself of his subjectivity, because God is, per se, his relin-
quished self, the possession of which he however again vindicates
to himself. As the action of the arteries drives the blood into the
extremities, and the action of the veins brings it back again, as life
in general consists in a perpetual systole and diastole; so is it in
religion. In the religious systole man propels his own nature from
himself, he throws himself outward; in the religious diastole he
receives the rejected nature into his heart again. God alone is the
being who acts of himself—this is the force of repulsion in religion;
God is the being who acts in me, with me, through me, upon me,
for me, is the principle of my salvation, of my good dispositions

and actions, consequently my own good principle and nature,—this is the force of attraction in religion.

The course of religious development which has been generally indicated consists specially in this, that man abstracts more and more from God, and attributes more and more to himself. This is especially apparent in the belief in revelation. That which to a later age or a cultured people is given by nature or reason, is to an earlier age, or to a yet uncultured people, given by God. Every tendency of man, however natural—even the impulse to cleanliness, was conceived by the Israelites as a positive divine ordinance. From this example we again see that God is lowered, is conceived more entirely on the type of ordinary humanity, in proportion as man detracts from himself. How can the self-humiliation of man go further than when he disclaims the capability of fulfilling spontaneously the requirements of common decency?* The Christian religion, on the other hand, distinguished the impulses and passions of man according to their quality, their character; it represented only good emotions, good dispositions, good thoughts, as revelations, operations—that is, as dispositions, feeling, thoughts,—of God; for what God reveals is a quality of God himself: that of which the heart is full overflows the lips; as is the effect such is the cause; as the revelation, such the being who reveals himself. A God who reveals himself in good dispositions is a God whose essential attribute is only moral perfection. The Christian religion distinguishes inward moral purity from external physical purity; the Israelites identified the two.† In relation to the Jewish religion, the Christian religion is one of criticism and freedom. The Israelite trusted himself to do nothing except what was commanded by God; he was without will even in external things; the authority of religion extended itself even to his food. The Christian religion, on the other hand, in all these external things made man dependent on himself, i.e., placed in man what the Israelite placed out of himself in God. Israel is the most complete presentation of Positivism in religion. In relation to the Israelite, the Christian is an *esprit fort,* a free-thinker. Thus do things change. What yesterday was still religion is no longer such today; and what today is atheism, tomorrow will be religion.

Translated by George Eliot

---

*Deut. xxiii. 12, 13.
†See, for example, Gen. 35. 2; Levit. 11. 44; 20. 26.

Preface to the Second Edition

The clamor excited by the present work has not surprised me, and hence it has not in the least moved me from my position. On the contrary, I have once more, in all calmness, subjected my work to the severest scrutiny, both historical and philosophical; I have, as far as possible, freed it from its defects of form, and enriched it with new developments, illustrations, and historical testimonies— testimonies in the highest degree striking and irrefragable. Now that I have thus verified my analysis by historical proofs, it is to be hoped that readers whose eyes are not sealed will be confined and will admit, even though reluctantly, that my work contains a faithful, correct translation of the Christian religion out of the oriental language of imagery into plain speech. And it has no pretension to be anything more than a close translation, or, to speak literally, an empirical or historico-philosophical analysis, a solution of the enigma of the Christian religion. The general propositions which I premise in the Introduction are no a priori, excogitated propositions, no products of speculation; they have arisen out of the analysis of religion; they are only, as indeed are all the fundamental ideas of the work, generalizations from the known manifestations of human nature, and in particular of the religious consciousness,—facts converted into thoughts, i.e., expressed in general terms, and thus made the property of the understanding. The ideas of my work are only conclusions, *consequences*, drawn from premises which are not themselves mere ideas, but objective facts either actual or historical—facts which had not their place in my head simply in virtue of their ponderous existence in folio. I unconditionally repudiate *absolute*, immaterial, self-sufficing speculation,—that speculation which draws its material from within. I differ *toto caelo* from those philosophers who pluck out their eyes that they may see better; for *my* thought I require the senses, especially sight; I found my ideas on materials which can be appropriated only through the activity of the senses. I do not generate the object from the thought, but the thought from the object; and I hold *that* alone to be an object which has an existence beyond one's own brain. I am an idealist only in the region of *practical* philosophy, that is, I do not regard the limits of the past and present as the limits of humanity, of the future; on the contrary, I firmly believe that many things—yes, many things—which with the short-sighted, pusillanimous practical men of today, pass for flights of imagination, for ideas never to be realized, for mere chimeras, will tomorrow, i.e., in the next century,—centuries in individual life are days in the life of humanity,—exist in full reality. Briefly, the "Idea" is to me only faith in the historical future, in the triumph of truth and virtue; it has for me only apolitical and moral significance; for in the sphere of strictly theoretical philosophy, I attach myself, in direct opposition to the Hegelian philosophy, only to *realism,* to materialism in the sense above indicated. The maxim hitherto adopted by speculative philosophy: All that is mine I carry with me, the old *omnia mea mecum porto,* I cannot, alas! appropriate. I have many things outside myself, which I cannot convey either in my pocket or my head, but which nevertheless I look upon as belonging to me, not indeed as a mere man—a view not now in question—but as a philosopher. I am nothing but a *natural philosopher in the domain of mind;* and the natural philosopher can do nothing without instruments, without material means. In this character I have written the present work, which consequently contains nothing else than the principle of a new philosophy verified practically, i.e., *in concreto,* in application to a special object, but an object which has a universal significance; namely, to religion, in which this principle is exhibited, developed, and thoroughly carried out. This philosophy is essentially distinguished from the systems hitherto prevalent, in that it corresponds to the real, complete nature of man; but for that very reason it is antagonistic to minds perverted and crippled by a superhuman, i.e., antihuman, antinatural religion and speculation. It does not, as I have already said elsewhere, regard the *pen* as the only fit organ for the revelation of truth, but the eye and ear, the hand and foot; it does not identify the *idea* of the fact with the fact itself, so as to reduce real existence to an existence on paper, but it separates the two, and precisely by this separation attains to the *fact itself*; it recognizes as the true thing not the thing as it is an object of the abstract reason, but as it is an object of the real, complete man, and hence as it is itself a real, complete thing. This philosophy does not rest on an Understanding per se, on an absolute, nameless understanding, belonging one knows not to whom, but on the understanding of man;—though not, I grant, on that of man enervated by speculation and dogma;—and it speaks the language of men, not an empty, unknown tongue. Yes, both in substance and in speech, it places philosophy in *the negation of philosophy,* i.e., it declares *that* alone to be the true philosophy which is converted *in succum et sanguinem,* which is incarnate in Man; and hence it finds its highest triumph in the fact that to all dull and pedantic minds, which place the *essence* of philosophy in the *show* of philosophy, it appears to be no philosophy at all.

This philosophy has for its principle, not the Substance of Spinoza, not the *ego* of Kant and Fichte, not the Absolute Identity of Schelling, not the Absolute Mind of Hegel, in short, no abstract, merely conceptional being, but a *real* being, the true *Ens realissimum*—man; its principle, therefore, is in the highest degree positive and real. It generates thought from the *opposite* of thought, from Matter, from existence, from the senses; it has relation to its object first through the senses, i.e., passively, before defining it in thought. Hence my work, as a specimen of this philosophy, so far from being a production to be placed in the category of Speculation,— although in another point of view it is the true, the incarnate result of prior philosophical systems,—is the direct opposite of speculation, nay, puts an end to it by explaining it. Speculation makes religion say only what it has *itself* thought, and expressed far better than religion; it assigns a meaning to religion without any reference to the *actual* meaning of religion; it does not look beyond itself. I, on the contrary, let religion itself speak; I constitute myself only its listener and interpreter, not its prompter. Not to invent, but to discover, "to unveil existence," has been my sole object; to *see* correctly, my sole endeavor. It is not I, but religion that worships man, although religion, or rather theology, denies this; it is not I, an insignificant individual, but religion itself that says: God is man, man is God; it is not I, but religion that denies the God who is *not* man, but only an *ens rationis,*—since it makes God become man, and then constitutes this God, not distinguished from man, having a human form, human feelings, and human thoughts, the object of its worship and veneration. I have only found the key to the cipher of the Christian religion, only extricated its true meaning from the web of contradictions and delusions called theology;—but in doing so I have certainly committed a sacrilege. If therefore my work is negative, irreligious, atheistic, let it be remembered that atheism—at least in the sense of this work—is the secret of religion itself; that religion itself, not indeed on the surface, but fundamentally, not intention or according to is own supposition, but in its heart, in its essence, believes in nothing else than the truth and divinity of human nature. Or let it be *proved* that the historical as well as the rational arguments of my work are false; let them be refuted—not, however, I entreat, by judicial denunciations, or theological jeremiads, by the trite phrases of speculation, or other pitiful expedients for which I have no name, but by *reasons,* and such reasons as I have not already thoroughly answered.

Certainly, my work is negative, destructive; but, be it observed, only in relation to the *un*human, not to the human elements of religion. It is therefore divided into two parts, of which the first is, as to its main idea, *positive,* the second, including the Appendix, not wholly, but in the main, *negative;* in both, however, the same positions are proved, only in a different or rather opposite manner. The first exhibits religion in its *essence,* its *truth,* the second exhibits it in its *contradictions;* the first is development, the second polemic; thus the one is, according to the nature of the case, calmer, the other more vehement. Development advances gently, contest impetuously, for development is self-contented at every stage, contest only at the last blow. Development is deliberate, but contest resolute. Development is *light,* contest *fire.* Hence results a difference between the two parts even as to their form. Thus in the first part I show that the true sense of Theology is Anthropology, that there is no distinction between the *predicates* of the divine and human nature, and, consequently, no distinction between the divine and human *subject*: I say *consequently,* for wherever, as is especially the case in theology, the predicates are not accidents, but express the essence of the subject, there is no distinction between subject and predicate, the one can be put in the place of the other; on which point I refer the reader to the Analytics of Aristotle, or even merely to the Introduction of Porphyry. In the second part, on the other hand, I show that the distinction which is made, or rather supposed to be made, between the theological and anthropological predicates resolves itself into an absurdity. Here is a striking example. In the first part I prove that the Son of God is *in religion* a real son, the son of God in the same sense in which man is the son of man, and I find therein the *truth*, the *essence* of religion, that it conceives and affirms a profoundly human relation as a divine relation; on the other hand, in the second part I show that the Son of God—not indeed in religion, but in theology, which is the reflection of religion upon itself,—is not a son in the natural, human sense, but in an entirely different manner, contradictory to Nature and reason, and therefore absurd, and I find in this negation of human sense and the human understanding, the negation of religion. Accordingly the first part is the *direct,* the second the *indirect* proof, that theology is anthropology: hence the second part necessarily has reference to the first; it has no independent significance; its only aim is to show that the sense in which religion is interpreted in the previous part of the work *must* be the true one, because the contrary is absurd. In brief, in the first part I am chiefly concerned with *religion,* in the second with *theology*: I say *chiefly,* for it was impossible to exclude theology from the first part, or religion from the second. A mere glance will show that my investigation includes *speculative* theology or philosophy, and not, as has been here and there erroneously supposed, *common* theology only, a kind of trash from which I rather keep as clear as possible, (though, for the rest, I am sufficiently well acquainted with it), confining myself always to the most essential, strict and necessary definition of the object, and hence to that definition which gives to an object the most general interest and raises it above the sphere of theology. But it is with theology that I have to do, not with theologians; for I can only undertake to characterize what is *primary,*—the *original,* not the copy, *principles,* not persons, *species,* not individuals, *objects of history,* not objects of the *chronique scandaleuse.*

If my work contained only the second part, it would be perfectly just to accuse it of a negative tendency, to represent the proposition: Religion is nothing, is an absurdity, as its essential purport. But I by no means say (that were an easy task!): God is nothing, the Trinity is nothing, the Word of God is nothing, etc. I only show that they are not *that* which the illusions of theology make them— not foreign, but native mysteries, the mysteries of human nature; I show that religion takes the apparent, the superficial in Nature and humanity for the essential, and hence conceives their true essence as a separate, special existence: that consequently, religion, in the definitions which it gives of God, e.g., of the Word of God—at least in those definitions which are not negative in the sense above alluded to—only defines or makes objective the true nature of the human word. The reproach that according to my book religion is an absurdity, a nullity, a pure illusion, would be well founded only if, according to it, that into which I resolve religion, which I prove to be its true object and substance, namely, *man—anthropology*, were an absurdity, a nullity, a pure illusion. But so far from giving a trivial or even a subordinate significance to anthropology,—a significance which is assigned to it only just so long as a theology stands above it and in opposition to it—I, on the contrary, while reducing theology to anthropology, exalt anthropology into theology, very much as Christianity, while lowering God into man, made man into God; though, it is true, this human God was by a further process made a transcendental, imaginary God, remote from man. Hence it is obvious that I do not take the word anthropology in the sense of the Hegelian or of any other philosophy, but in an infinitely higher and more general sense.

Religion is the dream of the human mind. But even in dreams we do not find ourselves in emptiness or in heaven, but on earth, in the realm of reality; we only see real things in the entrancing splendor of imagination and caprice, instead of in the simple daylight of reality and necessity. Hence I do nothing more to religion—and to speculative philosophy and theology also—than to open its eyes, or rather to turn its gaze from the internal toward the external, i.e., I change the object as it is in the imagination into the object as it is in reality.

But certainly for the present age, which prefers the sign to the thing signified, the copy to the original, fancy to reality, the appearance to the essence, this change, inasmuch as it does away with illusion, is an absolute annihilation, or at least a reckless profanation; for in these days *illusion* only is *sacred, truth profane*. Nay, sacredness is held to be enhanced in proportion as truth decreases and illusion increases, so that the highest degree of illusion comes to be the highest degree of sacredness. Religion has disappeared, and for it has been substituted, even among Protestants, the *appearance* of religion—the Church—in order at least that "the faith" may be imparted to the ignorant and indiscriminating multitude; *that* faith being still the Christian, because the Christian churches stand now as they did a thousand years ago, and now, as formerly, the *external signs* of the faith are in vogue. That which has no longer any existence in faith (the faith of the modern world is only an ostensible faith, a faith which does not believe what it fancies that it believes, and is only an undecided, pusillanimous unbelief) is still to pass current as *opinion*: that which is no longer sacred in itself and in truth is still at least to *seem* sacred. Hence the simulated religious indignation of the present age, the age of shows and illusion, concerning my analysis, especially of the Sacraments. But let it not be demanded of an author who proposes to himself as his goal not the favor of his contemporaries, but only the truth, the unveiled, naked truth, that he should have or feign respect towards an empty appearance, especially as the object which underlies this appearance is in itself the culminating point of religion, i.e., the point at which the religious slides into the irreligious. Thus much in justification, not in excuse, of my analysis of the Sacraments.

With regard to the true bearing of my analysis of the Sacraments, especially as presented in the concluding chapter, I only remark, that I therein illustrate by a palpable and visible example the essential purport, the peculiar theme of my work; that I therein call upon the senses themselves to witness to the truth of my analysis and my ideas, and demonstrate *ad oculos, ad tactum, ad gustum,* what I have taught *ad captum* throughout the previous pages. As, namely, the water of Baptism, the wine and bread of the Lord's Supper, taken in their natural power and significance, are and effect infinitely more than in a supernaturalistic, illusionary significance; so the object of religion in general, conceived in the sense of this work, i.e., the anthropological sense, is infinitely more productive and real, both in theory and practice, than when accepted in the sense of theology. For as that which is or is supposed to be imparted in the water, bread, and wine, over and above these natural substances themselves, is something in the imagination only, but in truth, in reality, nothing; so also the object of religion in general, the Divine essence, in distinction from the essence of Nature and Humanity,—that is to say, if its attributes, as understanding, love, etc., are and signify something else than these attributes as they belong to man and Nature,—is only something in the imagination, but in truth and reality nothing. Therefore—this is the moral of the fable—we should not, as is the case in theology and speculative philosophy, make real beings and things into arbitrary signs, vehicles, symbols, or predicates of a distinct, transcendent, absolute, i.e., abstract being; but we should accept and understand them in the significance which they have in themselves, which is identical with their qualities, with those conditions which make them what they are:—thus only do we obtain the key to a *real theory and practice*. I, in fact, put in the place of the barren baptismal water, the beneficent effect of real water. How "watery," how trivial! Yes, indeed, very trivial. But so Marriage, in its times, was a *very trivial truth,* which Luther, on the ground of his natural good sense, maintained in opposition to the seemingly holy illusion of celibacy. But while I thus view water as a real thing, I at the same time intend it as a vehicle, an image, an example, a symbol, of the "unholy" spirit of my work, just as the water of Baptism—the object of my analysis—is at once literal and symbolical water. It is the same with bread and wine. Malignity has hence drawn the conclusion that bathing, eating, and drinking are the *summa summarum,* the positive result of my work. I make no other reply than this: If the whole of religion is contained in the Sacraments, and there are consequently no other religious acts than those which are performed in Baptism and the Lord's Supper; *then* I grant that the entire purport and positive result of my work are bathing, eating, and drinking, since this work is nothing but a faithful, rigid, historico-philosophical analysis of religion—the revelation of religion to itself, the *awakening of religion to self-consciousness.*

I say an *historico-philosophical* analysis, in distinction from a merely *historical* analysis of Christianity. The historical critic—such a one, for example, as Daumer or Ghillany—shows that the Lord's Supper is a rite lineally descended from the ancient cultus of human sacrifice; that once, instead of bread and wine, real human flesh and blood were partaken. I, on the contrary, take as the object of my analysis and reduction only the Christian significance of the rite, that view of it which is *sanctioned* in Christianity, and I proceed on the supposition that only *that significance* which a dogma or institution has in Christianity (of course in ancient Christianity, not in modern), whether it may present itself in other religions or not, is also the *true origin* of that dogma or institution *in so far* as it is Christian. Again, the historical critic, as, for example, Lützelberger, shows that the narratives of the miracles of Christ resolve themselves into contradictions and absurdities, that they are later fabrications, and that consequently Christ was no miracle-worker, nor, in general, that which he is represented to be in the

Bible. I, on the other hand, do not inquire what the real, natural Christ was or may have been in distinction from what he has been made or has become in Supernaturalism; on the contrary, I accept the Christ of religion, but I show that this superhuman being is nothing else than a product and reflex of the supernatural human mind. I do not ask whether this or that, or any miracle *can* happen or not; I only show *what* miracle *is*, and I show it not a priori, but by examples of miracles narrated in the Bible as real events; in doing so, however, I answer or rather preclude the question as to the possibility or reality of necessity of miracle. Thus much concerning the distinction between me and the historical critics who have attacked Christianity. As regards my relation to Strauss and Bruno Bauer, in company with whom I am constantly named, I merely point out there that the distinction between our works is sufficiently indicated by the distinction between their objects, which is implied even in the title-page. Bauer takes for the object of his criticism the evangelical history, i.e., biblical Christianity, or rather biblical theology; Strauss, the System of Christian Doctrine and the Life of Jesus (which may also be included under the title of Christian Doctrine), i.e., dogmatic Christianity, or rather dogmatic theology; I, Christianity in general, i.e., the Christian *religion,* and consequently only Christian philosophy or theology. Hence I take my citations chiefly from men in whom Christianity was not merely a theory or a dogma, not merely theology, but religion. My principal theme is Christianity, is Religion, as it is the *immediate object,* the *immediate nature,* of man. Erudition and philosophy are to me only the *means* by which I bring to light the treasure hid in man.

I must further mention that the circulation which my work has had amongst the public at large was neither desired nor expected by me. It is true that I have always taken as the standard of the mode of teaching and writing, not the abstract, particular, professional philosopher, but universal man, that I have regarded *man* as the criterion of truth, and not this or that founder of a system, and have from the first placed the highest excellence of the philosopher in this, that he abstains, both as a man and as an author, from the ostentation of philosophy, i.e., that he is a philosopher only in reality, not formally, that he is a quiet philosopher, not a loud and still less a brawling one. Hence, in all my works, as well as in the present one, I have made the utmost clearness, simplicity, and definiteness a law to myself, so that they may be understood, at least in the main, by every cultivated and thinking man. But notwithstanding this, my work can be appreciated and fully understood only by the scholar, that is to say, by the scholar who loves truth, who is capable of forming a judgment, who is above the notions and prejudices of the learned and unlearned vulgar; for although a thoroughly independent production, it has yet its necessary logical basis in history. I very frequently refer to this or that historical phenomenon without expressly designating it, thinking this superfluous; and such references can be understood by the scholar alone. Thus, for example, in the very first chapter, where I develop the necessary consequences of the standpoint of Feeling, I allude to Jacobi and Schleiermacher; in the second chapter I allude chiefly to Kantism, Skepticism, Theism, Materialism, and Pantheism; in the chapter on the "Standpoint of Religion," where I discuss the contradictions between the religious or theological and the physical or natural-philosophical view of Nature, I refer to philosophy in the age of orthodoxy, and especially to the philosophy of Descartes and Leibniz, in which this contradiction presents itself in a peculiarly characteristic manner. The reader, therefore, who is unacquainted with the historical facts and ideas presupposed in my work, will fail to perceive on what my arguments and ideas hinge; no wonder if my positions often appear to him baseless, however firm the footing on which they stand. It is true that the subject of my work is of universal human interest; moreover, its fundamental ideas, though not in the form in which they are here expressed, or in which they could be expressed under existing circumstances, will one day become the common property of mankind: for nothing is opposed to them in the present day but empty, powerless illusions and prejudices in contradiction with the true nature of man. But in considering this subject in the first instance, I was under the necessity of treating it as a matter of science, of philosophy; and in rectifying the aberrations of Religion, Theology, and Speculation, I was naturally obliged to use their expressions, and even to appear to speculate, or—which is the same thing—to turn theologian myself, while I nevertheless only analyze speculation i.e., reduce theology to anthropology. My work as I said before, contains, and applies in the concrete, the principle of a new philosophy suited—not to the schools, but—to man. Yes, it contains that principle, but only by *evolving* it out of the very core of religion; hence, be it said in passing, the new philosophy can no longer, like the old Catholic and modern Protestant scholasticism, fall into the temptation to prove its agreement with religion by its agreement with Christian dogmas; on the contrary, being evolved from the nature of religion, it has in itself the true essence of religion,—is, in its very quality as a philosophy, a religion also. But a work which considers ideas in their genesis and explains and demonstrates them in strict sequence, is, by the very form which this purpose imposes upon it, unsuited to popular reading.

Lastly, as a supplement to this work with regard to many apparently unvindicated positions, I refer to my articles in the *Deutsches Jahrbuch,* January and February 1842, to my critiques and *Charakteristiken des modernen Afterchristenthums,* in previous numbers of the same periodical, and to my earlier works, especially the following: *P. Bayle. Ein Beitrag zur Geschichte der Philosophie und Menschheit,* Ansbach, 1838, and *Philosophie und Christenthum,* Mannheim, 1839. In these works I have sketched, with a few sharp touches, the historical solution of Christianity, and have shown that Christianity has in fact long vanished, not only from the reason but from the life of mankind, that it is nothing more than a *fixed idea,* in flagrant contradiction with our fire and life assurance companies, our railroads and steam-carriages, our picture and sculpture galleries, our military and industrial schools, our theatres and scientific museums.

Bruckberg, February 14, 1843.

Translated by George Eliot

Preliminary Theses on
the Reform of Philosophy

The secret of *theology* is *anthropology,* but *theology* itself is the secret of *speculative philosophy,* which thus turns out to be *speculative* theology. As such, it distinguishes itself from *ordinary* theology by the fact that it places the divine being back into this world—ordinary theology projects it into the beyond out of fear and ignorance; in contrast to ordinary theology, it *actualizes, determines,* and *realizes* the Divine Being.

*   *   *

Spinoza is actually the initiator of modern speculative philosophy; *Schelling,* its restorer; and *Hegel,* its consummator.

*   *   *

"Pantheism" is the *necessary consequence* of theology (or of theism); it is *consequent* theology. *"Atheism"* is the *necessary consequence* of *"Pantheism"*; it is consequent *"Pantheism."**

*   *   *

Christianity is the *contradiction* of *polytheism* and *monotheism.*

*   *   *

Pantheism is *monotheism* with the *predicate* of polytheism; i.e., pantheism makes the independent beings of polytheism into predicates or attributes of the one independent being. Thus Spinoza, taking thought as the sum of all thinking things and matter as the sum of all extended things, turned them into the attributes

---

*These *theological* designations are being used here in the sense of *trivial* nicknames.

of substance; i.e., of God. God is a thinking thing; God is an extended thing.

* * *

The philosophy of identity distinguished itself from that of Spinoza only by the fact that it infused into Spinoza's substance—this dead and phlegmatic thing—the Spirit of idealism. Hegel, in particular, turned self-activity, the power of self-differentiation, and self-consciousness into the attribute of the substance. The paradoxical statement of Hegel—"the consciousness of God is God's self-consciousness"—rests on *the same foundation* as the paradoxical statement of Spinoza—"the extension or matter is an attribute of substance"—and has no other meaning than self-consciousness is an attribute of the substance or of God; God is Ego. The consciousness that the theist ascribes to God in contradistinction to the real consciousness is only an idea without reality. But the statement of Spinoza—"matter is the *attribute* of substance"—says nothing more than this, that matter is substantial divine essence. Similarly, the statement of Hegel says nothing more than consciousness is divine essence.

* * *

The method of the reformative critique of *speculative philosophy* as such does not differ from that already used in the *Philosophy of Religion*. We need only turn the *predicate* into the *subject* and thus as *subject* into *object* and *principle*—that is, only *reverse* speculative philosophy. In this way, we have the concealed, pure, and untarnished truth.

* * *

"Atheism" is reversed "Pantheism."

* * *

Pantheism is the *negation of theology from the standpoint of theology.*

* * *

Just as according to Spinoza (*Ethics,* Part I. Definition 3 and Proposition 10) the attribute or the predicate of substance is the substance itself, so according to Hegel the *predicate* of the Absolute—that is, of the subject in general—is the *subject itself.* The Absolute, according to Hegel, is Being, Essence, or Concept (Spirit or Self-consciousness). The Absolute, conceived only as being, however, *nothing other than* being; the Absolute, in so far as it is thought of under this or that determination or category, loses itself *completely* in this category or determination, so that apart from it, it is a mere name. But, nevertheless, the Absolute *as subject* still constitutes that which lies at the base; the *true* subject or *that* through which the Absolute is not just a name but is *something*, is *determination*, and still has the meaning of a mere predicate, exactly like the predicate in Spinoza.

* * *

The Absolute or the infinite of speculative philosophy, looked at psychologically, is nothing other than that which is not determined, the indeterminate; namely, the abstraction from all that is determinate and posited as a being that is on the one hand distinct from this abstraction and on the other hand identified with it. Historically considered, it is, however, nothing other than the old theological-metaphysical being or un-being which is *not* finite, *not* human, *not* material, *not* determinate, and *not* created—the world-antecedent nothingness posited as *Deed*.

* * *

The Hegelian Logic is *theology* that has been turned into *reason* and *presence;* it is theology turned into *logic. Just as the Divine Being of theology is the ideal or abstract embodiment of all realities, i.e., of all determinations, of all finitudes, so too, it is the same with the Logic.* All that exists on earth finds itself back in the heaven of theology; likewise, *all that is in nature reappears in the heaven of the divine* Logic—quality, quantity, measure, essence, chemism, mechanism, and organism. In theology, we have everything *twice over,* first in abstracto and then in concreto; similarly, we have everything *twice over* in the Hegelian philosophy—as the object of logic, and then, again, as the object of the philosophy of nature and of the Spirit.

* * *

The essence of theology is the *transcendent;* i.e., the essence of man posited outside man. The essence of Hegel's *Logic* is *transcendent* thought; i.e., the thought of man *posited outside man.*

* * *

Just as theology *dichotomizes* and *externalizes* man in order to then identify his externalized essence with him, so similarly Hegel *pluralizes* and splits up the *simple, self-identical essence* of nature and man in order later to bring together forcibly what he has separated forcibly.

*   *   *

Metaphysics or logic is a *real* and *immanent science* only when it is *not separated* from the so-called *subjective spirit*. Metaphysics is *esoteric psychology*. What arbitrariness, what an act of violence it is to regard quality on its own account or sensation on its own account, to cleave both apart into two sciences, as if quality could be anything without sensation, and sensation anything without quality.

*   *   *

The *Absolute Spirit* of Hegel is none other than *abstract* spirit, i.e., *finite* spirit that has been separated from itself; just as the infinite being of theology is none other than the abstract *finite being*.

*   *   *

The Absolute Spirit according to Hegel reveals or realizes itself in art, religion, and philosophy. This simply means that the *spirit of art, religion, and philosophy is the Absolute Spirit*. But one cannot separate art and religion from human feeling, imagination, and perception, nor can one separate philosophy from thought. In short, one cannot separate the Absolute Spirit from the Subjective Spirit, or from the essence of man, without being thrown back to the standpoint of theology, without being deluded into regarding the Absolute Spirit as being *another* spirit that is distinct from the being of man, i.e., without making us accept the illusion of a ghost of ourselves existing outside ourselves.

*   *   *

The Absolute Spirit is the "deceased spirit" of theology that, as a *specter*, haunts the Hegelian philosophy.

*   *   *

Theology is *belief in ghosts*. Ordinary theology has its ghosts in the sensuous imagination, but *speculative* theology has its ghosts in non-sensuous abstraction.

*   *   *

To abstract means to posit the *essence* of nature *outside nature,* the *essence* of man *outside man,* the *essence* of thought *outside the act of thinking.* The Hegelian philosophy has alienated man *from himself* in so far as its whole system is based on these acts of abstraction. Although it again identifies what it separates, it does so only in a *separate* and *mediated* way. The Hegelian philosophy lacks *immediate unity, immediate certainty, immediate truth.*

* * *

The direct, crystal-clear, and undeceptive identification of the essence of man—which has been taken away from him through abstraction—*with* man, cannot be effected through a positive approach; it can only be derived from the Hegelian philosophy as its *negation*; it can only be *apprehended* at all if it is apprehended *as the total negation* of speculative philosophy, although it is the *truth* of this philosophy. It is true that everything is contained in Hegel's philosophy, but always together with its *negation,* its *opposite.*

* * *

The *obvious* proof that the Absolute Spirit is the so-called finite, subjective spirit, or, in other words, that the latter cannot be separated from the former, is *art.* Art is born out of the feeling that the life of this world is the true life, that the *finite* is the *infinite*; it is born out of enthusiasm for a *definite* and *real* being as the *highest* and the *Divine* Being. *Christian monotheism does not* contain *within itself the principle* of an *artistic* and *scientific* culture. Only *polytheism,* so-called *idolatry,* is the *source of art and science.*

The Greeks raised themselves to the perfection of the plastic arts only through the fact that to them the human form was *absolutely* and *unhesitatingly* the highest form—the form of divinity. The Christians were able to create poetry only at the point where they *practically negated Christian theology* and worshiped the *female principle* as the *divine* principle. As artists and poets, the Christians found themselves in contradiction to the essence of their religion as they conceived it and as it constituted the *object* of their consciousness. Petrarch *regretted,* from the point of view of religion, the poems in which he had deified his Laura. Why do the Christians not have, as do the pagans, works of art adequate to their religious ideas? Why do they not have a fully satisfying image of Christ? Because the religious art of the Christians founders on the fatal contradiction between their *consciousness* and *truth*. The essence of the Christian religion is, in truth, human essence; in the consciousness of the Christians it is, however, a *different*, a *non*human essence. Christ is supposed to be both man and not man; he is an ambiguity. Art, however, can represent only the true and the *unequivocal*.

*   *   *

The decisive consciousness—a consciousness that has become flesh and blood—that the human is the divine and the finite the infinite is the source of a new poetry and art which will exceed all previous poetry and art in energy, depth, and fire. The belief in the beyond is an absolutely unpoetical belief. Pain is the source of poetry. Only he who experiences the loss of a finite being as an infinite loss is capable of burning with lyrical fire. Only the painful stimulus of the memory of that which is *no more* is the first artist, the first idealist in man. But belief in the beyond turns every pain into mere appearance, into untruth.

*   *   *

A philosophy that derives the finite from the infinite and the determinate from the indeterminate *can never find its way to a true positing of the finite and the determinate*. That the finite is derived from the infinite means that the infinite, or the indeterminate, is determined, and hence *negated*; it is admitted that the infinite is *nothing without determination—that is, without finiteness*—and that it is the *finite* posited as the *reality* of the infinite. However, the negative unbeing, this nuisance of the absolute, still remains the underlying principle; the posited finiteness has, therefore, to be abolished again and again. The *finite* is the *negation* of the infinite, and, again, the *infinite* is the *negation* of the finite. The philosophy of the absolute is a *contradiction*.

*   *   *

Just as in theology, *man* is the *truth* and *reality* of God—for all predicates that realize God as God, or make God into a *real* being, predicates such as power, wisdom, goodness, love, even infinity and personality, which have as their condition the *distinction* from the finite, are posited first *in* and *with* man—likewise in speculative philosophy the *finite* is the *truth* of the infinite.

*   *   *

The truth of the finite is expressed by Absolute Philosophy only in an *indirect, inverted* way. If the infinite *has any meaning,* if it has *truth* and *reality* only when it is *determinate*—i.e., when it is posited not as infinite but as *finite*—then indeed the *finite* is the *infinite* in truth.

* * *

The task of true philosophy is not to cognize the infinite as the finite, but as the *non*finite; i.e., as the infinite. In other words, not to posit the finite in the infinite, but to posit the infinite in the finite.

* * *

The beginning of philosophy is neither God nor the Absolute, nor is it as being the *predicate* of the Absolute or of the Idea; rather the beginning of philosophy is the finite,* the determinate, and the *real.* The infinite cannot possibly be conceived without the finite. Can you think of quality and define it without thinking of a definite quality?

* * *

It is, therefore, not the indeterminate, but the determinate that comes first, since *determinate* quality is nothing but *real* quality; real quality precedes the quality which is imagined.

* * *

The *subjective* origin and course of philosophy is also its *objective* course and origin. Before you think quality, you already feel quality. *Suffering* precedes thinking.

* * *

The infinite is the *true essence* of the finite—the true finite. The *true* speculation or philosophy is nothing but what is *truly and universally empirical.*

* * *

The infinite in religion and philosophy is, and never was anything different from, a finite or a determinate of some kind, but *mys-*

---

*I am using the term *finite* throughout in the sense of Absolute Philosophy to which, in so far as it occupies the standpoint of the Absolute, the real appears as unreal and worthless, because it holds the unreal and the indeterminate to be the real. However, the finite and the worthless appear to it also as real when they are not viewed from the standpoint of the Absolute. This contradiction is conspicuous in the early philosophy of Schelling, but it also lies at the base of Hegelian philosophy.

tified; that is, it was a finite or a determinate with the *postulate* of being nothing finite and nothing determinate. Speculative philosophy has made itself guilty of the *same error* as theology; it has made the determinations of reality or finiteness into the determinations and predicates of the infinite through the *negation* of determinateness.

* * *

Honesty and uprightness are useful for all things—and that also applies to philosophy. Philosophy is, however, only honest and upright when it concedes the finiteness of its speculative infinity—when it concedes, e.g., that the mystery of nature in God is nothing but the mystery of human nature, that the *night* which it posits in God in order to produce out of it the light of consciousness is nothing but its own *dark, instinctual* feeling of the reality and indispensability of matter.

* * *

The course taken so far by all speculative philosophy from the abstract to the concrete, from the ideal to the real, is an inverted one. This way never leads one to the *true* and *objective reality,* but only to the *realization of one's own abstractions* and, precisely because of this, never to the true *freedom* of the Spirit; for *only the perception of things and beings in their objective reality can make man free and devoid of all prejudices.* The transition from the ideal to the real has its place only in practical philosophy.

* * *

Philosophy is the knowledge of *what* is. To think and know things and being *as* they are—that is the highest law, the highest task of philosophy.

* * *

To speak of what is *as* it is, or in other words, to speak *truly* of the true, *appears superficial;* to speak of what is *as it is not,* or in other words, to speak of the true in an *untrue, inverted* way, *appears* to be *profound.*

* * *

Truthfulness, simplicity, and *determinateness* are the formal characteristics of real philosophy.

* * *

Being, with which philosophy begins, cannot be separated from consciousness any more than consciousness can be separated from being. Just as the reality of feeling is quality and, inversely, feeling the reality of quality, so also is being the reality of consciousness, but also equally consciousness the reality of being—only consciousness is *real* being. The *real* unity of spirit and nature is consciousness alone.

* * *

All the determinations, forms, categories, or however one would like to put it that speculative philosophy has cast off from the Absolute and banished into the realm of the finite and the empirical contain within themselves precisely the *true essence* of the finite; i.e., the true infinite—the *true and ultimate mysteries* of philosophy.

* * *

Space and *time* are the forms of existence of all beings. Only existence in space and time is *existence*. The negation of space and time is always only the *negation of their limits, not of their being*. A non-temporal feeling, a non-temporal will, a non-temporal thought, a non-temporal being are all absurdities. He who is absolutely timeless has also no time, no urge to will and to think.

* * *

The negation of space and time in metaphysics, in the being of things, has the most pernicious practical consequences. Only he who *everywhere* occupies the standpoint of space and time has also *good sense* and *practical understanding* in life. Space and time are the primary criteria of praxis. A people that banishes time from its metaphysics and deifies the eternal—i.e., *abstract* and time-detached existence—excludes, in consequence, time from its politics, and worships the anti-historical principle of stability which is against right and reason.

* * *

Speculative philosophy has turned into a form, or into an attribute of the Absolute, the *development* which it has *detached from time*. This detachment of development from time is, however, truly a masterpiece of *speculative arbitrariness* and the conclusive proof of the fact that the speculative philosophers have done with their Absolute exactly what theologians have done with their God who possesses all emotions of men *without having emotion,* loves *without love,* and is angry *without anger.* Development without time amounts to development without development. The proposition that the Absolute Being unfolds itself is, moreover, true and rational only the *other way round.* It must, therefore, be formulated thus: Only a being that develops and unfolds itself in time is an absolute; i.e., a *true* and *actual* being.

*   *   *

Space and time are the forms of manifestation of the real infinite.

*   *   *

Where there is *no limit, no time,* and *no need, there is also no quality, no energy, no spirit, no fire,* and *no love.* Only that being which *suffers from need (notleidend)* is the *necessary (notwendig)* being. Existence *without need* is *superfluous* existence. Whatever is absolutely free from needs has no need of existence. Whether it is or is not is indifferent—indifferent to itself and indifferent to others. A being without need is a being without *ground.* Only that which can *suffer* deserves to exist. Only that being which *abounds in pain is the divine being.* A being *without suffering* is a being *without* being. A being without suffering is nothing but a being *without sensuousness, without matter.*

*   *   *

A philosophy that has no *passive principle* in it, a philosophy that speculates over existence *without time and duration,* over quality *without feeling,* over being *without being,* over life *without life*— i.e., without flesh and blood—such a philosophy, like the philosophy of the absolute, above all, has, due *necessarily* to its *one-sidedness,* the empirical as its opposite. Spinoza has no doubt made matter into an attribute of substance, but he does not take matter to be a principle of suffering. For Spinoza, matter is the attribute of substance precisely because it *does not* suffer, because it is unique, indivisible, and infinite, because it has the same determinations as its *opposite* attribute of thought; in short, because it is an *abstract* matter, matter *without matter,* just as essence in Hegel's *Logic* is the essence of nature and man, but *without essence, without nature,* and *without man.*

*   *   *

The philosopher must take into the *text* of philosophy that aspect of man which *does not* philosophize, but, rather, is *opposed* to philosophy and abstract thinking, or in other words, that which in Hegel has been reduced to a mere *footnote*. Only thus can philosophy become a *universal, free from contradictions, irrefutable,* and *irresistible power*. Philosophy has to begin then not so much *with itself* as with its own *antithesis*; i.e., with *non-philosophy*. This being which is distinguished from thought, which is unphilosophical, this absolutely *anti-scholastic* being in us is the principle of *sensualism*.

* * *

The essential tools and organs of philosophy are: the *head,* which is the source of activity, freedom, metaphysical infinity, and idealism, and the *heart,* which is the source of suffering, finiteness, needs, and sensualism. Or theoretically expressed: thought and sense perception, for *thought* is the *need* of the *head,* and sense perception, the *sense,* is the *need* of the *heart.* Thought is the principle of the schools; i.e., of the system; perception, the *principle of life.* When perceiving through the senses, I am *determined* by the object; when thinking, it is I who *determines* the object; in thought I am *ego,* in perception, *non-ego.* Only out of the *negation* of thought, out of *being determined* by the object, out of *passion,* out of the source of all pleasure and need is born true, objective thought, and true, objective philosophy. Perception gives being that is *immediately identical with existence;* thought gives being that is *mediated* through the *distinction* and *separation* from existence. *Life* and *truth* are, therefore, only to be found where essence is united with existence, thought with sense-perception, activity with passivity, and the *scholastic ponderousness of German metaphysics* with the *antischolastic, sanguine principle of French sensualism and materialism.*

* * *

What applies to philosophy, applies to the philosopher, and vice versa; the qualities of the philosopher, i.e., the *subjective conditions* and *elements* of philosophy, are also their *objective* conditions and elements. The true philosopher who is identical with life and man must be of Franco-German parentage. Do not be frightened, you chaste Germans, by this mixture. The *Acta Philosophorum* already spelled out this idea in the year 1716. "If we compare the *Germans* and the *French* with each other and ascertain that the latter have more agility in their temperament, and the former more weightiness, so one could justly say that the *temperamentum gallicogermanicum* is best suited for philosophy, or a child who had a *French* father and a *German* mother would (*caeteris paribus*) be endowed with a good *ingenium philosophicum*." Quite right; only we must make the mother French and the father German. The *heart*—the feminine principle, the *sense* of the finite, and the seat of materialism—is of *French disposition*; the *head*—the masculine principle and the seat of idealism—of German. The heart makes revolutions, the head reforms; the head brings things into existence, the heart sets them in *motion*. But only where there is movement, upsurge, passion, blood, and sensuousness is there also *spirit*. It was the *esprit* of a Leibniz, his sanguine *materialistic*-idealistic principle, that first pulled the Germans out of their philosophical pedantry and scholasticism.

* * *

In philosophy, the heart was hitherto regarded as the breastwork of theology. However, it is precisely the heart that is the positively *anti-theological* principle; in terms of theology it is the unbelieving, atheistic principle in man. For it believes in *nothing* except *itself*; it believes only in the unshakable, divine, and absolute reality of its *own* being. But the *head*, which *does not* understand the heart, transforms—since it is its business to separate and differentiate subject and object—the very being of the heart into a being that is *distinguished* from the heart; that is, *objective* and *external*. To be sure, the heart needs *another* being, but only one that is its own kind—i.e., not distinguished from the heart—and one that does not contradict the heart. Theology *denies* the *truth* of the *heart* or the *truth* of the *religious emotion*. The religious emotion, the heart, says, for example: God suffers. Theology, however, says: God does not suffer. That is, the heart denies the difference between God and man, but theology affirms it.

* * *

Theism rests on the *dichotomy* of the *head* and the *heart*; pantheism is the resolution of this dichotomy, but *within* dichotomy, for it makes the Divine Being immanent only as a *transcendent* being; anthropotheism is *without such dichotomy*. Anthropotheism is the heart raised to intellect; it speaks through the head in terms of the intellect only what the heart speaks in its own way. Religion is only emotion, feeling, heart, and love; i.e., the negation and *dissolution of God* in man. The new philosophy as the *negation of theology*, which denies the truth of religious emotion, is therefore a positing of religion. Anthropotheism is religion conscious of itself; it is religion that *understands itself*. Theology, on the other hand *negates* religion *under the appearance of positing* it.

* * *

Schelling and *Hegel* are opposites. Hegel represents the masculine principle of self-autonomy and self-activity; in short, the idealist principle. Schelling represents the feminine principle of receptivity and impressionability; in short, the materialist principle—he first imbibed Fichte, then Plato and Spinoza, and finally Böhme. Hegel lacks sense perception, Schelling the power of thought and the power to determine. Schelling is a thinker only of the *general*; when it comes to tackling the particular and the determinate, he lapses into the somnambulism of imagination. In Schelling, rationalism is only appearance; irrationalism the *truth*. The extent of Hegel's achievement is only an *abstract,* irrational principle; that of Schelling only a *mystical* and *imaginary* existence and reality that are opposed to a rational principle. Hegel compensates his lack of realism through robustly sensuous words; Schelling through fine words—Hegel expressed the uncommon in a common way, whereas Schelling expressed the common in an uncommon way. Hegel turns *things* into *mere thoughts,* whereas Schelling turns mere thoughts—for example, the aseity of God—into *things*. Hegel deludes thinking heads, Schelling only *unthinking* ones. Hegel turns unreason into reason; Schelling, conversely, reason into unreason. Schelling's is a philosophy in the element of dream; Hegel's in that of the concept. Schelling negates abstract thought through *fantasy*; Hegel through *abstract thought*. Hegel, as the *self-negation* of negative thought, or as the culmination of the old philosophy, is the negative beginning of the new philosophy. Schelling's is old philosophy *with the illusion and pretense* of being the new realistic philosophy.

* * *

The Hegelian philosophy is the resolution of the contradiction between thinking and being as, in particular, expressed by Kant; but, *nota bene,* the resolution of the contradiction still remains *within the contradiction*; i.e., within *one* element—*thought*. *Thought* is *being* in Hegel; i.e., *thought* is the *subject, being* the *predicate*. The *Logic* is thought in the element of thought, or thought thinking itself; it is thought as *subject without predicate,* or thought that is *subject* and *at the same time its own predicate*. But thought in the element of thought is still abstract; it therefore has to realize and externalize itself. This realized and externalized thought is nature, the real in general—being. But what is the truly real in this real? Thought! That is why it soon casts off from itself the predicate of reality in order to constitute a state without predicates as its true being. But this is exactly why Hegel remained unable to arrive at *being as being*; i.e., at free, independent being that is felicitous in itself. Hegel conceived objects only as the *predicates* of thought thinking itself. The admitted contradiction between the existing and conceived religion in Hegel's philosophy of religion is possible only because here, too, as elsewhere, thought is turned into the subject, but the object; i.e., religion, only into a mere *predicate* of thought.

* * *

He who clings to Hegelian philosophy also clings to theology. The Hegelian doctrine that nature or reality is posited by the Idea, is the *rational expression* of the theological doctrine that nature, the material being, has been created by God, the non-material; i.e., abstract, being. At the end of the *Logic,* the absolute Idea even comes to a nebulous "decision" to document with its own hands its descent from the theological heaven.

* * *

The Hegelian philosophy is the last refuge and the last rational mainstay of theology. Just as once the Catholic theologians became *de facto* Aristotelians in order to combat Protestantism, so now the Protestant theologians must *de jure* become *Hegelians* in order to combat "atheism."

* * *

The true relationship of thought to being is this only: *Being* is the *subject, thought* the *predicate*. Thought comes from being, but being does not come from thought. Being comes from itself and is through itself; being is given only through being; being has its ground within itself because only being is meaning, reason, necessity, and truth; in short, it is all in all. Being *is* because not-being is no being; i.e., nothing or *nonsense.*

*   *   *

The essence of being *as being* is the essence of nature. The temporal genesis applies only to the forms, not to the essence of nature.

*   *   *

Being is derived from thought only where the *true unity* of thought and being is *rent asunder,* where one, through abstraction, first takes away from being its *soul* and *essence* and then finds in this abstracted essence the *meaning* and *ground* of being thus emptied. Similarly, the world is, and must be, derived from God where one arbitrarily separates the essence of the world from the world.

*   *   *

He who directs his speculation toward finding a particular realistic principle of philosophy, like the so-called positive philosophers,

> is like an *animal,* on a barren *heath*
> driven by an *evil spirit* in a circle round and round
> and all about lies *beautiful, grazing ground.*

This beautiful, green grazing ground is nature and man, for both belong together. Behold nature, behold man! Here, before your eyes, are the mysteries of philosophy.

*   *   *

Nature is *being* that is *not distinguished* from *existence*; man is *being* that *distinguishes itself* from existence. The being that does not distinguish is the ground of the being that distinguishes; nature is, therefore, the ground of man.

*   *   *

The new and the only positive philosophy is the *negation of all scholastic philosophy,* although it contains the truth of the latter; it is the negation of philosophy as an *abstract, particular,* i.e., *scholastic,* quality; it has no *shibboleth,* no *particular* language, no *particular* name, no *particular* principle; it is *the thinking man* himself, i.e., man who *is* and *knows himself* as the self-conscious essence of nature, history, states, and religion; it is man who *is* and *knows himself* to be the *real* (not imaginary), absolute identity of all oppositions and contradictions, of all active and passive mental and sensuous, political and social, qualities; it is man who *knows* that the *pantheistic* being, which the speculative philosophers or rather theologians have *separated* from and objectified as an abstract being, is nothing but *his own indeterminate* being, but one that is capable of *infinite determinations*.

* * *

The new philosophy is the *negation of rationalism* as much as *mysticism*; of *pantheism* as much as *personalism*; of *atheism* as much as *theism*; it is the *unity of all these antithetical truths as an absolutely independent and pure truth.*

* * *

The new philosophy has already expressed itself as the philosophy of religion both positively and negatively in equal measure. One need only make the conclusions of its analysis into premises in order to recognize the principles of a positive philosophy. The new philosophy, however, does not court the favor of the public. Certain of itself, it scorns to *appear* as what it is; but precisely for that reason, it must be for our age—in whose most essential interests, appearance passes for essence, illusion for reality, and the name for the thing itself—that which it *is not*. That is the way opposites complement each other! Where *nothing* stands for *something* and *lies* for *truth*, it is only consistent that *something* must stand for *nothing* and *truth* for lies. And in a situation in which one undertakes the outrageous and unprecedented attempt to base philosophy exclusively on the *favor* and *opinion* of the *newspaper public*— and ironically at the very moment when philosophy is involved in a decisive and universal act of *self-disillusion*—in such a situation one can only seek, in an honest and Christian fashion, to *refute* philosophical works by publicly *slandering* them in the *Augsburger Allgemeine Zeitung*. O, how honorable and moral, indeed, are public affairs in Germany!

* * *

A new principle always makes its appearance with a new name; i.e., it elevates a name from a low, unprivileged station to the princely station—transforms it into the designation for the highest. If one were to *translate* the name of the new philosophy—the name "man"—by "*self-consciousness*," one would interpret the new philosophy in terms of the old and hence return it to the old standpoint; for the self-consciousness of the old philosophy *as divorced from man* is an *abstraction without reality.* Man *is* self-consciousness.

* * *

According to language, the name "man" is indeed a particular one, but according to truth it is the name of all names. The predicate "many-named" duly belongs to man; whatever man names or expresses, he always expresses his own essence. Language is, therefore, the criterion of judging how high or low the degree of the cultural development of mankind is. The name "God" is but the name for what man regards as the highest force and the highest being, i.e., for the highest feeling and the highest thought.

* * *

The word "man" commonly means only man with his needs, sensations, and opinions; it means man as person in distinction from man as mind; above all it means man as distinguished from his general public qualities on the whole, or man as distinguished from, say, the artist, thinker, writer, judge, etc.—as if it were not a *characteristic* and *essential quality of man* to be a judge and so on; as if man were *outside his own being* in art, science etc. Speculative philosophy has, theoretically, fixed the separation of essential qualities of man from man, thus deifying purely abstract qualities as independent beings. The Hegelian *Philosophy of Right* (§ 190), for example, has this: "In right, what we have before us is the *person*; in the sphere of morality, the *subject*; in the family, the family-member; in civil society as a whole, the burgher (as bourgeois). Here at the standpoint of needs what we have before us is the composite *idea* which we call *man*. It is thus here for the first time, and indeed properly only here, that we speak of man in this sense." In *this* sense: We speak in truth only and always of *one* and the *same* being; i.e., of man, even if we do so in a different sense and in a different quality, when we speak of the burgher, the subject, the family member, and the person.

* * *

All speculation concerning right, will, freedom, and personality without regard to man; i.e., outside of or even above man, is speculation *without unity, necessity, substance, ground,* and *reality.* Man is the existence of freedom, the existence of personality, and the existence of right. Only man is the *ground and base* of the Fichtean Ego, the *ground and base* of the Leibnizian Monad, and the *ground and base* of the Absolute.

*   *   *

All science must be grounded in *nature*. A doctrine remains a *hypothesis* as long as it has not found its *natural basis*. This is true particularly of the *doctrine of freedom*. Only the new philosophy will succeed in *naturalizing* freedom which was hitherto an *antihypothesis*, a *supernatural hypothesis*.

*   *   *

Philosophy must again unite itself with natural science, and *natural science with philosophy.* This unity, based on mutual need, on inner necessity, will be more durable, more felicitous and more fruitful than the previous *mésalliance* between philosophy and theology.

*   *   *

Man is the fundamental being of the state. The state is the realized, developed, and explicit totality of the human being. In the state, the essential qualities or activities of man are realized in particular estates (Ständen), but in the person of the head of state they are again resolved into an identity. It is the function of the head of state to represent all estates without distinction; to him, they are all equally necessary and equally entitled before him. The head of state represents universal man.

*   *   *

The Christian religion has linked the name of man with the name of God in the one name "God-man." It has, in other words, raised the name of man to an attribute of the highest being. The new philosophy has, in keeping with the truth, turned this attribute into substance, the predicate into the subject. The new philosophy is *the idea realized—the truth* of Christianity. But precisely because it contains within itself the *essence* of Christianity, it abandons the *name* of Christianity. Christianity has expressed the truth only *in contradiction to the truth*. The pure and unadulterated truth without contradiction is a *new truth*—a *new, autonomous deed* of mankind.

Translated by Zawar Hanfi

Principles of the Philosophy of the Future

1.

The task of the modern era was the realization and humanization of God—the transformation and dissolution of theology into anthropology.

*   *   *

32.

Taken in its reality or regarded as *real*, the real is the object of the senses—the *sensuous*. Truth, reality, and sensuousness are one and the same thing. Only a sensuous being is a *true* and *real* being. Only through the senses is an object given *in the true sense*, not through thought *for itself*. The object given by and identical with ideation is merely thought.

An object, i.e., a real object, is given to me only if a being is given to me in a way that it affects me, only if my own activity—when I proceed from the standpoint of thought—experiences the activity of another being as a *limit* or boundary to itself. The concept of the object is originally nothing else but the concept of another *I*—everything appears to man in childhood as a freely and arbitrarily acting being—which means that in principle the concept of the *object* is mediated through the concept of You, the *objective ego*. To use the language of Fichte, an object or an alter ego is given not to the ego, but to the non-ego in me; for only where I am transformed from an ego into a You—that is, where I am passive—does the idea of an activity *existing outside myself*, the idea of objectivity, really originate. But it is only through the senses that the ego is also non-ego.

A question characteristic of earlier abstract philosophy is the following: How can different independent entities or substances act upon one another, for example, the body upon the soul or ego? In so far as this question was an abstraction from sensuousness, in so far as the supposedly interacting substances were abstract entities, purely intellectual creatures, philosophy was unable to resolve it. The mystery of their interaction can be solved only by sensuousness. Only sensuous beings act upon one another. I am I—for myself—and at the same time You—for others. But I am You only in so far as I am a sensuous being. But the abstract intellect isolates being-for-itself as substance, ego, or God; it can, therefore, only arbitrarily connect being-for-others with being-for-self, for the necessity for this connection is sensuousness alone. But then it is precisely sensuousness from which the abstract intellect abstracts. What I think in isolation from sensuousness is what I think without and outside all connections. Hence the question: How can I think the unconnected to be at the same time connected?

33.

The new philosophy looks upon *being*—being as given to us not only as thinking, but also as really existing being—*as the object of being,* as *its own* object. Being as the object of being—and *this* alone is truly, and deserves the name of, being—is sensuous being; that is, the being involved in sense perception, feeling, and love. Or in other words, being is a *secret* underlying sense perception, feeling, and love.

Only in feeling and love has the demonstrative *this*—this person, this thing, that is, the particular—absolute value; only then is the *finite infinite:* In this and this alone does the infinite depth, divinity, and truth of love consist. In love alone resides the truth and reality of the God who counts the hairs on your head. The Christian God himself is only an abstraction from human love and an image of it. And since the demonstrative *this* owes its absolute value to love alone, it is only in love—not in abstract thought—that the secret of being is revealed. Love is passion, and passion alone is the distinctive mark of existence. Only that which is an object of passion, exists—whether as reality or possibility. Abstract thought, which is devoid of feeling and passion, abolishes *the distinction between being and nonbeing;* nonexistent for thought, this distinction is a reality for love. To love is nothing else than to become aware of this distinction. It is a matter of complete indifference to someone who loves nothing whether something exists or not, and be that what it may. But just as being as distinguished from nonbeing is given to me through love or feeling in general, so is everything else that is other than me given to me through love. Pain is a loud protest against identifying the subjective with the objective. The pain of love means that what is in the mind is not given in reality, or in other words, the subjective is here the objective, the concept itself the object. But this is precisely what ought not to be, what is a contradiction, an untruth, a misfortune—hence, the desire for that true state of affairs in which the subjective and the objective are not identical. Even physical pain clearly expresses this distinction. The pain of hunger means that there is nothing objective inside the stomach, that the stomach is, so to speak, its own object, that its empty walls grind against each other instead of grinding some content. Human feelings have, therefore, no empirical or anthropological significance in the sense of the old transcendental philosophy; they have, rather, an ontological and metaphysical significance: Feelings, everyday feelings, contain the deepest and highest truths. Thus, for example, love is the true *ontological* demonstration of the existence of objects apart from our head: There is no other proof of being except love or feeling in general. Only that whose *being brings you joy* and whose *not-being, pain,* has existence. The difference between subject and object, being and nonbeing is as *happy* a difference as it is *painful.*

34.

The new philosophy bases itself on the *truth of love,* on the *truth of feeling.* In love, in feeling in general, *every human being confesses to the truth of the new philosophy.* As far as its basis is concerned, the new philosophy is nothing but *the essence of feeling raised to consciousness*—it only *affirms in the form and through the medium of reason what every man*—every *real* man—*admits in his heart.* It is the heart made aware of itself as reason. The *heart demands real* and *sensuous objects, real and sensuous beings.*

35.

The *old* philosophy maintained that that which *could not be thought of also did not exist;* the *new* philosophy maintains that that which is not loved or *cannot be loved does not exist.* But that which cannot be loved can also not be adored. That which is the *object of religion* can alone be the object of philosophy.

Love is not only objectively but also subjectively the criterion of being, the criterion of truth and reality. *Where there is no love there is also no truth.* And only he who *loves* something *is* also something—*to be nothing* and *to love nothing* is one and the same thing. The more one is, the more one loves, and vice versa.

36.

The old philosophy had its point of departure in the proposition: I am an abstract, a merely thinking being to which the body does not belong. The new philosophy proceeds from the principle: I am a real and sensuous *being; indeed, the whole of my body is my ego, my being itself.* The old philosopher, therefore, thought in a *constant contradiction to and conflict with the senses* in order to avoid sensuous conceptions, or in order not to pollute abstract concepts. In contrast, the new philosopher thinks *in peace and harmony with the senses.* The old philosophy conceded the truth of sensuousness *only in a concealed way,* only in terms of the *concept,* only *unconsciously* and *unwillingly,* only because it had to. This is borne out even by its concept of God as the being who encompasses all other beings within himself, for he was held to be distinct from a merely conceived being; that is, he was held to be existing outside the mind, outside thought—a really objective, sensuous being. In contrast, the new philosophy *joyfully* and *consciously* recognizes the truth of sensuousness: It is a *sensuous* philosophy with an *open heart.*

37.

The philosophy of the modern era was in search of something *immediately certain.* Hence, it rejected the *baseless* thought of the Scholastics and grounded philosophy on *self-consciousness.* That is, it posited the *thinking* being, the *ego,* the *self-conscious mind* in place of the merely conceived being or in place of God, the highest and ultimate being of all Scholastic philosophy; for a being who thinks is infinitely closer to a thinking being, infinitely more actual and certain than a being who is only conceived. Doubtful is the existence of God, doubtful is in fact anything I could think of; but indubitable is that I am, I who think and doubt. Yet this self-consciousness in modern philosophy is again something that is only conceived, only mediated through abstraction, and hence something that can be doubted. *Indubitable* and *immediately certain* is only that which is *the object of the senses, of perception and feeling.*

38.

True and *divine* is only that which *requires no proof,* that which is *certain immediately through itself,* that which *speaks immediately for itself* and carries the affirmation of its being within itself; in short, that which is *purely and simply unquestionable, indubitable, and as clear as the sun.* But only the sensuous is as clear as the sun. When sensuousness begins all doubts and quarrels cease. The secret of *immediate* knowledge is *sensuousness.*

All is mediated, says the Hegelian philosophy. But something is *true* only when it is no longer mediated; that is, when it is immediate. Thus, new historical epochs originate only when something, having so far existed in the mediated form of conception, becomes the object of immediate and sensuous certainty; that is, only when something—erstwhile only thought—becomes a *truth.* To make out of mediation a divine necessity or an essential quality of truth is mere scholasticism. The necessity of mediation is only a *limited* one; it is necessary only where a *wrong presupposition* is involved; where a different truth or doctrine, contradicting an established one which is still held to be valid and respected, arises. A truth that *mediates itself* is a truth that still has its opposite clinging to it. The opposite is taken as the starting point, but is later on discarded. Now, if it is all along something to be discarded or negated, why should I then proceed from it rather than from its negation? Let us illustrate this by an example. God as God is an abstract being; he particularizes, determines, or realizes himself in the world and in man. This is what makes him concrete and hereby is his abstract being negated. But why should I not proceed directly from the concrete? Why, after all, should that which owes its truth and certainty only to itself not stand higher than that whose certainty depends on the nothingness of its opposite? Who would, therefore, give mediation the status of necessity or make a principle of truth out of it? Only he who is still imprisoned in that which is to be negated; only he who is still *in conflict and strife with himself;* only he who has *not yet fully made up his mind*—in short, only he who regards truth as a matter of talent, of a particular, albeit outstanding faculty, but not of genius, not of the whole man. Genius is immediate sensuous knowledge. Talent is merely head, but genius is flesh and blood. That which is only an object of thought for talent is an object of the senses for genius.

39.

The old absolute philosophy drove away the senses into the region of appearance and finitude; and yet contradicting itself, it determined the *absolute,* the *divine* as an *object of art.* But an object of art is—in a mediated form in the spoken, in an unmediated form in the plastic arts—an object of vision, hearing, and feeling. Not only is the finite and phenomenal being, but also the divine, the true being, an object of the senses—*the senses are the organs of the absolute.* Art "presents the truth by means of the sensuous"— properly understood and expressed, this means that *art presents the truth of the sensuous.*

40.

What applies to art, applies to *religion.* The *essence of the Christian religion* is not ideation but *sensuous perception*—the form and *organ of the highest and Divine Being.* But if sensuous perception is taken to be the *organ of the Divine and True Being, the Divine Being is expressed and acknowledged as a sensuous being, just as the sensuous is expressed and acknowledged as the Divine Being; for subject and object correspond to each other.*

"And the word became flesh and dwelt among us, and we *saw* its glory." Only for later generations is the object of the Christian religion an object of conception and fantasy; but this goes together with a restoration of the original sensuous perception. In Heaven, Christ or God is the object of *immediate sensuous* perception; there he turns from an *object of conception and thought*—that is, from a *spiritual being* which he is for us here—into a *sensuous, feelable, visible being.* And—remembering that the goal corresponds to the origin—this is, therefore, the essence of Christianity. Speculative philosophy has, therefore, grasped and presented art and religion not in the true light, not in the light of reality, but only in the twilight of reflection insofar as in keeping with its principle—abstraction from sensuousness—it dissolved sensuousness into the formal determinateness of art and religion: Art is God *in* the formal determinateness of sensuous perception, whereas religion is God *in* that of conception. But that which appears to reflection as a mere form is in truth essence. Where God appears and is worshiped *in* the fire, there it is that fire is in actual truth worshiped as God.

God *in* the fire is nothing else than the being of fire which is so striking to men because of its effects and qualities; *God in man* is nothing else than *the being of man*. And, similarly, that which art represents in the form of sensuousness is nothing else than *the very essence of sensuousness that is inseparable from this form*.

41.

It is not only "external" things that are objects of the senses. *Man,* too, is *given to himself only through the senses;* only as a sensuous object is he an object for himself. The *identity* of *subject and object*—in self-consciousness only an abstract thought—has the character of *truth* and reality only in *man's sensuous perception of* man.

We feel not only stones and wood, not only flesh and bones, but also feelings when we press the hands or lips of a feeling being; we perceive through our ears not only the murmur of water and the rustle of leaves, but also the soulful voice of love and wisdom; we see not only mirror-like surfaces and specters of color, but we also gaze into the gaze of man. Hence, not only that which is external, but also that which is internal, not only flesh, but also spirit, not only things, but also the *ego* is an object of the senses. All is therefore capable of being perceived through the senses, even if only a mediated and not immediate way, even if not with the help of crude and vulgar senses, but only through those that are cultivated; even if not with the eyes of the anatomist and the chemist, but only with those of the philosopher. Empiricism is therefore perfectly justified in regarding ideas as originating from the senses; but what it forgets is that the most essential sensuous object for man is *man himself;* that only in man's glimpse of man does the spark of consciousness and intellect spring. And this goes to show that idealism is right in so far as it sees the origin of ideas *in* man; but it is wrong in so far as it derives these ideas from man understood as an isolated being, as mere soul existing for himself; in one word, it is wrong when it derives the ideas from an ego that is not given in the context of its togetherness with a perceptibly given You. Ideas spring only from conversation and communication. Not alone but only within a dual relationship does one have concepts and reason in general. It takes two human beings to give birth to a man, to physical as well as spiritual man; the togetherness of man with man is the first principle and the criterion of truth and universality. Even the certitude of those things that exist outside me is given to me through the certitude of the existence of other men besides myself. That which is seen by me alone is open to question, but that which is seen also by another person is certain.

42.

The *distinction* between *essence* and *appearance, cause* and *effect, substance* and *accident, necessity* and *contingency, speculative* and *empirical* does not mean that there are two different realms or worlds—the supersensuous world which is essence, and the sensuous world which is appearance; rather, *this distinction is internal to sensuousness itself.* Let us take an example from the natural sciences. In Linne's system of plants the first groups are determined according to the number of filaments. But in the eleventh group where twelve to twenty stamens occur—and more so in the group of twenty stamens and polystamens—the numerical determinations become irrelevant; counting is of no use any more. Here in one and the same area we have, therefore, before us the difference between definite and indefinite, necessary and indifferent, rational and irrational multiplicity. This means that we *need not go beyond sensuousness* to arrive, *in the sense of the Absolute Philosophy,* at the *limit of the merely sensuous and empirical;* all we have to do is *not separate the intellect from the senses* in order to find the supersensuous—spirit and reason—*within the sensuous.*

43.

The *sensuous* is *not* the *immediate* in the sense of speculative philosophy; i.e., *in the sense* in which it is the *profane,* the *readily obvious,* the *thoughtless,* the *self-evident.* According to speculative philosophy the immediate sensuous perception comes *later* than conception and fantasy. Man's *first* conception is itself only a conception based on imagination and fantasy. The task of philosophy and science consists, therefore, *not* in *turning away* from *sensuous*—i.e., *real* things—but in *turning towards* them—*not* in transforming *objects* into *thoughts* and ideas, but in making *visible*—i.e., *objective*—*what is invisible to common eyes.*

In the beginning men see things *as they appear to them,* not as they are. What they see in things is not they themselves, but their own ideas about them; they transpose their own being into things, and do not distinguish between an object and the idea of it. To the subjective and uncultivated man, imagined reality is *closer* than actually perceived reality, for in perceiving it he is compelled to move out of himself, but in imagining it he *remains inside himself.*

And just as it is with imagination, so it is with thought. Initially and for far longer, men occupy themselves with heavenly, with divine things rather than with earthly things; that is, initially and for far longer they occupy themselves with things *translated into thoughts* rather than with *things in the original,* with things in their *own innate* language. Only in the modern era has mankind—as once in Greece after a foregoing era of the oriental dreamworld—found its way back to a *sensuous;* i.e., *unadulterated and objective* perception of the sensuous or the real. But with this, it has also found its way *back to itself,* for a man who occupies himself only with creatures of the imagination and abstract thought is himself only an abstract or fantastic, not a *real,* not a truly human being. The reality of man depends on the reality of his objects. If you *have* nothing, you *are* nothing.

44.

Space and *time* are not *mere forms of appearance:* They are *essential conditions, rational forms, and laws of being as well as of thought.* "Here-being" is the being that comes first, the being that is the first to be determined. *Here* I am—that is the first sign of a *real* and *living* being. The index finger shows the way from nothingness to being. Saying *here* is the first boundary, the first demarcation. I am here, you are there; in between there is a distance separating us; this is what makes it possible for both of us to exist without jeopardizing each other; there is enough room. The sun is not where Mercury is, and Mercury is not where Venus is; the eye is not where the ear is, and so on. Where there is no space, there is also no place for *any system.* The *first determination of reason* upon which every other determination rests is to *situate* things. Although space immediately presupposes its differentiation into places, the organizing work of nature begins with a distribution of locations. Only in space does reason orient itself. The first question asked by awakening consciousness, the first question of practical wisdom is: Where am I? The first virtue that we inculcate in the child, the raw material of man, is that of being limited by space and time, and the first difference that we teach it is the difference of place, the difference between what is proper and what is improper. What the distinction of place means is indifferent to the unfinished man; like the fool, he does everything at all places without distinction. Fools, therefore, achieve reason when they recover the sense for time and place. To put different things in different places, to allot different places to things that differ in quality—that is the condition for all economy including even that of the mind. Not to put in the text what belongs to the footnotes, not to put at the beginning what is to be put at the end, in short, spatial differentiation and limitation belong also to the wisdom of the writer.

It is true that we are speaking here of a definite kind of place; but even so the question is nothing else than that of the determination of place. And I cannot separate place from space were I to grasp space in its *reality*. The concept of space arises in me when I ask: Where? This question as to where is universal and applies to every place without distinction; and yet it is particular. As the positing of the particular "where" is simultaneously a positing of the universal "where," so the universality of space is posited with the particularity of place. But precisely for that reason the general concept of space can be a real and concrete concept only if it includes the particularity of place. Hegel attributes to space—as to nature in general—a *negative* determination. Nevertheless, "here-being" is positive. I am *not* there *because* I *am here*—this not-being-there is therefore only a consequence of the positive and emphatic here-being. The separation of here from there is by no means a limit in itself; only your imagination regards it as such. That they are separate is something that *ought to be* the case, something that does not contradict but corresponds to reason. But this separation is a negative determination in Hegel because it is a separation of that which *ought not to be* separate—because the logical concept, understood as absolute self-identity, is what Hegel regards as the truth; space is to him the *negation* of the Idea, of reason, and hence the only means by which reason can be put back into the Idea is to *negate* it (the Idea). But far from being the negation of reason, space is the first sphere of reason, for it is space that makes room for the idea, for reason. Where there are no spatial distinctions, there are also no logical distinctions. Or vice versa—should we depart, like Hegel, from Logic to space—where there is no distinction, there is no space. Distinctions in thought arise out of the activity of distinguishing; whatever arises out of the activity of distinguishing is spatially set apart. Spatial distinctions are, therefore, the *truth* of logical distinctions. But only that which exists separately can also be thought as forming a sequence. *Real* thought is thought in time and space. Even the negation of time and space (duration) must fall *within* time and space themselves. Only in order to *gain time* and *space,* do we wish to save them.

45.

Things in thought should not be different from what they are in reality. What is *separate in reality* should *not* be *identical in thought.* To *exclude* thinking or ideas—the intellectual world of the neo-Platonists—from the *laws of reality* is the *privilege* of *theological capriciousness.* The *laws of reality* are also the *laws of thought.*

46.

The *immediate unity of opposite* determinations is *possible* and *valid* only in *abstraction.* In *reality,* contradictory statements are always linked by means of an intermediary concept. This intermediary concept is the *object* to which those statements refer; it is their *subject.*

Nothing is therefore easier than to demonstrate the unity of opposite predicates; all one needs is to abstract from the object underlying the predicates or from the subject of these predicates. Once the object has thus vanished, the boundary between the opposites also vanishes; having no ground to stand on and nothing to hold on to, they immediately collapse and lose themselves in indistinction. If, for example, I regard being only as such, that is, if I abstract from every determination whatsoever, being will be the same for me as nothing. Determinateness is indeed the only difference or boundary between being and nothing. If I disregard *that which is,* what then is this mere "is" about? But what applies to *this* particular case of opposites and their identity applies to all other opposites in speculative philosophy.

47.

The only means by which *opposite* or *contradictory determinations* are *united* in one and the same being in a way corresponding to reality is in *time.*

This is true at least in the case of living beings. Only here, for example in man, does the contradiction appear that I am now filled and swayed by this determination—this particular feeling, this particular intention—and now by another, opposite determination. Only where one idea ousts another, where one feeling drives the other out, where nothing is finally settled, where no lasting determination emerges, where the soul continually alternates between opposite states—there alone does the soul find itself in the hellish pain of contradiction. Were I to unite contradictory determinations within myself, the result would be their mutual neutralization and loss of character, not unlike the opposite elements of a chemical process which lose their difference in a neutral product. But the pain of contradiction consists precisely in the fact that I passionately am and want to be at the present moment what I equally emphatically am not and do not want to be in the following, in the fact that positing and negating follow each other, both opposing each other and *each, with the exclusion of the other,* affecting me with all its determinateness and sharpness.

48.

The *real* can be *presented* in *thought not as a whole* but only *in parts.* This distinction is normal; it lies in the nature of thought whose essence is generality as distinct from reality whose essence is individuality. That in spite of this distinction no *formal contradiction* may arise between *thought* and *reality* can be achieved only if thought does not proceed *in a straight line* or *within its self-identity, but is interrupted by sensuous perception.* Only that thought which is *determined* and *rectified* by *sensuous perception* is *real objective* thought—the thought of *objective truth.*

The most important thing to realize is that absolute thought, that is, thought which is isolated and cut off from sensuousness, *cannot get beyond formal identity—the identity of thought with itself;* for although thought or concept is determined as the unity of opposite determinations, the fact remains that these determinations are themselves only abstractions, thought-determinations—hence, always repetitions of the self-identity of thought, only *multipla* of identity as the absolutely true point of departure. The Other as counterposed to the Idea, but posited by the Idea itself, is not truly and in reality distinguished from it, not allowed to exist outside the Idea, or if it is, then only *pro forma,* only in appearance to demonstrate the liberality of the Idea; for the *Other* of the Idea is *itself Idea* with the only difference that it does not yet have the form of the Idea, that it is not yet posited and realized as such. Thought *confined to itself* is thus unable to arrive at anything positively distinct from and opposed to itself; for that very reason it also has no other criterion of truth except that something does not contradict the Idea or thought—only a formal, subjective criterion that is not in a position to decide whether the truth of thought is also the truth of reality. The criterion which alone can decide this question is *sensuous perception*. One should always hear the opponent. And sensuous perception is precisely the *antagonist* of thought. Sensuous perception takes things in a *broad* sense, but thought takes them in the *narrowest* sense; perception leaves things in their *unlimited freedom,* but thought imposes on them *laws* that are only too often *despotic;* perception introduces clarity into the head, but without *determining* or *deciding* anything; thought performs a determining function, but it also often makes the mind narrow; perception in itself has no *principles* and thought in itself has no *life;* the rule is the *way of thought* and *exception* to the rule is *that of perception.* Hence, just as true perception is perception determined by thought, so true thought is the thought that has been enlarged and opened up by perception so as to correspond to the essence of reality. The thought that is identical, and exists in an uninterrupted continuity, with itself, lets the world circle, in contradiction to reality, around itself as its center; but the thought that is *interrupted* through the observation as to the irregularity of this movement, or through the anomaly of perception, transforms this circular movement into an *elliptical* one in accordance with the truth. The *circle* is the symbol, the coat of arms of *speculative* philosophy, of the thought that has *only itself* to support itself. The Hegelian philosophy, too, as we know, is a circle of circles, although in relation to the planets it declares—and led to this by empirical evidence—the circular course to be "the course of a *defectively regular* movement"; in contrast to the circle, the *ellipse* is the symbol, the coat of arms of *sensuous* philosophy, of thought that is based on *perception.*

49.

Only those determinations are productive of *real* knowledge which *determine the object by the object itself;* that is, *by its own individual* determinations but *not* those that are *general,* as for example the logico-metaphysical determinations that, being applicable to *all objects without distinction, determine no object.*

Hegel was therefore quite justified in transforming the logico-metaphysical determinations from determinations of objects into independent determinations—namely, into the determinations of the Concept—quite justified in turning them from predicates—this is what they were in the old metaphysics—into subjects, thus attributing to metaphysics or logic the significance of a self-sufficient divine knowledge. But it is a contradiction when these logico-metaphysical shadows are made, in the concrete sciences in exactly the same way as in the old metaphysics, into the determinations of real things—something that is naturally possible only in so far as either the concrete determinations—that is, those that are appropriate because of their derivation from the object—are connected with the logico-metaphysical determinations, or the object is reduced to wholly *abstract* determinations in which it is *no longer recognizable.*

50.

The real in its reality and totality, the object of the new philosophy, is the object also of a *real* and *total* being. The new philosophy therefore regards as its *epistemological principle,* as its *subject, not the ego, not the absolute*—i.e., abstract spirit, *in short, not reason for itself alone*—but the *real* and the *whole being of man. Man* alone is the *reality,* the *subject of reason.* It is man who thinks, not the ego, not reason. The new philosophy does not depend on the divinity; i.e., the truth of reason for itself alone. Rather, it depends on the *divinity; i.e., the truth of the whole man.* Or, to put it more appropriately, the new philosophy is certainly based on reason as well, but on a reason whose *being* is the same as the *being of man;* that is, it is based not on an empty, colorless, nameless reason, but on a reason that is *of the very blood of man.* If the motto of the old philosophy was: "The rational alone is the true and real," the motto of the new philosophy is: "The *human* alone is the true and *real,*" for the human alone is the rational; *man is the measure of reason.*

51.

The *unity* of *thought* and *being* has *meaning* and *truth* only if *man* is comprehended as the *basis and subject of this unity.* Only a *real being* cognizes *real things;* only where thought is not its own subject but the *predicate* of a *real* being is it *not separated from being.* The unity of thought and being is therefore not formal, meaning that *being as a determination* does not belong to *thought in and for itself;* rather, this unity depends on the *object,* the *content* of thought.

From this arises the following categorical imperative: Desire not to be a philosopher if being a philosopher means being different to man; do not be anything more than a *thinking man;* think not as a thinker, that is, not as one confined to a faculty which is *isolated* in so far as it is *torn away* from the totality of the real being of man; think as a *living real* being, in which capacity you are exposed to the vivifying and refreshing waves of the ocean of the world; think as one who exists, as one who is *in the world* and is part of the world, not as one in the vacuum of abstraction, not as a solitary monad, not as an absolute monarch, not as an unconcerned, extra-worldly God; only then can you be sure that being and thought are united in all your thinking. How should thought as the activity of a real being not grasp real things and entities? Only when thought is cut off from man and confined to itself do embarrassing, fruitless, and, from the standpoint of an isolated thought, unresolvable questions arise: How does thought reach being, reach the object? For *confined to itself,* that is, posited *outside man,* thought is outside all ties and connections with the world. You elevate yourself to an object only in so far as you lower yourself so as to be an object for others. You think only because *your thoughts* themselves can be thought, and they are true only if they pass the test of objectivity, that is, when someone else, to whom they are given as objects, acknowledges them as such. You see because you are yourself a visible being, you feel because you are yourself a feelable being. Only to an open mind does the world stand open, and the *openings of the mind* are only the senses. But the thought that exists in isolation, that is *enclosed in itself,* is *detached from the senses, cut off from man,* is *outside* man—that thought is *absolute subject* which cannot or ought not to be an object for others. But precisely for that reason, and despite all efforts, it is *forever unable to cross over to the object, to being;* it is like a head separated from the body, which must remain unable to seize hold of an object because it lacks the means, the organs to do so.

52.

The new philosophy is the *complete* and *absolute dissolution of theology into anthropology,* a dissolution *in which all contradictions have been overcome;* for the new philosophy is the dissolution of theology not only in reason—this was effected by the old philosophy—but also in the *heart;* in short, in the *whole* and *real* being of man. In this regard, it is only the *necessary outcome* of the old philosophy; for that which was once dissolved in reason must dissolve itself in *life*, in the *heart*, in the *blood* of man; but as a *new* and *independent* truth, the new philosophy is also the truth of the old philosophy, for only *a truth that has become flesh and blood is the truth*. The old philosophy *necessarily* relapsed into theology, for that which is sublated only *in reason*, only in the concept, still has an *antithesis* in the *heart*. The new philosophy, on the other hand, *cannot suffer such a relapse* because there is nothing to relapse into; that which is dead in both body and soul cannot return even as a ghost.

53.

It is *by no means only through thinking that man is distinguished from the animal*. Rather, his *whole being* constitutes *his distinction from the animal*. It is true that he who does not think is not a man; but this is so not because thinking is the cause, but only because it is a *necessary consequence* and *quality* of man's being.

Hence, here too we need not go beyond the realm of sensuousness in order to recognize man as a being superior to animals. Man is not a particular being like the animal; rather, he is a *universal* being; he is therefore not a limited and unfree but an unlimited and free being, for universality, being without limit, and freedom are inseparable. And this freedom is not the property of just one *special* faculty, say, the will, nor does this universality reside in a special faculty of thinking called reason; this freedom, this universality applies to the *whole* being of man. The senses of the animal are certainly keener than those of man, but they are so only in relation to certain things that are necessarily linked with the needs of the animal; and they are keener precisely because of the determination that they are limited by being exclusively directed towards some definite objects. Man does not possess the sense of smell of a hunting dog or a raven, but because his sense of smell encompasses all kinds of smell, it is free and also indifferent to particular smells. But where a sense is elevated above the limits of particularity and above being tied down to needs, it is elevated to an *independent*, to a *theoretical* significance and dignity—*universal* sense is *intellect*, and *universal* sensuousness is *intellectuality*. Even the lowest senses—smell and taste—are elevated in man to intellectual and scientific activities. The smell and taste of things are objects of natural science. Indeed, even the *stomach* of man, no matter how contemptuously we look down upon it, is something *human* and not animal because it is universal; that is, not limited to certain kinds of food. That is why man is free from that ferocious voracity with which the animal hurls itself on its prey. Leave a man his head, but give him the stomach of a lion or a horse, and he will certainly cease to be a man. A limited stomach is compatible only with a limited, that is, animal sense. Man's moral and rational relationship to his stomach consists therefore in his according it a human and not a beastly treatment. He who thinks that what is important to mankind is stomach, and that stomach is something animal, also authorizes man to be bestial in his eating.

54.

The new philosophy makes *man, together with nature* as the basis of man, the *exclusive, universal,* and *highest object* of philosophy; it makes *anthropology, together with physiology,* the *universal science.*

55.

Art, religion, philosophy, and *science* are only expressions or manifestations of the *true being of man.* A man is truly and perfectly man only when he possesses an *aesthetic* or *artistic, religious* or *moral, philosophical* or *scientific sense. And only he who excludes from himself nothing that is essentially human is,* strictly speaking, man. *Homo sum, humani nihil a me alienum puto*—this sentence, taken in its *universal* and *highest meaning,* is the *motto* of the *new philosophy.*

56.

The *philosophy of Absolute Identity* has *completely mislocated the standpoint of truth.* The *natural standpoint* of man, the standpoint of the *distinction* between "*I*" and "*You,*" between *subject* and *object* is the *true,* the *absolute* standpoint and, hence, also the *standpoint of philosophy.*

57.

The *true unity of head and heart* does not consist in wiping out or covering up their difference, but rather in the recognition that *the essential object of the heart* is also *the essential object of the head,* or in the identity of the *object.* The new philosophy, which makes the essential and highest object of the heart—man—also the essential and highest object of the intellect, lays the foundation of a rational unity of head and heart, of thought and life.

58.

Truth does not exist in thought, nor in cognition confined to itself. *Truth is only the totality of man's life and being.*

59.

The single man *in isolation* possesses in himself the *essence* of man neither as a *moral* nor as a *thinking* being. The *essence* of man is contained only in the community, in the *unity of man with man*— a unity, however, that rests on the *reality* of the *distinction* between "I" and "You."

60.

Solitude means being *finite* and *limited, community* means being *free* and *infinite.* For *himself* alone, man is just man (in the ordinary sense); but man *with* man—*the unity of "I" and "You"*—that is God.

61.

The *absolute* philosopher said, or at least thought of himself— naturally as a *thinker* and not as a man—"La vérité c'est moi," in a way analogous to the absolute monarch claiming, *"L'état c'est moi,"* or the absolute God claiming, *"L'être c'est moi."* The human philosopher, on the other hand, says: *Even in thought, even as a philosopher, I am a man in togetherness with men.*

62.

The *true* dialectic is *not a monologue of the solitary thinker with himself;* it is a *dialogue between "I" and "You."*

63.

The *Trinity* was the *highest mystery,* the *central point* of the *absolute philosophy* and *religion.* But the secret of the Trinity, as demonstrated historically and philosophically in the *Essence of Christianity,* is the secret of *communal* and *social life*—the secret of the *necessity of a "You" for an "I."* It is the truth that *no being whatsoever,* be it man or God and be it called "spirit" or "I," can be a *true, perfect,* and *absolute* being *in isolation,* that the *truth* and *perfection* are only the *union* and *unity* of beings that are similar in essence. Hence, the highest and ultimate principle of philosophy is *the unity of man with man.* All essential relationships—the principles of various sciences are only *different kinds and modes of this unity.*

64.

The old philosophy possesses a *double truth;* first, its *own* truth—*philosophy*—which is not concerned with man, and second, the truth *for man—religion.* The new philosophy as the philosophy of man, on the other hand, is also essentially the *philosophy for man;* it has, without in the least compromising the dignity and autonomy of theory—indeed it is in perfect harmony with it—essentially a *practical* tendency, and is practical in the highest sense. The new philosophy takes the place of religion; it has within itself the *essence* of religion; in truth, it is *itself religion.*

65.

All attempts undertaken so far to reform philosophy are not very different from the old philosophy to the extent that they are *species* belonging to the same *genus.* The most indispensable condition for a really new—i.e., independent—philosophy corresponding to the need of mankind and of the future is, however, that it distinguish itself *in essence* from the old philosophy.

Translated by Zawar Hanfi

KARL MARX

I. PRACTICAL PHILOSOPHY
AS PROFESSION

Reflections of a Young Man on the Choice of a Profession

Nature herself has determined the sphere of activity in which the animal should move, and it peacefully moves within that sphere, without attempting to go beyond it, without even an inkling of any other. To man, too, the Deity gave a general aim, that of ennobling mankind and himself, but he left it to man to seek the means by which this aim can be achieved; he left it to him to choose the position in society most suited to him, from which he can best uplift himself and society.

This choice is a great privilege of man over the rest of creation, but at the same time it is an act which can destroy his whole life, frustrate all his plans, and make him unhappy. Serious consideration of this choice, therefore, is certainly the first duty of a young man who is beginning his career and does not want to leave his most important affairs to chance.

Everyone has an aim in view, which to him at least seems great, and actually is so if the deepest conviction, the innermost voice of the heart declares it so, for the Deity never leaves mortal man wholly without a guide; he speaks softly but with certainty.

But this voice can easily be drowned, and what we took for inspiration can be the product of the moment, which another moment can perhaps also destroy. Our imagination, perhaps, is set on fire, our emotions excited, phantoms flit before our eyes, and we plunge headlong into what impetuous instinct suggests, which we imagine the Deity himself has pointed out to us. But what we ardently embrace soon repels us and we see our whole existence in ruins.

We must therefore seriously examine whether we have really been inspired in our choice of a profession, whether an inner voice approves it, or whether this inspiration is a delusion, and what we took to be a call from the Deity was self-deception. But how can we recognize this except by tracing the source of the inspiration itself?

What is great glitters, its glitter arouses ambition, and ambition can easily have produced the inspiration, or what we took for inspiration; but reason can no longer restrain the man who is tempted by the demon of ambition, and he plunges headlong into what impetuous instinct suggests: he no longer chooses his position in life, instead it is determined by chance and illusion.

Nor are we called upon to adopt the position which offers us the most brilliant opportunities; that is not the one which, in the long series of years in which we may perhaps hold it, will never tire us, never dampen our zeal, never let our enthusiasm grow cold, but one in which we shall soon see our wishes unfulfilled, our ideas unsatisfied, and we shall inveigh against the Deity and curse mankind.

But it is not only ambition which can arouse sudden enthusiasm for a particular profession; we may perhaps have embellished it in our imagination, and embellished it so that it appears the highest that life can offer. We have not analysed it, not considered the whole burden, the great responsibility it imposes on us; we have seen it only from a distance, and distance is deceptive.

Our own reason cannot be counsellor here; for it is supported neither by experience nor by profound observation, being deceived by emotion and blinded by fantasy. To whom then should we turn our eyes? Who should support us where our reason forsakes us?

Our parents, who have already travelled life's road and experienced the severity of fate—our heart tells us.

And if then our enthusiasm still persists, if we still continue to love a profession and believe ourselves called to it after we have examined it in cold blood, after we have perceived its burdens and become acquainted with its difficulties, then we ought to adopt it, then neither does our enthusiasm deceive us nor does overhastiness carry us away.

But we cannot always attain the position to which we believe we are called; our relations in society have to some extent already begun to be established before we are in a position to determine them.

Our physical constitution itself is often a threatening obstacle, and let no one scoff at its rights.

It is true that we can rise above it; but then our downfall is all the more rapid, for then we are venturing to build on crumbling ruins, then our whole life is an unhappy struggle between the mental and the bodily principle. But he who is unable to reconcile the warring elements within himself, how can he resist life's tempestuous stress, how can he act calmly? And it is from calm alone that great and fine deeds can arise; it is the only soil in which ripe fruits successfully develop.

Although we cannot work for long and seldom happily with a physical constitution which is not suited to our profession, the thought nevertheless continually arises of sacrificing our well-being to duty, of acting vigorously although we are weak. But if we have chosen a profession for which we do not possess the talent, we can never exercise it worthily, we shall soon realize with shame our own incapacity and tell ourselves that we are useless created beings, members of society who are incapable of fulfilling their vocation. Then the most natural consequence is self-contempt, and what feeling is more painful and less capable of being made up for by all that the outside world has to offer? Self-contempt is a serpent that ever gnaws at one's breast, sucking the life-blood from one's heart and mixing it with the poison of misanthropy and despair.

An illusion about our talents for a profession which we have closely examined is a fault which takes its revenge on us ourselves, and even if it does not meet with the censure of the outside world it gives rise to more terrible pain in our hearts than such censure could inflict.

If we have considered all this, and if the conditions of our life permit us to choose any profession we like, we may adopt the one that assures us the greatest worth, one which is based on ideas of whose truth we are thoroughly convinced, which offers us the widest scope to work for mankind, and for ourselves to approach closer to the general aim for which every profession is but a means—perfection.

Worth is that which most of all uplifts a man, which imparts a higher nobility to his actions and all his endeavours, which makes him invulnerable, admired by the crowd and raised above it.

But worth can be assured only by a profession in which we are not servile tools, but in which we act independently in our own sphere. It can be assured only by a profession that does not demand reprehensible acts, even if reprehensible only in outward appearance, a profession which the best can follow with noble pride. A profession which assures this in the greatest degree is not always the highest, but is always the most to be preferred.

But just as a profession which gives us no assurance of worth degrades us, we shall as surely succumb under the burdens of one which is based on ideas that we later recognise to be false.

There we have no recourse but to self-deception, and what a desperate salvation is that which is obtained by self-betrayal!

Those professions which are not so much involved in life itself as concerned with abstract truths are the most dangerous for the young man whose principles are not yet firm and whose convictions are not yet strong and unshakeable. At the same time these professions may seem to be the most exalted if they have taken deep root in our hearts and if we are capable of sacrificing our lives and all endeavors for the ideas which prevail in them.

They can bestow happiness on the man who has a vocation for them, but they destroy him who adopts them rashly, without reflection, yielding to the impulse of the moment.

On the other hand, the high regard we have for the ideas on which our profession is based gives us a higher standing in society, enhances our own worth, and makes our actions unchallengeable.

One who chooses a profession he values highly will shudder at the idea of being unworthy of it; he will act nobly if only because his position in society is a noble one.

But the chief guide which must direct us in the choice of a profession is the welfare of mankind and our own perfection. It should not be thought that these two interests could be in conflict, that one would have to destroy the other; on the contrary, man's nature is so constituted that he can attain his own perfection only by working for the perfection, for the good, of his fellow men.

If he works only for himself, he may perhaps become a famous man of learning, a great sage, an excellent poet, but he can never be a perfect, truly great man.

History calls those men the greatest who have ennobled themselves by working for the common good; experience acclaims as happiest the man who had made the greatest number of people happy; religion itself teaches us that the ideal being whom all strive to copy sacrificed himself for the sake of mankind, and who would dare to set at nought such judgments?

If we have chosen the position in life in which we can most of all work for mankind, no burdens can bow us down, because they are sacrifices for the benefit of all; then we shall experience no petty, limited, selfish joy, but our happiness will belong to millions, our deeds will live on quietly but perpetually at work, and over our ashes will be shed the hot tears of noble people.

Translated by Clemens Dutt

Letter to Arnold Ruge

Kreuznach, September 1843

I am glad that you have made up your mind and, ceasing to look back at the past, are turning your thoughts ahead to a new enterprise. And so—to Paris, to the old university of philosophy—*absit omen!** —and the new capital of the new world! What is necessary comes to pass. I have no doubt, therefore, that it will be possible to overcome all obstacles, the gravity of which I do not fail to recognise.

But whether the enterprise comes into being or not, in any case I shall be in Paris by the end of this month, since the atmosphere here makes one a serf, and in Germany I see no scope at all for free activity.

In Germany, everything is forcibly suppressed; a real anarchy of the mind, the reign of stupidity itself, prevails there, and Zurich obeys orders from Berlin. It therefore becomes increasingly obvious that a new rallying point must be sought for truly thinking and independent minds. I am convinced that our plan would answer a real need, and after all it must be possible for real needs to be fulfilled in reality. Hence I have no doubt about the enterprise, if it is undertaken seriously.

The internal difficulties seem to be almost greater than the external obstacles. For although no doubt exists on the question of "Whence," all the greater confusion prevails on the question of "Whither." Not only has a state of general anarchy set in among the reformers, but everyone will have to admit to himself that he

---

*May it not be an ill omen!

has no exact idea what the future ought to be. On the other hand, it is precisely the advantage of the new trend that we do not dogmatically anticipate the world, but only want to find the new world through criticism of the old one. Hitherto philosophers have had the solution of all riddles lying in their writing-desks, and the stupid, exoteric world had only to open its mouth for the roast pigeons of absolute knowledge to fly into it. Now philosophy has become mundane, and the most striking proof of this is that philosophical consciousness itself has been drawn into the torment of the struggle, not only externally but also internally. But, if constructing the future and settling everything for all times are not our affair, it is all the more clear what we have to accomplish at present: I am referring to *ruthless criticism of all that exists,* ruthless both in the sense of not being afraid of the results it arrives at and in the sense of being just as little afraid of conflict with the powers that be.

Therefore I am not in favor of raising any dogmatic banner. On the contrary, we must try to help the dogmatists to clarify their propositions for themselves. Thus, *communism,* in particular, is a dogmatic abstraction; in which connection, however, I am not thinking of some imaginary and possible communism, but actually existing communism as taught by Cabet, Dézamy, Weitling, etc. This communism is itself only a special expression of the humanistic principle, an expression which is still infected by its antithesis— the private system. Hence the abolition of private property and communism are by no means identical, and it is not accidental but inevitable that communism has seen other socialist doctrines—such as those of Fourier, Proudhon, etc.—arising to confront it because it is itself only a special, one-sided realization of the socialist principle.

And the whole socialist principle in its turn is only one aspect that concerns the *reality* of the true human being. But we have to pay just as much attention to the other aspect, to the theoretical existence of man, and therefore to make religion, science, etc., the object of our criticism. In addition, we want to influence our contemporaries, particularly our German contemporaries. The question arises: how are we to set about it? There are two kinds of facts which are undeniable. In the first place religion, and next to it, politics, are the subjects which form the main interest of Germany today. We must take these, in whatever form they exist, as our point of departure, and not confront them with some ready-made system such as, for example, the *Voyage en Icarie.**

Reason has always existed, but not always in a reasonable form. The critic can therefore start out from any form of theoretical and practical consciousness and from the forms *peculiar* to existing reality develop the true reality as its obligation and its final goal. As far as real life is concerned, it is precisely the *political state*—in all its *modern* forms—which, even where it is not yet consciously imbued with socialist demands, contains the demands of reason. And the political state does not stop there. Everywhere it assumes that reason has been realized. But precisely because of that it everywhere becomes involved in the contradiction between its ideal function and its real prerequisites.

From this conflict of the political state with itself, therefore, it is possible everywhere to develop the social truth. Just as *religion* is a register of the theoretical struggles of mankind, so the *political state* is a register of the practical struggles of mankind. Thus, the political state expresses, within the limits of its form *sub specie rei publicae,*† all social struggles, needs and truths. Therefore, to take as the object of criticism a most specialized political question—such as the difference between a system based on social estate and one based on representation—is in no way below the *hauteur des principes.*§ For this question only expresses in a *political* way the difference between rule by man and rule by private property. Therefore the critic not only can, but must deal with these political questions (which according to the extreme Socialists are altogether unworthy of attention). In analyzing the superiority of the representative system over the social-estate system, the critic *in a practical way wins the interest* of a large party. By raising the representative system from its political form to the universal form and by bringing out the true significance underlying this system, the critic at the same time compels this party to go beyond its own confines, for its victory is at the same time its defeat.

Hence, nothing prevents us from making criticism of politics, participation in politics, and therefore *real* struggles, the starting point of our criticism, and from identifying our criticism with them. In that case we do not confront the world in a doctrinaire

---

*Étienne Cabet, *Voyage en Icarie. Roman philosophique et social.*
†As a particular kind of state.
§Level of principles.

way with a new principle: Here is the truth, kneel down before it! We develop new principles for the world out of the world's own principles. We do not say to the world: cease your struggles, they are foolish; we will give you the true slogan of struggle. We merely show the world what it is really fighting for, and consciousness is something that it *has to* acquire, even if it does not want to.

The reform of consciousness consists *only* in making the world aware of its own consciousness, in awakening it out of its dream about itself, in *explaining* to it the meaning of its own actions. Our whole object can only be—as is also the case of Feuerbach's criticism of religion—to give religious and philosophical questions the form corresponding to man who has become conscious of himself.

Hence, our motto must be: reform of consciousness not through dogmas, but by analyzing the mystical consciousness that is unintelligible to itself, whether it manifests itself in a religious or a political form. It will then become evident that the world has long dreamed of possessing something of which it has only to be conscious in order to possess it in reality. It will become evident that it is not a question of drawing a great mental dividing line between past and future, but of *realizing* the thoughts of the past. Lastly, it will become evident that mankind is not beginning a *new* work, but is consciously carrying into effect its old work.

In short, therefore, we can formulate the trend of our journal as being: self-clarification (critical philosophy) to be gained by the present time of its struggles and desires. This is a work for the world and for us. It can be only the work of united forces. It is a matter of a *confession,* and nothing more. In order to secure remission of its sins, mankind has only to declare them for what they actually are.

Translated by Jack Cohen

Contribution to the Critique of Hegel's Philosophy of Law

For Germany the *criticism of religion* is in the main complete, and criticism of religion is the premise of all criticism.

The *profane* existence of error is discredited after its *heavenly oratio pro aris et focis** has been disproved. Man, who looked for a superhuman being in the fantastic reality of heaven and found nothing there but the *reflection* of himself, will no longer be disposed to find but the *semblance* of himself, only an inhuman being, where he seeks and must seek his true reality.

The basis of irreligious criticism is: *Man makes religion,* religion does not make man. Religion is the self-consciousness and self-esteem of man who has either not yet found himself or has already lost himself again. But *man* is no abstract being encamped outside the world. Man is *the world of man,* the state, society. This state, this society, produce religion, an *inverted world-consciousness,* because they are an *inverted world.* Religion is the general theory of that world, its encyclopaedic compendium, its logic in a popular form, its spiritualistic *point d'honneur,* its enthusiasm, its moral sanction, its solemn complement, its universal source of consolation and justification. It is the *fantastic realization* of the human essence because the *human essence* has no true reality. The struggle against religion is therefore indirectly a fight against *the world* of which religion is the spiritual *aroma.*

Religious distress is at the same time the *expression* of real distress and also the *protest* against real distress. Religion is the sigh

---

*Speech for the altars and hearths.

of the oppressed creature, the heart of a heartless world, just as it is the spirit of spiritless conditions. It is the *opium* of the people.

To abolish religion as the *illusory* happiness of the people is to demand their *real* happiness. The demand to give up illusion about the existing state of affairs is the *demand to give up a state of affairs which needs illusions*. The criticism of religion is therefore *in embryo the criticism of the vale of tears*, the *halo* of which is religion.

Criticism has torn up the imaginary flowers from the chain not so that man shall wear the unadorned, bleak chain but so that he will shake off the chain and pluck the living flower. The criticism of religion disillusions man to make him think and act and shape his reality like a man who has been disillusioned and has come to reason, so that he will revolve round himself and therefore round his true sun. Religion is only the illusory sun which revolves round man as long as he does not revolve round himself.

The *task of history*, therefore, once the *world beyond the truth* has disappeared, is to establish the *truth of this world*. The immediate *task of philosophy*, which is at the service of history, once the *holy form* of human self-estrangement has been unmasked, is to unmask self-estrangement in its *unholy forms*. Thus the criticism of heaven turns into the criticism of the earth, the *criticism of religion* into the *criticism of law* and the *criticism of theology* into the *criticism of politics*.

The following exposition—a contribution to that task—deals immediately not with the original, but with a copy, the German *philosophy* of state and of law, for no other reason than that it deals with *Germany*.

If one wanted to proceed from the *status quo* itself in Germany, even in the only appropriate way, i.e., negatively, the result would still be an *anachronism*. Even the negation of our political present is a reality already covered with dust in the historical lumber-room of modern nations. If I negate powdered pigtails, I am still left with unpowdered pigtails. If I negate the German state of affairs in 1843, then, according to the French computation of time, I am hardly in the year 1789, and still less in the focus of the present.

Yes, German history flatters itself with a movement which no people in the firmament of history went through before it or will go through after it. For we shared the restorations of the modern nations although we had not shared their revolutions. We underwent a restoration, first because other nations dared to carry out a revolution and second because other nations suffered a counter-revolution, the first time because our rulers were afraid, and the second because our rulers were not afraid. We—and our shepherds first and foremost—never found ourselves in the company of freedom except once—on the *day of its burial.*

A school which legitimates the baseness of today by the baseness of yesterday, a school that declares rebellious every cry of the serf against the knout once that knout is a time-honored, ancestral historical one, a school to which history only shows its *posterior* as the God of Israel did to his servant Moses*—the *historical school of law*—would hence have invented German history had it not been an invention of German history. For every pound of flesh cut from the heart of the people the historical school of law— Shylock, but Shylock the bondsman—swears on its bond, its historical bond, its Christian-Germanic bond.

Good-natured enthusiasts, Germanomaniacs by extraction and free-thinkers by reflection, on the contrary, seek our history of freedom beyond our history in the primeval Teutonic forests. But what difference is there between the history of our freedom and the history of the boar's freedom if it can be found only in the forests? Besides, it is common knowledge that the forest echoes back what you shout into it. So let us leave the ancient Teutonic forests in peace!

War on the German conditions! By all means! They are *below the level of history, beneath any criticism,* but they are still an object of criticism like the criminal who is below the level of humanity but still an object for the *executioner.* In the struggle against those conditions criticism is no passion of the head, it is the head of passion. It is not a lancet, it is a weapon. Its object is its *enemy,* which it wants not to refute but to *exterminate.* For the spirit of those conditions is refuted. In themselves they are not objects *worthy of thought,* but *phenomena* which are as despicable as they are despised. Criticism does not need to make things clear to itself as regards this subject-matter, for it has already dealt with it. Criticism appears no longer as an *end in itself,* but only as a *means.* Its essential sentiment is *indignation,* its essential activity is *denunciation.*

It is a case of describing the dull reciprocal pressure of all social spheres on one another, a general inactive ill humor, a limitedness

---

*The Holy Bible, Exodus 33:23.

which recognizes itself as much as it misjudges itself, within the frame of a government system which, living on the preservation of all wretchedness, is itself nothing but *wretchedness in office*. . . .

It is asked: Can Germany attain a practice *à la hauteur des principes,* i.e., a *revolution* which will raise it not only to the *official level* of the modern nations but to the *height of humanity* which will be the near future of those nations?

The weapon of criticism cannot, of course, replace criticism by weapons, material force must be overthrown by material force; but theory also becomes a material force as soon as it has gripped the masses. Theory is capable of gripping the masses as soon as it demonstrates *ad hominem,* and it demonstrates *ad hominem* as soon as it becomes radical. To be radical is to grasp the root of the matter. But for man the root is man himself. The evident proof of the radicalism of German theory, and hence of its practical energy, is that it proceeds from a resolute *positive* abolition of religion. The criticism of religion ends with the teaching that *man is the highest being for man,* hence with the *categorical imperative to overthrow all relations* in which man is a debased, enslaved, forsaken, despicable being, relations which cannot be better described than by the exclamation of a Frenchman when it was planned to introduce a tax on dogs: Poor dogs! They want to treat you like human beings!

Even historically, theoretical emancipation has specific practical significance for Germany. For Germany's *revolutionary* past is theoretical, it is the *Reformation.* As the revolution then began in the brain of the *monk,* so now it begins in the brain of the *philosopher.*

Luther, we grant, overcame the bondage of piety by replacing it by the bondage of *conviction.* He shattered faith in authority because he restored the authority of faith. He turned priests into laymen because he turned laymen into priests. He freed man from outer religiosity because he made religiosity the inner man. He freed the body from chains because he enchained the heart.

But if Protestantism was not the true solution it was at least the true setting of the problem. It was no longer a case of the layman's struggle against the *priest outside himself* but of his struggle against his own *priest inside himself,* his *priestly nature.* And if the Protestant transformation of the German laymen into priests emancipated the lay popes, the *princes,* with the whole of their priestly clique, the privileged and philistines, the philosophical transformation of priestly Germans into men will emancipate the *people*. But *secularization* will not stop at the *pillaging of churches* practised mainly by hypocritical Prussia any more than emancipation stops at princes. The Peasant War, the most radical fact of German history, came to grief because of theology. Today, when theology itself has come to grief, the most unfree fact of German history, our *status quo*, will be shattered against philosophy. On the eve of the Reformation official Germany was the most unconditional slave of Rome. On the eve of its revolution it is the unconditional slave of less than Rome, of Prussia and Austria, of country squires and philistines.

A major difficulty, however, seems to stand in the way of a *radical* German revolution.

For revolutions require a *passive* element, a *material* basis. Theory can be realized in a people only insofar as it is the realization of the needs of that people. But will the enormous discrepancy between the demands of German thought and the answers of German reality be matched by a corresponding discrepancy between civil society and the state and between civil society and itself? Will the theoretical needs be immediate practical needs? It is not enough for thought to strive for realization, reality must itself strive toward thought.

Where, then, is the *positive* possibility of a German emancipation?

Answer: In the formation of a class with *radical chains*, a class of civil society which is not a class of civil society, an estate which is the dissolution of all estates, a sphere which has a universal character by its universal suffering and claims no *particular right* because no *particular wrong* but *wrong generally* is perpetrated against it; which can no longer invoke a *historical* but only a *human* title; which does not stand in any one-sided antithesis to the consequences but in an all-round antithesis to the premises of the German state; a sphere, finally, which cannot emancipate itself without emancipating itself from all other spheres of society and thereby emancipating all other spheres of society, which, in a word, is the *complete loss* of man and hence can win itself only through the *complete rewinning of man*. This dissolution of society as a particular estate is the *proletariat*.

The proletariat is coming into being in Germany only as a result of the rising *industrial* development. For it is not the *naturally arising* poor but the *artificially impoverished*, not the human masses mechanically oppressed by the gravity of society but the masses resulting from the *drastic dissolution* of society, mainly of the middle estate, that form the proletariat, although it is obvious that gradually the naturally arising poor and the Christian–Germanic serfs also join its ranks.

By proclaiming the *dissolution of the hitherto existing world order* the proletariat merely states the *secret of its own existence*, for it *is in fact* the dissolution of that world order. By demanding the *negation of private property*, the proletariat merely raises to the rank of a *principle of society* what society has made the principle of the *proletariat*, what, without its own cooperation, is already incorporated in *it* as the negative result of society. In regard to the world which is coming into being the proletarian then finds himself possessing the same right as the *German king* in regard to the world which has come into being when he calls the people *his* people as he calls the horse *his* horse. By declaring the people his private property the king simply states that the property owner is king.

As philosophy finds its *material* weapons in the proletariat, so the proletariat finds its *spiritual* weapons in philosophy. And once the lightning of thought has squarely struck this ingenuous soil of the people the emancipation of the *Germans* into *human beings* will take place.

Let us sum up the result:

The only *practically* possible liberation of Germany is liberation that proceeds from the standpoint of *the* theory which proclaims man to be the highest being for man. In Germany emancipation from the *Middle Ages* is possible only as emancipation from the *partial* victories over the Middle Ages as well. In Germany *no* kind of bondage can be broken without breaking *every* kind of bondage. The *thorough* Germany cannot make a revolution without making a *thoroughgoing* revolution. The *emancipation of the German* is the *emancipation of the human being*. The *head* of this emancipation is *philosophy*, its *heart* is the *proletariat*. Philosophy cannot be made a reality without the abolition of the proletariat, the proletariat cannot be abolished without philosophy being made a reality.

When all inner requisites are fulfilled the *day of German resurrection* will be proclaimed by the *ringing call of the Gallic cock*.

Written at the end of 1843–January 1844

Translator unknown

Critical Battle against
French Materialism

To the critical history of French materialism we shall oppose a brief outline of its ordinary, mass-type history. We shall acknowledge with due respect the abyss between history as it really happened and history as it takes place according to the decree of *"Absolute Criticism,"* the creator equally of the old and of the new. And finally, obeying the prescriptions of *criticism*, we shall make the "Why?," "Whence?," and "Whither?" of critical history the "object of a persevering study."

"Speaking *exactly* and in the *prosaic sense*," the French Enlightenment of the eighteenth century, and in particular *French materialism,* was not only a struggle against the existing political institutions and the existing religion and theology; it was just as much an *open, clearly expressed* struggle against the *metaphysics of the seventeenth century,* and against *all metaphysics,* in particular that of *Descartes, Malebranche, Spinoza* and *Leibniz. Philosophy* was counterposed to *metaphysics,* just as *Feuerbach,* in his first resolute attack on *Hegel,* counterposed *sober philosophy* to *wild speculation.* Seventeenth century *metaphysics,* driven from the field by the French Enlightenment, notably, by *French materialism* of the eighteenth century, experienced a *victorious and substantial restoration* in *German philosophy,* particularly in the *speculative German philosophy* of the nineteenth century. After *Hegel* linked it in a masterly fashion with all subsequent metaphysics and with German idealism and founded a metaphysical universal kingdom, the attack on theology again corresponded, as in the eighteenth century, to an attack on *speculative metaphysics* and *metaphysics in general.* It will be defeated forever by *materialism,* which has now been perfected by the work of *speculation* itself and coincides with *humanism.* But just as *Feuerbach* is the representative of *materialism* coinciding with *humanism* in the *theoretical* domain, French and English *socialism* and *communism* represent *materialism* coinciding with *humanism* in the *practical* domain.

"Speaking *exactly* and in the *prosaic sense*," there are *two trends* in *French materialism;* one traces its origin to *Descartes,* the other to *Locke.* The latter is *mainly* a *French* development and leads directly to *socialism.* The former, *mechanical* materialism, merges with French *natural science* proper. The two trends intersect in the course of development. We have no need here to go more deeply into the French materialism that derives directly from *Descartes,* anymore than into the French school of *Newton* and the development of French natural science in general.

We shall therefore merely say the following:

Descartes in his *physics* endowed *matter* with self-creative power and conceived *mechanical* motion as the manifestation of its life. He completely separated his *physics* from his *metaphysics. Within* his physics, *matter* is the sole *substance,* the sole basis of being and of knowledge.

Mechanical French materialism adopted *Descartes's physics* in opposition to his metaphysics. His followers were by profession *anti-metaphysicians,* i.e., *physicists.*

This school begins with the *physician Le Roy,* reaches its zenith with the physician *Cabanis,* and the physician *La Mettrie* is its centre. Descartes was still living when Le Roy, like *La Mettrie* in the eighteenth century, transposed the Cartesian structure of the *animal* to the human soul and declared that the soul is a *modus of the body* and *ideas* are *mechanical motions.* Le Roy even thought Descartes had kept his real opinion secret. Descartes protested. At the end of the eighteenth century *Cabanis* perfected Cartesian materialism in his treatise: *Rapports du physique et du moral de l'homme.*

Cartesian materialism still exists today in France. It has achieved great successes in *mechanical natural science* which, "speaking *exactly* and in the *prosaic sense*," will be least of all reproached with *romanticism.*

The *metaphysics* of the seventeenth century, represented in France by *Descartes,* had *materialism* as its *antagonist* from its very birth. The latter's opposition to Descartes was personified by

Gassendi, the restorer of *Epicurean* materialism. French and English materialism was always closely related to *Democritus* and *Epicurus.* Cartesian metaphysics had another opponent in the *English* materialist *Hobbes.* Gassendi and Hobbes triumphed over their opponent long after their death at the very time when metaphysics was already officially dominant in all French schools.

Voltaire pointed out that the indifference of the French of the eighteenth century to the disputes between the Jesuits and the Jansenists was due less to philosophy than to *Law's* financial speculations. So the downfall of seventeenth-century metaphysics can be explained by the materialistic theory of the eighteenth century only in so far as this theoretical movement itself is explained by the practical nature of French life at that time. This life was turned to the immediate present, to worldly enjoyment and worldly interests, to the *earthly* world. Its anti-theological, anti-metaphysical, materialistic practice demanded corresponding anti-theological, anti-metaphysical, materialistic theories. Metaphysics had *in practice* lost all credit. Here we have only to indicate briefly the *theoretical* course of events.

In the seventeenth century metaphysics (cf. Descartes, Leibniz, and others) still contained a *positive,* secular element. It made discoveries in mathematics, physics and other exact sciences which seemed to come within its scope. This semblance was done away with as early as the beginning of the eighteenth century. The positive sciences broke away from metaphysics and marked out their independent fields. The whole wealth of metaphysics now consisted only of beings of thought and heavenly things, at the very time when real beings and earthly things began to be the centre of all interest. Metaphysics had become insipid. In the very year in which Malebranche and Arnauld, the last great French metaphysicians of the seventeenth century, died, *Helvétius* and *Condillac* were born.

The man who deprived seventeenth-century metaphysics and metaphysics in general of all *credit* in the domain of *theory* was *Pierre Bayle.* His weapon was *skepticism,* which he forged out of metaphysics' own magic formulas. He himself proceeded at first from Cartesian metaphysics. Just as *Feuerbach* by combating speculative theology was driven further to combat *speculative philosophy,* precisely because he recognised in speculation the last prop of theology, because he had to force theology to retreat from pseudoscience to *crude,* repulsive *faith,* so Bayle too was driven by religious doubt to doubt about the metaphysics which was the prop of that faith. He therefore critically investigated metaphysics in its entire historical development. He became its historian in order to write the history of its death. He refuted chiefly *Spinoza* and *Leibniz.*

Pierre Bayle not only prepared the reception of materialism and of the philosophy of common sense in France by shattering metaphysics with his skepticism. He heralded the *atheistic society* which was soon to come into existence by *proving* that a society consisting only of atheists is *possible,* that an atheist *can* be a man worthy of respect, and that it is not by atheism but by superstition and idolatry that man debases himself.

To quote a French writer, *Pierre Bayle* was *"the last metaphysician in the sense of the seventeenth century* and *the first philosopher in the sense of the eighteenth century."*

Besides the negative refutation of seventeenth-century theology and metaphysics, a *positive, anti-metaphysical* system was required. A book was needed which would systematize and theoretically substantiate the life practice of that time. *Locke's* treatise *An Essay Concerning Humane Understanding* came from across the Channel as if in answer to a call. It was welcomed enthusiastically like a long-awaited guest.

The question arises: Is *Locke* perhaps a disciple of *Spinoza?* "Profane" history can answer:

Materialism is the *natural-born* son of *Great Britain.* Already the British schoolman, *Duns Scotus,* asked, *"whether it was impossible for matter to think?"*

In order to effect this miracle, he took refuge in God's omnipotence, i.e., he made *theology* preach *materialism.* Moreover, he was a *nominalist. Nominalism,* the *first form* of materialism, is chiefly found among the *English* schoolmen.

The real progenitor of *English materialism* and all *modern experimental* science is *Bacon.* To him natural philosophy is the only true philosophy, and *physics* based upon the experience of the senses is the chiefest part of natural philosophy. *Anaxagoras* and his *homoeomeriae, Democritus* and his atoms, he often quotes as his authorities. According to him the *senses* are infallible and the *source* of all knowledge. All science is based on *experience,* and consists in subjecting the data furnished by the senses to a *rational method* of investigation. Induction, analysis, comparison, observation, experiment, are the principal forms of such a rational method. Among the qualities inherent in *matter, motion* is the first and foremost, not only in the form of *mechanical* and *mathematical* motion, but chiefly in the form of an *impulse,* a *vital spirit, a tension*—or a *Qual,* to use a term of Jakob Böhme's—of matter. The primary forms of matter are the living, individualizing *forces of being* inherent in it and producing the distinctions between the species.

In *Bacon,* its first creator, materialism still holds back within itself in a naive way the germs of a many-sided development. On the one hand, matter, surrounded by a sensuous, poetic glamour, seems to attract man's whole entity by winning smiles. On the other, the aphoristically formulated doctrine pullulates with inconsistencies imported from theology.

In its further evolution, materialism becomes *one-sided. Hobbes* is the man who *systematizes Baconian* materialism. Knowledge based upon the senses loses its poetic blossom. It passes into the abstract experience of the *geometrician. Physical* motion is sacrificed to *mechanical* or *mathematical* motion; *geometry* is proclaimed as the queen of sciences. Materialism takes to *misanthropy.* If it is to overcome its opponent, *misanthropic, fleshless* spiritualism, and that on the latter's own ground, materialism has to chastise its own flesh and turn *ascetic.* Thus it passes into an *intellectual entity;* but thus, too, it evolves all the consistency, regardless of consequences, characteristic of the intellect.

Hobbes, as Bacon's continuator, argues thus: if all human knowledge is furnished by the senses, then our concepts, notions, and ideas are but the phantoms of the real world, more or less divested of its sensual form. Philosophy can but give names to these phantoms. One name may be applied to more than one of them. There may even be names of names. But it would imply a contradiction if, on the one hand, we maintained that all ideas had their origin in the world of sensation, and, on the other, that a word was more than a word; that besides the beings known to us by our senses, beings which are one and all individuals, there existed also beings of a general, not individual, nature. An *unbodily substance* is the same absurdity as an *unbodily body. Body, being, substance,* are but different terms for the same *reality.* It is impossible to separate thought from matter *that* thinks. This matter is the substratum of all changes going on in the world. The word *infinite* is *meaningless,* unless it states that our mind is capable of performing an endless process of addition. Only material things being perceptible, knowable to us, we cannot know *anything* about the existence of God. My own existence alone is certain. Every human passion is a mechanical movement which has a beginning and an end. The objects of impulse are what we call good. Man is subject to the same laws as nature. Power and freedom are identical.

Hobbes had systematized Bacon without, however, furnishing a proof for Bacon's fundamental principle, the origin of all human knowledge and ideas from the world of sensation.

It was *Locke* who, in his *Essay on the Humane Understanding,* supplied this proof.

Hobbes had shattered the *theistic* prejudices of Baconian materialism; Collins, Dodwell, Coward, Hartley, Priestley, similarly shattered the last theological bars that still hemmed in Locke's sensationalism. At all events, for materialists, deism is but an easygoing way of getting rid of religion.

We have already mentioned how opportune Locke's work was for the French. Locke founded the philosophy of *bon sens,* of common sense; i.e., he said indirectly that there cannot be any philosophy at variance with the healthy human senses and reason based on them.

Locke's *immediate* pupil, *Condillac,* who translated him into *French,* at once applied Locke's sensualism against seventeenth-century *metaphysics.* He proved that the French had rightly rejected this metaphysics as a mere botch work of fancy and theological prejudice. He published a refutation of the systems of *Descartes, Spinoza, Leibniz* and *Malebranche.*

In his *Essai sur l'origine des connaissances humaines* he expounded Locke's ideas and proved that not only the soul, but the senses too, not only the art of creating ideas, but also the art of sensuous perception, are matters of *experience* and *habit.* The whole development of man therefore depends on *education* and *external circumstances.* It was only by *eclectic* philosophy that Condillac was ousted from the French schools.

The difference between *French* and *English* materialism reflects the difference between the two nations. The French imparted to English materialism wit, flesh and blood, and eloquence. They gave it the temperament and grace that it lacked. They *civilized* it.

In *Helvétius,* who also based himself on Locke, materialism assumed a really French character. Helvétius conceived it immediately in its application to social life (Helvétius, *De l'homme*). The sensory qualities and self-love, enjoyment and correctly understood personal interest are the basis of all morality. The natural equality of human intelligences, the unity of progress of reason and progress of industry, the natural goodness of man, and the omnipotence of education, are the main features in his system.

In *La Mettrie's* works we find a synthesis of Cartesian and English materialism. He makes use of Descartes's physics in detail. His *L'homme machine* is a treatise after the model of Descartes's animal-machine. The physical part of Holbach's *Système de la nature* is also a result of the combination of French and English materialism, while the moral part is based essentially on the morality of Helvétius. *Robinet (De la nature),* the French materialist who had the most connection with metaphysics and was therefore praised by Hegel, refers explicitly to *Leibniz.*

We need not dwell on Volney, Dupuis, Diderot and others, any more than on the physiocrats, after we have proved the dual origin of French materialism from Descartes's physics and English materialism, and the opposition of French materialism to seventeenth-century *metaphysics,* to the metaphysics of Descartes, Spinoza, Malebranche, and Leibniz. This opposition only became evident to the Germans after they themselves had come into opposition to *speculative metaphysics.*

Just as *Cartesian* materialism passes into *natural science proper,* the other trend of French materialism leads directly to *socialism* and *communism.*

There is no need for any great penetration to see from the teaching of materialism on the original goodness and equal intellectual endowment of men, the omnipotence of experience, habit and education, and the influence of environment on man, the great significance of industry, the justification of enjoyment, etc., how necessarily materialism is connected with communism and socialism. If man draws all his knowledge, sensation, etc., from the world of the senses and the experience gained in it, then what has to be done is to arrange the empirical world in such a way that man experiences and becomes accustomed to what is truly human in it and that he becomes aware of himself as man. If correctly understood interest is the principle of all morality, man's private interest must be made to coincide with the interest of humanity. If man is unfree in the materialistic sense, i.e., is free not through the negative power to avoid this or that, but through the positive power to assert his true individuality, crime must not be punished in the individual, but the anti-social sources of crime must be destroyed, and each man must be given social scope for the vital manifestation of his being. If man is shaped by environment, his environment must be made human. If man is social by nature, he will develop his true nature only in society, and the power of his nature must be measured not by the power of the separate individual but by the power of society.

These and similar propositions are to be found almost literally even in the oldest French materialists. This is not the place to assess them. The apologia of vices by *Mandeville,* one of Locke's early English followers, is typical of the socialist tendencies of materialism. He proves that in *modern* society vice is *indispensable* and *useful.* This was by no means an apologia for modern society.

Fourier proceeds directly from the teaching of the French materialists. The *Babouvists* were crude, uncivilized materialists, but developed communism, too, derives *directly* from *French materialism.* The latter returned to its mother-country, *England,* in the form *Helvétius* gave it. *Bentham* based his system of *correctly understood interest* on Helvétius's morality, and *Owen* proceeded from *Bentham's* system to found English communism. Exiled to England, the Frenchman *Cabet* came under the influence of communist ideas there and on his return to France became the most popular, if the most superficial, representative of communism. Like Owen, the more scientific French Communists, *Dézamy, Gay,* and others, developed the teaching of *materialism* as the teaching of *real humanism* and the *logical* basis of *communism.*

Translated by Richard Dixon and Clemens Dutt

Theses on Feuerbach

1.

The chief defect of all previous materialism (that of Feuerbach included) is that things [*Gegenstand*], reality, sensuousness are conceived only in the form of the *object, or of contemplation,* but not as *sensuous human activity, practice,* not subjectively. Hence, in contradistinction to materialism, the *active* side was set forth abstractly by idealism—which, of course, does not know real, sensuous activity as such. Feuerbach wants sensuous objects, really distinct from conceptual objects, but he does not conceive human activity itself as *objective* activity. In *Das Wesen des Christenthums,* he therefore regards the theoretical attitude as the only genuinely human attitude, while practice is conceived and defined only in its dirty-Jewish* form of appearance. Hence he does not grasp the significance of "revolutionary," of "practical-critical," activity.

2.

The question whether objective truth can be attributed to human thinking is not a question of theory but is a *practical* question. Man must prove the truth, i.e., the reality and power, the this-worldliness of his thinking in practice. The dispute over the reality or non-reality of thinking which is isolated from practice is a purely *scholastic* question.

3.

The materialist doctrine concerning the changing of circumstances and upbringing forgets that circumstances are changed by men and that the educator must himself be educated. This doctrine must,

---

*Cf. "On the Jewish Question" (1844), Marx's polemic in which he stereotypically portrays the Jewish people as being obsessed with money, transforming humanity and nature into commodities.

therefore, divide society into two parts, one of which is superior to society.

The coincidence of the changing of circumstances and of human activity or self-change can be conceived and rationally understood only as *revolutionary practice*.

4.

Feuerbach starts out from the fact of religious self-estrangement, of the duplication of the world into a religious world and a secular one. His work consists in resolving the religious world into its secular basis. But that the secular basis lifts off from itself and establishes itself as an independent realm in the clouds can only be explained by the inner strife and intrinsic contradictoriness of this secular basis. The latter must, therefore, itself be both understood in its contradiction and revolutionized in practice. Thus, for instance, once the earthly family is discovered to be the secret of the holy family, the former must then itself be destroyed in theory and in practice.

5.

Feuerbach, not satisfied with *abstract thinking*, wants [*sensuous*] *contemplation;* but he does not conceive sensuousness as *practical, human-sensuous activity.*

6.

Feuerbach resolves the essence of religion into the essence of *man*. But the essence of man is no abstraction inherent in each single individual. In its reality it is the ensemble of the social relations.

Feuerbach, who does not enter upon a criticism of this real essence, is hence obliged:

(1) To abstract from the historical process and to define the religious sentiment [*Gemüt*] by itself, and to presuppose an abstract—*isolated*—human individual.

(2) Essence, therefore, can be regarded only as "species," as an inner, mute, general character which unites the many individuals *in a natural way.*

7.

Feuerbach, consequently, does not see that the "religious sentiment" is itself a social product, and that the abstract individual which he analyzes belongs to a particular form of society.

8.

All social life is essentially *practical*. All mysteries which lead theory to mysticism find their rational solution in human practice and in the comprehension of this practice.

9.

The highest point reached by contemplative materialism, that is, materialism which does not comprehend sensuousness as practical activity, is the contemplation of single individuals and of civil society.

10.

The standpoint of the old materialism is civil society; the standpoint of the new is human society, or social humanity.

11.

The philosophers have only *interpreted* the world in various ways; the point is to *change* it.

Written in 1845

Translated by Clemens Dutt

II. EMANCIPATION: LABOR, PRIVATE PROPERTY, AND THE PROLETARIAT

Letter to P. V. Annenkov in Paris

Brussels, 28 December 1846

You would long since have had a reply to your letter of 1 November had not my bookseller delayed sending me Mr. Proudhon's book, *Philosophie de la misère,* until last week. I skimmed through it in two days so as to be able to give you my opinion straight away. Having read the book very cursorily, I cannot go into details but can only let you have the general impression it made on me. Should you so desire, I could go into it in greater detail in another letter.

To be frank, I must admit that I find the book on the whole poor, if not very poor. You yourself make fun in your letter of the "little bit of German philosophy" paraded by Mr. Proudhon in this amorphous and overweening work, but you assume that the economic argument has remained untainted by the philosophic poison. Therefore I am by no means inclined to ascribe the faults of the economic argument to Mr. Proudhon's philosophy. Mr. Proudhon does not provide a false critique of political economy because his philosophy is absurd—he produces an absurd philosophy because he has not understood present social conditions in their *engrènement,** to use a word which Mr. Proudhon borrows from Fourier, like so much else.

Why does Mr. Proudhon speak of God, of universal reason, of mankind's impersonal reason which is never mistaken, which has at all times been equal to itself and of which one only has to be correctly aware in order to arrive at truth? Why does he indulge in feeble Hegelianism in order to set himself up as an *esprit fort?*

---

*intermeshing.

He himself provides the key to this enigma. Mr. Proudhon sees in history a definite series of social developments; he finds progress realized in history; finally, he finds that men, taken as individuals, did not know what they were about, were mistaken as to their own course, i.e., that their social development appears at first sight to be something distinct, separate and independent of their individual development. He is unable to explain these facts, and the hypothesis of universal reason made manifest is ready to hand. Nothing is easier than to invent mystical causes, i.e., phrases in which common sense is lacking.

But in admitting his total incomprehension of the historical development of mankind—and he admits as much in making use of high-flown expressions such as universal reason, God, etc.—does not Mr. Proudhon admit, implicitly and of necessity, his inability to understand *economic development?*

What is society, irrespective of its form? The product of man's interaction upon man. Is man free to choose this or that form of society? By no means. If you assume a given state of development of man's productive faculties, you will have a corresponding form of commerce and consumption. If you assume given stages of development in production, commerce or consumption, you will have a corresponding form of social constitution, a corresponding organization, whether of the family, of the estates or of the classes—in a word, a corresponding civil society. If you assume this or that civil society, you will have this or that political system, which is but the official expression of civil society. This is something Mr. Proudhon will never understand, for he imagines he's doing something great when he appeals from the state to civil society, i.e., to official society from the official epitome of society.

Needless to say, man is not free to choose *his productive forces*— upon which his whole history is based—for every productive force is an acquired force, the product of previous activity. Thus the productive forces are the result of man's practical energy, but that energy is in turn circumscribed by the conditions in which man is placed by the productive forces already acquired, by the form of society which exists before him, which he does not create, which is the product of the preceding generation. The simple fact that every succeeding generation finds productive forces acquired by the preceding generation and which serve it as the raw material of further production, engenders a relatedness in the history of man, engenders a history of mankind, which is all the more a history of mankind as man's productive forces, and hence his social relations, have expanded. From this it can only be concluded that the social history of man is never anything else than the history of his individual development, whether he is conscious of this or not. His material relations form the basis of all his relations. These material relations are but the necessary forms in which his material and individual activity is realized.

Mr. Proudhon confuses ideas and things. Man never renounces what he has gained, but this does not mean that he never renounces the form of society in which he has acquired certain productive forces. On the contrary. If he is not to be deprived of the results obtained or to forfeit the fruits of civilization, man is compelled to change all his traditional social forms as soon as the mode of commerce ceases to correspond to the productive forces acquired. Here I use the word *commerce* in its widest sense—as we would say *Verkehr* in German. For instance, privilege, the institution of guilds and corporations, the regulatory system of the Middle Ages, were the only social relations that corresponded to the acquired productive forces and to the pre-existing social conditions from which those institutions had emerged. Protected by the corporative and regulatory system, capital had accumulated, maritime trade had expanded, colonies had been founded—and man would have lost the very fruits of all this had he wished to preserve the forms under whose protection those fruits had ripened. And, indeed, two thunderclaps occurred, the revolutions of 1640 and of 1688. In England, all the earlier economic forms, the social relations corresponding to them, and the political system which was the official expression of the old civil society, were destroyed. Thus, the economic forms in which man produces, consumes and exchanges are *transitory and historical*. With the acquisition of new productive faculties man changes his mode of production and with the mode of production he changes all the economic relations which were but the necessary relations of that particular mode of production.

It is this that Mr. Proudhon has failed to understand, let alone demonstrate. Unable to follow the real course of history, Mr. Proudhon provides a phantasmagoria which he has the presumption to present as a dialectical phantasmagoria. He no longer feels any need to speak of the seventeenth, eighteenth or nineteenth centuries, for his history takes place in the nebulous realm of the imagination and soars high above time and place. In a word it is Hegelian trash, it is not history, it is not profane history—history of mankind, but sacred history—history of ideas. As seen by him, man is but the instrument used by the idea or eternal reason in order to unfold itself. The *evolutions* of which Mr. Proudhon speaks are presumed to be evolutions such as take place in the mystical bosom of the absolute idea. If the veil of this mystical language be rent, it will be found that what Mr. Proudhon gives us is the order in which economic categories are arranged within his mind. It would require no great effort on my part to prove to you that this arrangement is the arrangement of a very disorderly mind. . . .

In order to explain this system of antagonisms, let us take an example.

Monopoly is good because it is an economic category, hence an emanation of God. *Competition* is good because it, too, is an economic category. But what is not good is the reality of monopoly and the reality of competition. And what is even worse is that monopoly and competition mutually devour each other. What is to be done about it? Because these two eternal thoughts of God contradict each other, it seems clear to him that, in God's bosom, there is likewise a synthesis of these two thoughts in which the evils of monopoly are balanced by competition and vice versa. The result of the struggle between the two ideas will be that only the good aspects will be thrown into relief. This secret idea need only be wrested from God and put into practice and all will be for the best: the synthetic formula concealed in the night of mankind's impersonal reason must be revealed. Mr. Proudhon does not hesitate for a moment to act as revealer.

But take a brief glance at real life. In present-day economic life you will find, not only competition and monopoly, but also their synthesis, which is not a *formula* but a *movement*. Monopoly produces competition, competition produces monopoly. That equation, however, far from alleviating the difficulties of the present situation, as bourgeois economists suppose, gives rise to a situation even more difficult and involved. Thus, by changing the basis upon which the present economic relations rest, by abolishing the present *mode* of production, you abolish not only competition, monopoly and their antagonism, but also their unity, their synthesis, the movement whereby a true balance is maintained between competition and monopoly.

Let me now give you an example of Mr. Proudhon's dialectics.

Freedom and *slavery* constitute an antagonism. There is no need for me to speak either of the good or of the bad aspects of freedom.

As for slavery, there is no need for me to speak of its bad aspects. The only thing requiring explanation is the good side of slavery. I do not mean indirect slavery, the slavery of proletariat; I mean direct slavery, the slavery of blacks in Surinam, in Brazil, in the southern regions of North America.

Direct slavery is as much the pivot upon which our present-day industrialism turns as are machinery, credit, etc. Without slavery there would be no cotton, without cotton there would be no modern industry. It is slavery which has given value to the colonies, it is the colonies which have created world trade, and world trade is the necessary condition for large-scale machine industry. Consequently, prior to the slave trade, the colonies sent very few products to the Old World, and did not noticeably change the face of the world. Slavery is therefore an economic category of paramount importance. Without slavery, North America, the most progressive nation, would be transformed into a patriarchal country. Only wipe North America off the map and you will get anarchy, the complete decay of trade and modern civilization. But to do away with slavery would be to wipe America off the map. Being an economic category, slavery has existed in all nations since the beginning of the world. All that modern nations have achieved is to disguise slavery at home and import it openly into the New World. After these reflections on slavery, what will the good Mr. Proudhon do? He will seek the synthesis of liberty and slavery, the true golden mean, in other words the balance between slavery and liberty.

Mr. Proudhon understands perfectly well that men manufacture worsted, linens and silks; and whatever credit is due for understanding such a trifle! What Mr. Proudhon does not understand is that, according to their faculties, men also produce the *social relations* in which they produce worsted and linens. Still less does Mr. Proudhon understand that those who produce social relations in conformity with their material productivity also produce the *ideas, categories,* i.e., the ideal abstract expressions of those same social relations. Indeed, the categories are no more eternal than the relations they express. They are historical and transitory products. To Mr. Proudhon, on the contrary, the prime cause consists in abstractions and categories. According to him it is these and not men which make history. *The abstraction, the category regarded as such,* i.e., as distinct from man and his material activity, is, of course, immortal, immutable, impassive. It is nothing but an entity of pure reason, which is only another way of saying that an abstraction, regarded as such, is abstract. An admirable *tautology!*

Hence, to Mr. Proudhon, economic relations seen in the form of categories, are eternal formulas without origin or progress.

To put it another way: Mr. Proudhon does not directly assert that to him *bourgeois life* is an *eternal truth:* he says so indirectly, by deifying the categories which express bourgeois relations in the form of thought. He regards the products of bourgeois society as spontaneous entities, endowed with a life of their own, eternal, the moment these present themselves to him in the shape of categories, of thought. Thus he fails to rise above the bourgeois horizon. Because he operates with bourgeois thoughts and assumes them to be eternally true, he looks for the synthesis of those thoughts, their balance, and fails to see that their present manner of maintaining a balance is the only possible one.

In fact he does what all good bourgeois do. They all maintain that competition, monopoly, etc., are, in principle—i.e. regarded as abstract thoughts—the only basis for existence, but leave a great deal to be desired in practice. What they all want is competition without the pernicious consequences of competition. They all want the impossible, i.e., the conditions of bourgeois existence without the necessary consequences of those conditions. They all fail to understand that the bourgeois form of production is an historical and transitory form, just as was the feudal form. This mistake is due to the fact that, to them, bourgeois man is the only possible basis for any society, and that they cannot envisage a state of society in which man will have ceased to be bourgeois.

Hence Mr. Proudhon is necessarily *doctrinaire.* The historical movement by which the present world is convulsed resolves itself, so far as he is concerned, into the problem of discovering the right balance, the synthesis of two bourgeois thoughts. Thus, by subtlety, the clever fellow discovers God's secret thought, the unity of two isolated thoughts which are isolated thoughts only because Mr. Proudhon has isolated them from practical life, from present-day production, which is the combination of the realities they express. In place of the great historical movement which is born of the conflict between the productive forces already acquired by man, and his social relations which no longer correspond to those productive forces, in the place of the terrible wars now imminent between the various classes of a nation and between the various nations, in place of practical and violent action on the part of the masses, which is alone capable of resolving those conflicts, in place of that movement—vast, prolonged and complex—Mr. Proudhon puts the cacky-dauphin movement of his own mind. Thus it is the savants, the men able to filch from God his inmost thoughts, who make history. All the lesser fry have to do is put their revelations into practice.

Now you will understand why Mr. Proudhon is the avowed enemy of all political movements. For him, the solution of present-day problems does not consist in public action but in the dialectical rotations of his brain. Because to him the categories are the motive force, it is not necessary to change practical life in order to change the categories; on the contrary, it is necessary to change the categories, whereupon actual society will change as a result.

In his desire to reconcile contradictions Mr. Proudhon does not ask himself whether the very basis of those contradictions ought not to be subverted. He is exactly like the political doctrinaire who wants a king and a chamber of deputies and a chamber of peers as integral parts of social life, as eternal categories. Only he seeks a new formula with which to balance those powers (whose balance consists precisely in the actual movement in which one of those powers is now the conqueror, now the slave, of the other). In the eighteenth century, for instance, a whole lot of mediocre minds busied themselves with finding the true formula with which to maintain a balance between the social estates, the nobility, the king, the parliaments, etc., and the next day there was neither king, nor parliament, nor nobility. The proper balance between the aforesaid antagonisms consisted in the convulsion of all the social relations which served as a basis for those feudal entities and for the antagonism between those feudal entities.

Because Mr. Proudhon posits on the one hand eternal ideas, the categories of pure reason, and, on the other, man and his practical life which, according to him, is the practical application of these categories, you will find in him from the very outset a *dualism* between life and ideas, between soul and body—a dualism which recurs in many forms. So you now see that the said antagonism is nothing other than Mr. Proudhon's inability to understand either the origin or the profane history of the categories he has deified.

My letter is already too long for me to mention the absurd case Mr. Proudhon is conducting against communism. For the present you will concede that a man who has failed to understand the present state of society must be even less able to understand either the movement which tends to overturn it or the literary expression of that revolutionary movement.

The *only point* upon which I am in complete agreement with Mr. Proudhon is the disgust he feels for socialist sentimentalizing. I anticipated him in provoking considerable hostility by the ridicule I directed at ovine, sentimental, utopian socialism. But is not Mr. Proudhon subject to strange delusions when he opposes his petty-bourgeois sentimentality, by which I mean his homilies about home, conjugal love and suchlike banalities, to socialist sentimentality which—as for instance in Fourier's case—is infinitely more profound than the presumptuous platitudes of our worthy Proudhon? He himself is so well aware of the emptiness of his reasoning, of his complete inability to discuss such things, that he indulges in tantrums, exclamations and *irae hominis probi,* that he fumes, curses, denounces, cries pestilence and infamy, thumps his chest and glorifies himself before God and man as being innocent of socialist infamies! It is not as a critic that he derides socialist sentimentalities, or what he takes to be sentimentalities. It is as a saint, a pope, that he excommunicates the poor sinners and sings the praises of the petty bourgeoisie and of the miserable patriarchal amorous illusions of the domestic hearth. Nor is this in any way fortuitous. Mr. Proudhon is, from top to toe, a philosopher, an economist of the petty bourgeoisie. In an advanced society and because of his situation, *a petty bourgeois* becomes a socialist on the one hand, and economist on the other, i.e., he is dazzled by the magnificence of the upper middle classes and feels compassion for the sufferings of the people. He is at one and the same time bourgeois and man of the people. In his heart of hearts he prides himself on his impartiality, on having found the correct balance, allegedly distinct from the happy medium. A petty bourgeois of this kind deifies *contradiction*, for contradiction is the very basis of his being. He is nothing but social contradiction in action. He must justify by means of theory what he is in practice, and Mr. Proudhon has the merit of being the scientific exponent of the French petty bourgeoisie, which is a real merit since the petty bourgeoisie will be an integral part of all the impending social revolutions.

With this letter I should have liked to send you my book on political economy, but up till now I have been unable to have printed either this work or the critique of German philosophers and socialists* which I mentioned to you in Brussels. You would

---

*K. Marx and F. Engels, *The German Ideology.*

never believe what difficulties a publication of this kind runs into in Germany, on the one hand from the police, on the other from the booksellers, who are themselves the interested representatives of all those tendencies I attack. And as for our own party, not only is it poor, but there is a large faction in the German communist party which bears me a grudge because I am opposed to its utopias and its declaiming.

Ever yours
Charles Marx

Translated by Peter and Betty Ross

On Estranged Labor

We have proceeded from the premises of political economy. We have accepted its language and its laws. We presupposed private property, the separation of labor, capital and land, and of wages, profit of capital and rent of land—likewise division of labor, competition, the concept of exchange-value, etc. On the basis of political economy itself, in its own words, we have shown that the worker sinks to the level of a commodity and becomes indeed the most wretched of commodities; that the wretchedness of the worker is in inverse proportion to the power and magnitude of his production; that the necessary result of competition is the accumulation of capital in a few hands, and thus the restoration of monopoly in a more terrible form; and that finally the distinction between capitalist and land rentier, like that between the tiller of the soil and the factory worker, disappears and that the whole of society must fall apart into the two classes—the *property owners* and the propertyless *workers*.

Political economy starts with the fact of private property; it does not explain it to us. It expresses in general, abstract formulas the *material* process through which private property actually passes, and these formulas it then takes for *laws*. It does not *comprehend* these laws, i.e., it does not demonstrate how they arise from the very nature of private property. Political economy throws no light on the cause of the division between labor and capital, and between capital and land. When, for example, it defines the relationship of wages to profit, it takes the interest of the capitalists to be the ultimate cause, i.e., it takes for granted what it is supposed to explain. Similarly, competition comes in everywhere. It is explained from external circumstances. As to how far these external and apparently accidental circumstances are but the expression of a necessary course of development, political economy teaches us nothing. We have seen how exchange itself appears to it as an accidental fact. The only wheels which political economy sets in motion are *greed* and the *war amongst the greedy—competition.*

Precisely because political economy does not grasp the way the movement is connected, it was possible to oppose, for instance, the doctrine of competition to the doctrine of monopoly, the doctrine of the freedom of the crafts to the doctrine of the guild, the doctrine of the division of landed property to the doctrine of the big estate— for competition, freedom of the crafts and the division of landed property were explained and comprehended only as accidental, premeditated, and violent consequences of monopoly, of the guild system, and of feudal property, not as their necessary, inevitable and natural consequences.

Now, therefore, we have to grasp the intrinsic connection between private property, avarice, the separation of labor, capital and landed property; the connection of exchange and competition, of value and the devaluation of men, of monopoly and competition, etc.—we have to grasp this whole estrangement connected with the *money* system.

Do not let us go back to a fictitious primordial condition as the political economist does, when he tries to explain. Such a primordial condition explains nothing; it merely pushes the question away into a grey nebulous distance. The economist assumes in the form of a fact, of an event, what he is supposed to deduce—namely, the necessary relationship between two things—between, for example, division of labor and exchange. Thus the theologian explains the origin of evil by the fall of man; that is, he assumes as a fact, in historical form, what has to be explained.

We proceed from an *actual* economic fact.

The worker becomes all the poorer the more wealth he produces, the more his production increases in power and size. The worker becomes an ever cheaper commodity the more commodities he creates. The *devaluation* of the world of men is in direct proportion to the *increasing value* of the world of things. Labor produces not only commodities: it produces itself and the worker as a *commodity*—and this at the same rate at which it produces commodities in general.

This fact expresses merely that the object which labor produces—labor's product—confronts it as *something alien,* as a *power independent* of the producer. The product of labor is labor which has been embodied in an object, which has become material: it is the *objectification* of labor. Labor's realization is its objectification. Under these economic conditions this realization of labor appears as *loss of realization* for the workers; objectification as *loss of the object and bondage to it;* appropriation as *estrangement, as alienation.*

So much does labor's realization appear as loss of realization that the worker loses realization to the point of starving to death. So much does objectification appear as loss of the object that the worker is robbed of the objects most necessary not only for his life but for his work. Indeed, labor itself becomes an object which he can obtain only with the greatest effort and with the most irregular interruptions. So much does the appropriation of the object appear as estrangement that the more objects the worker produces the less he can possess and the more he falls under the sway of his product, capital.

All these consequences are implied in the statement that the worker is related to the *product of his labor* as to an *alien* object. For on this premise it is clear that the more the worker spends himself, the more powerful becomes the alien world of objects which he creates over and against himself, the poorer he himself— his inner world—becomes, the less belongs to him as his own. It is the same in religion. The more man puts into God, the less he retains in himself. The worker puts his life into the object; but now his life no longer belongs to him but to the object. Hence, the greater this activity, the more the worker lacks objects. Whatever the product of his labor is, he is not. Therefore the greater this product, the less is he himself. The *alienation* of the worker in his product means not only that his labor becomes an object, an *external* existence, but that it exists *outside him,* independently, as something alien to him, and that it becomes a power on its own confronting him. It means that the life which he has conferred on the object confronts him as something hostile and alien.

Let us now look more closely at the *objectification,* at the production of the worker; and in it at the *estrangement,* the *loss* of the object, of his product.

The worker can create nothing without *nature,* without the *sensuous external world.* It is the material on which his labor is realized, in which it is active, from which and by means of which it produces.

But just as nature provides labor with [the] *means of life* in the sense that labor cannot *live* without objects on which to operate, on the other hand, it also provides the *means of life* in the more restricted sense, i.e., the means for the physical subsistence of the *worker* himself.

Thus the more the worker by his labor *appropriates* the external world, sensuous nature, the more he deprives himself of *means of life* in two respects: first, in that the sensuous external world more and more ceases to be an object belonging to his labor—to be his labor's *means of life;* and secondly, in that it more and more ceases to be *means of life* in the immediate sense, means for the physical subsistence of the worker.

In both respects, therefore, the worker becomes a servant of his object, first, in that he receives an *object of labor,* i.e., in that he receives *work;* and secondly, in that he receives *means of subsistence.* This enables him to exist, first, as a *worker;* and, second, as a *physical subject.* The height of this servitude is that it is only as a *worker* that he can maintain himself as a *physical subject,* and that it is only as a *physical subject* that he is a worker.

(According to the economic laws the estrangement of the worker in his object is expressed thus: the more the worker produces, the less he has to consume; the more values he creates, the more value-less, the more unworthy he becomes; the better formed his product, the more deformed becomes the worker; the more civilized his object, the more barbarous becomes the worker; the more powerful labor becomes, the more powerless becomes the worker; the more ingenious labor becomes, the less ingenious becomes the worker and the more he becomes nature's servant.)

Political economy conceals the estrangement inherent in the nature of labor by not considering the direct *relationship between the* worker (labor) *and production.* It is true that labor produces wonderful things for the rich—but for the worker it produces privation. It produces palaces—but for the worker, hovels. It produces beauty—but for the worker, deformity. It replaces labor by machines, but it throws one section of the workers back to a barbarous type of labor, and it turns the other section into a machine. It produces intelligence—but for the worker, stupidity, cretinism.

The direct relationship of labor to its products is the relationship of the worker to the objects of his production. The relationship of the man of means to the objects of production and to production itself is only a *consequence* of this first relationship—and confirms it. We shall consider this other aspect later. When we ask, then, what is the essential relationship of labor we are asking about the relationship of the *worker* to production.

Till now we have been considering the estrangement, the alienation of the worker only in one of its aspects, i.e., the worker's *relationship to the products of his labor.* But the estrangement is manifested not only in the result but in the *act of production,* within the *producing activity* itself. How could the worker come to face the product of his activity as a stranger, were it not that in the very act of production he was estranging himself from himself? The product is after all but the summary of the activity, of production. If then the product of labor is alienation, production itself must be active alienation, the alienation of activity, the activity of alienation. In the estrangement of the object of labor is merely summarized the estrangement, the alienation, in the activity of labor itself.

What, then, constitutes the alienation of labor?

First, the fact that labor is *external* to the worker, i.e., it does not belong to his intrinsic nature; that in his work, therefore, he does not affirm himself but denies himself, does not feel content but unhappy, does not develop freely his physical and mental energy but mortifies his body and ruins his mind. The worker therefore only feels himself outside his work, and in his work feels outside himself. He feels at home when he is not working, and when he is working he does not feel at home. His labor is therefore not voluntary, but coerced; it is *forced labor.* It is therefore not the satisfaction of a need; it is merely a *means* to satisfy needs external to it. Its alien character emerges clearly in the fact that as soon as no physical or other compulsion exists, labor is shunned like the plague. External labor, labor in which man alienates himself, is a labor of self-sacrifice, of mortification. Lastly, the external character of labor for the worker appears in the fact that it is not his own, but someone else's, that it does not belong to him, that in it he belongs, not to himself, but to another. Just as in religion the spontaneous activity of the human imagination, of the human brain and the human heart, operates on the individual independently of him—that is, operates as an alien, divine or diabolical activity—so is the worker's activity not his spontaneous activity. It belongs to another; it is the loss of his self.

As a result, therefore, man (the worker) only feels himself freely active in his animal functions—eating, drinking, procreating, or at most in his dwelling and in dressing-up, etc.; and in his human functions he no longer feels himself to be anything but an animal. What is animal becomes human and what is human becomes animal.

Certainly eating, drinking, procreating, etc., are also genuinely human functions. But taken abstractly, separated from the sphere of all other human activity and turned into sole and ultimate ends, they are animal functions.

We have considered the act of estranging practical human activity, labor, in two of its aspects. (1) The relation of the worker to the *product of labor* as an alien object exercising power over him. This relation is at the same time the relation to the sensuous external world, to the objects of nature, as an alien world inimically opposed to him. (2) The relation of labor to the *act of production* within the *labor* process. This relation is the relation of the worker to his own activity as an alien activity not belonging to him; it is activity as suffering, strength as weakness, begetting as emasculating, the worker's *own* physical and mental energy, his personal life—for what is life but activity?—as an activity which is turned against him, independent of him and not belonging to him. Here we have *self-estrangement,* as previously we had the estrangement of the *thing.*

We have still a third aspect of *estranged labor* to deduce from the two already considered.

Man is a species-being, not only because in practice and in theory he adopts the species (his own as well as those of other things) as his object, but—and this is only another way of expressing it—also because he treats himself as the actual, living species; because he treats himself as a *universal* and therefore a free being.

The life of the species, both in man and in animals, consists physically in the fact that man (like the animal) lives on inorganic nature; and the more universal man (or the animal) is, the more universal is the sphere of inorganic nature on which he lives. Just as plants, animals, stones, air, light, etc., constitute theoretically a part of human consciousness, partly as objects of natural science, partly as objects of art—his spiritual inorganic nature, spiritual nourishment which he must first prepare to make palatable and digestible—so also in the realm of practice they constitute a part of human life and human activity. Physically man lives only on these products of nature, whether they appear in the form of food, heating, clothes, a dwelling, etc. The universality of man appears in practice precisely in the universality which makes all nature his *inorganic* body—both inasmuch as nature is (1) his direct means of life, and (2) the material, the object, and the instrument of his life activity. Nature is man's *inorganic body*—nature, that is, insofar as it is not itself human body. Man *lives* on nature—means that nature is his *body,* with which he must remain in continuous interchange if he is not to die. That man's physical and spiritual life is linked to nature means simply that nature is linked to itself, for man is a part of nature.

In estranging from man (1) nature, and (2) himself, his own active functions, his life activity, estranged labor estranges the *species* from man. It changes for him the *life of the species* into a means of individual life. First it estranges the life of the species and individual life, and secondly it makes individual life in its abstract form the purpose of the life of the species, likewise in its abstract and estranged form.

For labor, *life activity, productive life* itself, appears to man in the first place merely as a *means* of satisfying a need—the need to maintain physical existence. Yet the productive life is the life of the species. It is life-engendering life. The whole character of a species—its species-character—is contained in the character of its life activity; and free, conscious activity is man's species-character. Life itself appears only as a *means to life.*

The animal is immediately one with its life activity. It does not distinguish itself from it. It is *its life activity.* Man makes his life activity itself the object of his will and of his consciousness. He has conscious life activity. It is not a determination with which he directly merges. Conscious life activity distinguishes man immediately from animal life activity. It is just because of this that he is a species-being. Or it is only because he is a species-being that he is a conscious being, i.e., that his own life is an object for him. Only because of that is his activity free activity. Estranged labor reverses this relationship, so that it is just because man is a conscious being that he makes his life activity, his *essential being,* a mere means to his *existence.*

In creating a *world of objects* by his practical activity, in his *work upon* inorganic nature, man proves himself a conscious species-being, i.e., as a being that treats the species as its own essential being, or that treats itself as a species-being. Admittedly animals also produce. They build themselves nests, dwellings, like the bees, beavers, ants, etc. But an animal only produces what it immediately needs for itself or its young. It produces one-sidedly, while man produces universally. It produces only under the dominion of immediate physical need, while man produces even when he is free from physical need and only truly produces in freedom therefrom. An animal produces only itself, while man reproduces the whole of nature. An animal's product belongs immediately to its physical body, while man freely confronts his product. An animal forms objects only in accordance with the standard and the need of the species to which it belongs, while man knows how to produce in accordance with the standard of every species, and knows how to apply everywhere the inherent standard to the object. Man therefore also forms objects in accordance with the laws of beauty.

It is just in his work upon the objective world, therefore, that man really proves himself to be a *species-being*. This production is his active species-life. Through this production, nature appears as *his* work and his reality. The object of labor is, therefore, the *objectification of man's species-life:* for he duplicates himself not only, as in consciousness, intellectually, but also actively, in reality, and therefore he sees himself in a world that he has created. In tearing away from man the object of his production, therefore, estranged labor tears from him his *species-life,* his real objectivity as a member of the species, and transforms his advantage over animals into the disadvantage that his inorganic body, nature, is taken away from him.

Similarly, in degrading spontaneous, free activity to a means, estranged labor makes man's species-life a means to his physical existence.

The consciousness which man has of his species is thus transformed by estrangement in such a way that species[-life] becomes for him a means.

Estranged labor turns thus:

(3) *Man's species-being,* both nature and his spiritual species-property, into a being *alien* to him, into a *means* for his *individual existence*. It estranges from man his own body, as well as external nature and his spiritual aspect, his *human* aspect.

(4) An immediate consequence of the fact that man is estranged from the product of his labor, from his life activity, from his species-being is the *estrangement of man* from *man*. When man confronts himself, he confronts the *other* man. What applies to a man's relation to his work, to the product of his labor and to

himself, also holds of a man's relation to the other man, and to the other man's labor and object of labor.

In fact, the proposition that man's species-nature is estranged from him means that one man is estranged from the other, as each of them is from man's essential nature.

The estrangement of man, and in fact every relationship in which man [stands] to himself, is realized and expressed only in the relationship in which a man stands to other men.

Hence within the relationship of estranged labor each man views the other in accordance with the standard and the relationship in which he finds himself as a worker.

We took our departure from a fact of political economy—the estrangement of the worker and his product. We have formulated this fact in conceptual terms as *estranged, alienated* labor. We have analyzed this concept—hence analyzing merely a fact of political economy.

Let us now see, further, how the concept of estranged, alienated labor must express and present itself in real life.

If the product of labor is alien to me, if it confronts me as an alien power, to whom, then, does it belong?

If my own activity does not belong to me, if it is an alien, a coerced activity, to whom, then, does it belong?

To a being *other* than myself.

Who is this being?

The *gods?* To be sure, in the earliest times the principal production (for example, the building of temples, etc., in Egypt, India and Mexico) appears to be in the service of the gods, and the product belongs to the gods. However, the gods on their own were never the lords of labor. No more was *nature*. And what a contradiction it would be if, the more man subjugated nature by his labor and the more the miracles of the gods were rendered superfluous by the miracles of industry, the more man were to renounce the joy of production and the enjoyment of the product to please these powers.

The *alien* being, to whom labor and the product of labor belongs, in whose service labor is done and for whose benefit the product of labor is provided, can only be *man* himself.

If the product of labor does not belong to the worker, if it confronts him as an alien power, then this can only be because it belongs to some *other man than the worker*. If the worker's activity is a torment to him, to another it must give *satisfaction* and pleasure. Not the gods, not nature, but only man himself can be this alien power over man.

We must bear in mind the previous proposition that man's relation to himself only becomes for him *objective* and *actual* through his relation to the other man. Thus, if the product of his labor, his labor objectified, is for him an *alien, hostile,* powerful object independent of him, then his position toward it is such that someone else is master of this object, someone who is alien, hostile, powerful, and independent of him. If he treats his own activity as an unfree activity, then he treats it as an activity performed in the service, under the dominion, the coercion, and the yoke of another man.

Every self-estrangement of man, from himself and from nature, appears in the relation in which he places himself and nature to men other than and differentiated from himself. For this reason religious self-estrangement necessarily appears in the relationship of the layman to the priest, or again to a mediator, etc., since we are here dealing with the intellectual world. In the real practical world self-estrangement can only become manifest through the real practical relationship to other men. The medium through which estrangement takes place is itself *practical.* Thus through estranged labor man not only creates his relationship to the object and to the act of production as to powers that are alien and hostile to him; he also creates the relationship in which other men stand to his production and to his product, and the relationship in which he stands to these other men. Just as he creates his own production as the loss of his reality, as his punishment; his own product as a loss, as a product not belonging to him; so he creates the domination of the person who does not produce over production and over the product. Just as he estranges his own activity from himself, so he confers upon the stranger an activity which is not his own.

We have until now considered this relationship only from the standpoint of the worker and later we shall be considering it also from the standpoint of the non-worker.

Through *estranged, alienated labor,* then, the worker produces the relationship to this labor of a man alien to labor and standing outside it. The relationship of the worker to labor creates the relation to it of the capitalist (or whatever one chooses to call the master of labor). *Private property* is thus the product, the result, the necessary consequence, of *alienated labor,* of the external relation of the worker to nature and to himself.

Private property thus results by analysis from the concept of *alienated labor,* i.e., of *alienated man,* of estranged labor, of estranged life, of *estranged* man.

True, it is as a result of the *movement of private property* that we have obtained the concept of *alienated labor (of alienated life)* in political economy. But analysis of this concept shows that though private property appears to be the reason, the cause of alienated labor, it is rather its consequence, just as the gods are *originally* not the cause but the effect of man's intellectual confusion. Later this relationship becomes reciprocal.

Only at the culmination of the development of private property does this, its secret, appear again, namely, that on the one hand it is the *product* of alienated labor, and that on the other it is the *means* by which labor alienates itself, the *realization of this alienation.*

This exposition immediately sheds light on various hitherto unsolved conflicts.

(1) Political economy starts from labor as the real soul of production; yet to labor it gives nothing, and to private property everything. Confronting this contradiction, Proudhon has decided in favor of labor against private property. We understand, however, that this apparent contradiction is the contradiction of *estranged labor* with itself, and that political economy has merely formulated the laws of estranged labor.

We also understand, therefore, that *wages* and *private property* are identical. Indeed, where the product, as the object of labor, pays for labor itself, there the wage is but a necessary consequence of labor's estrangement. Likewise, in the wage of labor, labor does not appear as an end in itself but as the servant of the wage. We shall develop this point later, and meanwhile will only draw some conclusions.

An enforced *increase of wages* (disregarding all other difficulties, including the fact that it would only be by force, too that such an increase, being an anomaly, could be maintained) would therefore be nothing but better *payment for the slave,* and would not win either for the worker or for labor their human status and dignity.

Indeed, even the *equality of wages,* as demanded by Proudhon, only transforms the relationship of the present-day worker to his labor into the relationship of all men to labor. Society is then conceived as an abstract capitalist.

Wages are a direct consequence of estranged labor, and estranged labor is the direct cause of private property. The downfall of the one must therefore involve the downfall of the other.

(2) From the relationship of estranged labor to private property it follows further that the emancipation of society from private property, etc., from servitude, is expressed in the *political* form of the *emancipation of the workers;* not that *their* emancipation alone is at stake, but because the emancipation of the workers contains universal human emancipation—and it contains this, because the whole of human servitude is involved in the relation of the worker to production, and all relations of servitude are but modifications and consequences of this relation.

Just as we have derived the concept of *private property* from the concept of *estranged, alienated labor* by *analysis,* so we can develop every *category* of political economy with the help of these two factors; and we shall find again in each category, e.g., trade, competition, capital, money, only a *particular* and *developed expression* of these first elements.

Before considering this phenomenon, however, let us try to solve two other problems.

(1) To define the general *nature of private property,* as it has arisen as a result of estranged labor, in its relation to *truly human* and *social property.*

(2) We have accepted the *estrangement of labor,* its *alienation,* as a fact, and we have analyzed this fact. How, we now ask, does *man* come to *alienate,* to estrange, his *labor?* How is this estrangement rooted in the nature of human development? We have already gone a long way to the solution of this problem by *transforming* the question of the *origin of private property* into the question of the relation of *alienated labor* to the course of humanity's development. For when one speaks of *private property,* one thinks of dealing with something external to man. When one speaks of labor, one is directly dealing with man himself. This new formulation of the question already contains its solution.

As to (1): The general nature of private property and its relation to truly human property.

Alienated labor has resolved itself for us into two components which depend on one another, or which are but different expressions of one and the same relationship. *Appropriation* appears as *estrangement,* as *alienation;* and *alienation* appears as *appropriation, estrangement* as truly *becoming a citizen.*

Translated by Martin Milligan and Dirk J. Struik

Private Property
and Communism

The antithesis between *lack of property* and *property,* so long as it is not comprehended as the antithesis of *labor* and *capital,* still remains an indifferent antithesis, not grasped in its *active connection,* in its *internal* relation, not yet grasped as a *contradiction.* It can find expression in this *first* form even without the advanced development of private property (as in ancient Rome, Turkey, etc.). It does not yet *appear* as having been established by private property itself. But labor, the subjective essence of private property as exclusion of property, and capital, objective labor as exclusion of labor, constitute *private property* as its developed state of contradiction—hence a dynamic relationship driving toward resolution.

The transcendence of self-estrangement follows the same course as self-estrangement. *Private property* is first considered only in its objective aspect—but nevertheless with labor as its essence. Its form of existence is therefore *capital,* which is to be annulled "as such" (Proudhon). Or a *particular form* of labor—labor leveled down, fragmented, and therefore unfree—is conceived as the source of private property's *perniciousness* and of its existence in estrangement from men. For instance, *Fourier,* who, like the Physiocrats, also conceives *agricultural labor* to be at least the *exemplary* type, whereas *Saint-Simon* declares in contrast that *industrial labor* as such is the essence, and accordingly aspires to the *exclusive* rule of the industrialists and the improvement of the workers' condition. Finally, *communism* is the *positive* expression of annulled private property—at first as *universal* private property. By embracing this relation as a *whole,* communism is:

(1) In its first form only a *generalization* and *consummation* of it [of this relation]. As such it appears in a twofold form: on the one hand, the dominion of *material* property bulks so large that it wants to destroy *everything* which is not capable of being possessed by all as *private property*. It wants to disregard talent, etc., in an *arbitrary* manner. For it the sole purpose of life and existence is direct, physical *possession*. The category of the *worker* is not done away with, but extended to all men. The relationship of private property persists as the relationship of the community to the world of things. Finally, this movement of opposing universal private property to private property finds expression in the brutish form of opposing to *marriage* (certainly a *form of exclusive private property)* the *community of women,* in which a woman becomes a piece of *communal* and *common* property. It may be said that this idea of the *community of women gives away the secret* of this as yet completely crude and thoughtless communism. Just as woman passes from marriage to general prostitution,* so the entire world of wealth (that is, of man's objective substance) passes from the relationship of exclusive marriage with the owner of private property to a state of universal prostitution with the community. This type of communism—since it negates the *personality* of man in every sphere—is but the logical expression of private property, which is this negation. General *envy* constituting itself as a power is the disguise in which *greed* reestablishes itself and satisfies itself, only in *another* way. The thought of every piece of private property as such is *at least* turned against *wealthier* private property in the form of envy and the urge to reduce things to a common level, so that this envy and urge even constitute the essence of competition. Crude communism is only the culmination of this envy and of this leveling-down proceeding from the *preconceived* minimum. It has a *definite, limited standard.* How little this annulment of private property is really an appropriation is in fact proved by the abstract negation of the entire world of culture and civilization, the regression to the *unnatural* simplicity of the *poor* and crude man who has few needs and who has not only failed to go beyond private property, but has not yet even reached it.

The community is only a community of *labor,* and equality of *wages* paid out by communal capital—by the *community* as the

---

*Prostitution is only a *specific* expression of the *general* prostitution of the *laborer,* and since it is a relationship in which falls not the prostitute alone, but also the universal capitalist. Both sides of the relationship are raised to an *imagined* universality—*labor* as the category in which every person is placed, and *capital* as the acknowledged universality and power of the community.

In the approach to *woman* as the *spoil* and handmaid of communal lust is expressed the infinite degradation in which man exists for himself, for the secret of this approach has its *unambiguous*, decisive, *plain* and undisguised expression in the relation of *man* to *woman* and in the manner in which the *direct* and *natural* species-relationship is conceived. The direct, natural, and necessary relation of person to person is the *relation of man to woman*. In this *natural* species-relationship man's relation to nature is immediately his relation to man, just as his relation to man is immediately his relation to nature—his own *natural* destination. In this relationship, therefore, is *sensuously manifested*, reduced to an observable *fact*, the extent to which the human essence has become nature to man, or to which nature to him has become the human essence of man. From this relationship one can therefore judge man's whole level of development. From the character of this relationship follows how much *man* as a *species-being*, as *man*, has come to be himself and to comprehend himself; the relation of man to woman is the *most natural* relation of human being to human being. It therefore reveals the extent to which man's *natural* behavior has become *human*, or the extent to which the *human* essence in him has become a *natural* essence—the extent to which his *human nature* has come to be *natural* to him. This relationship also reveals the extent to which man's *need* has become a *human* need; the extent to which, therefore, the *other* person as a person has become for him a need—the extent to which he in his individual existence is at the same time a social being.

The first positive annulment of private property—*crude* communism—is thus merely a *manifestation* of the vileness of private property, which wants to set itself up as the *positive community system*.

(2) Communism still political in nature—democratic or despotic; with the abolition of the state, yet still incomplete, and being still affected by private property, i.e., by the estrangement of man. In both forms communism already is aware of being reintegration

---

one who prostitutes—and the latter's abomination is still greater—the capitalist, etc., also comes under this head.

or return of man to himself, the transcendence of human self-estrangement; but since it has not yet grasped the positive essence of private property, and just as little the *human* nature of need, it remains captive to it and infected by it. It has, indeed, grasped its concept, but not its essence.

(3) *Communism* as the *positive* transcendence of *private property* as *human self-estrangement,* and therefore as the real *appropriation* of the *human* essence by and for man; communism therefore as the complete return of man to himself as a *social* (i.e., human) being—a return accomplished consciously and embracing the entire wealth of previous development. This communism, as fully developed naturalism, equals humanism, and as fully developed humanism equals naturalism; it is the *genuine* resolution of the conflict between man and nature and between man and man—the true resolution of the strife between existence and essence, between objectification and self-confirmation, between freedom and necessity, between the individual and the species. Communism is the riddle of history solved, and it knows itself to be this solution.

The entire movement of history, just as its [communism's] *actual* act of genesis—the birth act of its empirical existence—is, therefore, also for its thinking consciousness the *comprehended* and *known* process of its *becoming.* Whereas the still immature communism seeks a *historical* proof for itself—a proof in the realm of what already exists—among disconnected historical phenomena opposed to private property, tearing single phases from the historical process and focusing attention on them as proofs of its historical pedigree (a hobby-horse ridden hard especially by Cabet, Villegardelle, etc.). By so doing it simply makes clear that by far the greater part of this process contradicts its own claim, and that, if it has ever existed, precisely its being in the *past* refutes its pretention to *reality.*

It is easy to see that the entire revolutionary movement necessarily finds both its empirical and its theoretical basis in the movement of *private property*—more precisely, in that of the economy.

This *material,* immediately *perceptible* private property is the material perceptible expression of *estranged human* life. Its movement—production and consumption—is the *perceptible* revelation of the movement of all production until now, i.e., the realization or the reality of man. Religion, family, state, law, morality, science, art, etc., are only *particular* modes of production, and fall under its general law. The positive transcendence of *private property,* as the appropriation of *human* life, is therefore the positive transcendence of all estrangement—that is to say, the return of man from religion, family, state, etc., to his *human,* i.e., *social,* existence. Religious estrangement as such occurs only in the realm of *consciousness,* of man's inner life, but economic estrangement is that of *real life;* its transcendence therefore embraces both aspects. It is evident that the *initial* stage of the movement amongst the various peoples depends on whether the true *recognized* life of the people manifests itself more in consciousness or in the external world—is more ideal or real. Communism begins from the outset *(Owen)* with atheism; but atheism is at first far from being *communism;* indeed, that atheism is still mostly an abstraction.

The philanthropy of atheism is therefore at first only *philosophical,* abstract philanthropy, and that of communism is at once *real* and directly bent on *action.*

We have seen how on the assumption of positively annulled private property man produces man—himself and the other man: how the object, being the direct manifestation of his individuality, is simultaneously his own existence for the other man, the existence of the other man, and that existence for him. Likewise, however, both the material of labor and man as the subject, are the point of departure as well as the result of the movement (and precisely in this fact, that they must constitute the *point of departure,* lies the historical *necessity* of private property). Thus the *social* character is the general character of the whole movement: *just as* society itself produces *man as man,* so is society *produced* by him. Activity and enjoyment, both in their content and in their *mode of existence,* are *social: social* activity and *social* enjoyment. The *human* aspect of nature exists only for *social* man; for only then does nature exist for him as a *bond* with *man*—as his existence for the other and the other's existence for him—and as the life-element of human reality. Only then does nature exist as the *foundation* of his own *human* existence. Only here has what is to him his *natural* existence become his *human* existence, and nature become man for him. Thus *society* is the complete unity of man with nature—the true resurrection of nature—the accomplished naturalism of man and the accomplished humanism of nature.

Social activity and social enjoyment exist by no means *only* in the form of some *directly* communal activity and directly *communal* enjoyment, although *communal* activity and *communal* enjoyment—i.e., activity and enjoyment which are manifested and affirmed in *actual* direct *association* with other men—will occur wherever such a *direct* expression of sociability stems from the true character of the activity's content and is appropriate to the nature of the enjoyment.

But also when I am active *scientifically,* etc.—an activity which I can seldom perform in direct community with others—then my activity is *social,* because I perform it as a *man.* Not only is the material of my activity given to me as a social product (as is even the language in which the thinker is active): my *own* existence *is* social activity, and therefore that which I make of myself, I make of myself for society and with the consciousness of myself as a social being.

My *general* consciousness is only the *theoretical* shape of that of which the *living* shape is the *real* community, the social fabric, although at the present day *general* consciousness is an abstraction from real life and as such confronts it with hostility. The *activity* of my general consciousness, as an activity, is therefore also my *theoretical* existence as a social being.

Above all we must avoid postulating "society" again as an abstraction *vis-à-vis* the individual. The individual *is the social being.* His manifestations of life—even if they may not appear in the direct form of *communal* manifestations of life carried out in association with others—*are* therefore an expression and confirmation of *social life.* Man's individual and species-life are not *different,* however much—and this is inevitable—the mode of existence of the individual is a more *particular* or more *general* mode of the life of the species, or the life of the species is a more *particular* or more *general* individual life.

In his *consciousness of species* man confirms his real *social life* and simply repeats his real existence in thought, just as conversely the being of the species confirms itself in species consciousness and exists for itself in its generality as a thinking being.

Man, much as he may therefore be a *particular* individual (and it is precisely his particularity which makes him an individual, and a real *individual* social being), is just as much the *totality*—the ideal totality—the subjective existence of imagined and experienced society for itself; just as he exists also in the real world both as awareness and real enjoyment of social existence, and as a totality of human manifestation of life.

Thinking and being are thus certainly *distinct,* but at the same time they are in *unity* with each other.

Death seems to be a harsh victory of the species over the *particular* individual and to contradict their unity. But the particular individual is only a *particular species-being,* and as such mortal.

(4) Just as *private property* is only the perceptible expression of the fact that man becomes *objective* for himself and at the same time becomes to himself a strange and inhuman object; just as it expresses the fact that the manifestation of his life is the alienation of his life, that his realization is his loss of reality, is an *alien* reality: so, the positive transcendence of private property—i.e., the *perceptible* appropriation for and by man of the human essence and of human life, of objective man, of human *achievements*— should not be conceived merely in the sense of *immediate,* one-sided *enjoyment,* merely in the sense of *possessing,* of *having.* Man appropriates his comprehensive essence in a comprehensive manner, that is to say, as a whole man. Each of his *human* relations to the world—seeing, hearing, smelling, tasting, feeling, thinking, observing, experiencing, wanting, acting, loving—in short, all the organs of his individual being, like those organs which are directly social in their form, are in their *objective* orientation, or in their *orientation to the object,* the appropriation of the object, the appropriation of *human* reality. Their orientation to the object is the *manifestation of the human reality,** it is human *activity* and human *suffering,* for suffering, humanly considered, is a kind of self-enjoyment of man.

Private property has made us so stupid and one-sided that an object is only *ours* when we have it—when it exists for us as capital, or when it is directly possessed, eaten, drunk, worn, inhabited, etc.,—in short, when it is *used* by us. Although private property itself again conceives all these direct realizations of possession only as *means of life,* and the life which they serve as means is the *life of private property*—labor and conversion into capital.

In the place of *all* physical and mental senses there has therefore come the sheer estrangement of *all* these senses, the sense of *having.* The human being had to be reduced to this absolute poverty in order that he might yield his inner wealth to the outer world.

The abolition of private property is therefore the complete *emancipation* of all human senses and qualities, but it is this emancipation precisely because these senses and attributes have become,

---

*For this reason it is just as highly varied as the *determinations* of human *essence* and *activities*.

subjectively and objectively, *human.* The eye has become a *human* eye, just as its *object* has become a social, *human* object—an object made by man for man. The *senses* have therefore become directly in their practice *theoreticians.* They relate themselves to the *thing* for the sake of the thing, but the thing itself is an *objective human* relation to itself and to man,* and vice versa. Need or enjoyment has consequently lost its *egotistical* nature, and nature has lost its mere *utility* by use becoming *human* use.

In the same way, the senses and enjoyment of other men have become my *own* appropriation. Besides these direct organs, therefore, *social* organs develop in the *form* of society; thus, for instance, activity in direct association with others, etc., has become an organ for *expressing* my own *life,* and a mode of appropriating *human* life.

It is obvious that the *human* eye enjoys things in a way different from the crude, nonhuman eye; the human *ear* different from the crude ear, and so forth.

We have seen that man does not lose himself in his object only when the object becomes for him a *human* object or objective man. This is possible only when the object becomes for him a *social* object, he himself for himself a social being, just as society becomes a being for him in this object.

On the one hand, therefore, it is only when the objective world becomes everywhere for man in society the world of man's essential powers—human reality, and for that reason the reality of his *own* essential powers—that all *objects* become for him the *objectification* of himself, become objects which confirm and realize his individuality, become *his* objects: that is, *man himself* becomes the object. The *manner* in which they become *his* depends on the *nature of the objects* and on the nature of the *essential power* corresponding to *it;* for it is precisely the *determinate nature* of this relationship which shapes the particular, *real* mode of affirmation. To the *eye* an object comes to be other than it is to the *ear,* and the object of the eye *is* another object than the object of the *ear.* The specific character of each essential power is precisely its *specific essence,* and therefore also the specific mode of its objectification, of its *objectively actual,* living *being.* Thus man is affirmed in the objective world not only in the act of thinking, but with *all* his senses.

---

*In practice I can relate myself to a thing humanly only if the thing relates itself humanly to the human being.

On the other hand, let us look at this in its subjective aspect. Just as only music awakens in man the sense of music, and just as the most beautiful music has *no* sense for the unmusical ear—is [no] object for it, because my object can only be the confirmation of one of my essential powers—it can therefore only exist for me insofar as my essential power exists for itself as a subjective capacity; because the meaning of an object for me goes only so far as *my* sense goes (has only a meaning for a sense corresponding to that object)—for this reason the *senses* of the social man *differ* from those of the non-social man. Only through the objectively unfolded richness of man's essential being is the richness of subjective *human* sensibility (a musical ear, an eye for beauty of form—in short, *senses* capable of human gratification, senses affirming themselves as essential powers of *man*) either cultivated or brought into being. For not only the five senses but also the so-called mental senses, the practical senses (will, love, etc.), in a word, *human* sense, the human nature of the senses, comes to be by virtue of *its* object, by virtue of *humanized* nature. The *forming* of the five senses is a labor of the entire history of the world down to the present. The *sense* caught up in crude practical need has only a *restricted* sense. For the starving man, it is not the human form of food that exists, but only its abstract existence as food. It could just as well be there in its crudest form, and it would be impossible to say wherein this feeding activity differs from that of *animals*. The care-burdened, poverty-stricken man has no *sense* for the finest play; the dealer in minerals sees only the commercial value but not the beauty and the specific character of the mineral: he has no mineralogical sense. Thus, the objectification of the human essence, both in its theoretical and practical aspects, is required to make man's *sense human,* as well as to create the *human sense* corresponding to the entire wealth of human and natural substance.

(Just as through the movement of *private property,* of its wealth as well as its poverty—of its material and spiritual wealth and poverty—the budding society finds at hand all the material for this *development,* so *established* society produces man in this entire richness of his being—produces the *rich* man *profoundly endowed with all the senses*—as its enduring reality.)

We see how subjectivity and objectivity, spirituality and materiality, activity and suffering, lose their antithetical character, and thus their existence as such antitheses only within the framework of society; we see how the resolution of the *theoretical* antitheses is *only* possible in a *practical* way, by virtue of the practical energy of man. Their resolution is therefore by no means merely a problem of understanding, but a *real* problem of life, which *philosophy* could not solve precisely because it conceived this problem as *merely* a theoretical one.

We see how the history of *industry* and the established *objective* existence of industry are the *open* book of *man's essential powers,* the perceptibly existing human *psychology.* Hitherto this was not conceived in its connection with man's *essential being,* but only in an external relation of utility, because, moving in the realm of estrangement, people could only think of man's general mode of being—religion or history in its abstract-general character as politics, art, literature, etc.—as the reality of man's essential powers and *man's species-activity.* We have before us the *objectified essential powers* of man in the form of *sensuous, alien, useful objects* in the form of estrangement, displayed in *ordinary material industry* (which can be conceived either as a part of that general movement, or that movement can be conceived as a *particular* part of industry, since all human activity hitherto has been labor—that is, industry—activity estranged from itself).

A *psychology* for which this book, the part of history existing in the most perceptible and accessible form, remains a closed book, cannot become a genuine, comprehensive and *real* science. What indeed are we to think of a science which *airily* abstracts from this large part of human labor and which fails to feel its own incompleteness, while such a wealth of human endeavor, unfolded before it, means nothing more to it than, perhaps, what can be expressed in one word—*"need," "vulgar need?"*

The *natural sciences* have developed an enormous activity and have accumulated an ever-growing mass of material. Philosophy, however, has remained just as alien to them as they remain to philosophy. Their momentary unity was only a *chimerical illusion.* The will was there, but the power was lacking. Historiography itself pays regard to natural science only occasionally, as a factor of enlightenment, utility, and of some special great discoveries. But natural science has invaded and transformed human life all the more *practically* through the medium of industry; and has prepared human emancipation, although its immediate effect had to be the furthering of the dehumanization of man. *Industry* is the *actual,* historical relationship of nature, and therefore of natural science, to man. If, therefore, industry is conceived as the *exoteric* revelation of man's *essential powers,* we also gain an understanding of the *human* essence of nature or the *natural* essence of man. In consequence, natural science will lose its abstractly material—or rather, its idealistic—tendency, and will become the basis of *human* science, as it has already become—albeit in an estranged form—the basis of actual human life, and to assume *one* basis for life and a different basis for *science* is as a matter of course a lie. (The nature which develops in human history—the genesis of human society—is man's *real* nature; hence nature as it develops through industry, even though in an *estranged* form, is true *anthropological* nature.)

Sense-perception (see Feuerbach) must be the basis of all science. Only when it proceeds from sense-perception in the twofold form of *sensuous* consciousness and *sensuous* need—that is, only when science proceeds from nature—is it *true* science. All history is the history of preparing and developing *man* to become the object of *sensuous* consciousness, and turning the requirements of "man as man" into his needs. History itself is a *real* part of *natural history*—of nature developing into man. Natural science will in time incorporate into itself the science of man, just as the science of man will incorporate into itself natural science: there will be *one* science.

Man is the immediate object of natural science; for immediate, *sensuous nature* for man is, immediately, human sensuousness (the expressions are identical)—presented immediately in the form of the *other* man sensuously present for him. Indeed, his own sense-perception first exists as human sensuousness for himself through the *other* man. But *nature* is the immediate object of the *science of man:* the first object of man—man—is nature, sensuousness; and the particular human sensuous essential powers can only find their self-understanding in the science of the natural world in general, just as they can find their objective realization only in *natural* objects. The element of thought itself—the element of thought's living expression—*language*—is of a sensuous nature. The *social* reality of nature, and *human* natural science, or the *natural science of man,* are identical terms.

(It will be seen how in place of the *wealth* and *poverty* of political economy come the *rich human being* and the rich *human* need. The *rich* human being is simultaneously the human being *in need of* a totality of human manifestations of life—the man in whom his own realization exists as an inner necessity, as *need.* Not only *wealth,* but likewise the *poverty* of man—under the assumption of socialism—receives in equal measure a *human* and therefore social significance. Poverty is the passive bond which causes the human being to experience the need of the greatest wealth—the *other* human being. The dominion of the objective being in me, the sensuous outburst of my life activity, is *passion,* which thus becomes here the *activity* of my being.)

(5) A *being* only considers himself independent when he stands on his own feet; and he only stands on his own feet when he owes his *existence* to himself. A man who lives by the grace of another regards himself as a dependent being. But I live completely by the grace of another if I owe him not only the maintenance of my life, but if he has, moreover, *created* my *life*—if he is the *source* of my life. When it is not of my own creation, my life has necessarily a source of this kind outside of it. The *Creation* is therefore an idea very difficult to dislodge from popular consciousness. The fact that nature and man exist on their own account is *incomprehensible* to it, because it contradicts everything *tangible* in practical life.

The creation of the *earth* has received a mighty blow from *geognosy*—i.e., from the science which presents the formation of the earth, the development of the earth, as a process, as a self-generation. *Generatio aequivoca* is the only practical refutation of the theory of creation.

Now it is certainly easy to say to the single individual what Aristotle has already said: You have been begotten by your father and your mother; therefore in you the mating of two human beings—a species-act of human beings—has produced the human being. You see, therefore, that even physically man owes his existence to man. Therefore you must not only keep sight of the *one* aspect—the *infinite* progression which leads you further to inquire: Who begot my father? Who his grandfather? etc. You must also hold on to the *circular movement* sensuously perceptible in that progress by which man repeats himself in procreation, *man* thus always remaining the subject. You will reply, however: I grant you this circular movement; now grant me the progress which drives me ever further until I ask: Who begot the first man, and nature as a whole? I can only answer you: Your question is itself a product of abstraction. Ask yourself how you arrived at that question. Ask yourself whether your question is not posed from a standpoint to which I cannot reply, because it is wrongly put. Ask yourself whether that progress as such exists for a reasonable mind. When you ask about the creation of nature and man, you are abstracting, in so doing, from man and nature. You postulate them as *nonexistent*, and yet you want me to prove them to you as *existing*. Now I say to you: Give up your abstraction and you will also give up your question. Or if you want to hold on to your abstraction, then be consistent, and if you think of man and nature as *nonexistent*, then think of yourself as non-existent, for you too are surely nature and man. Don't think, don't ask me, for as soon as you think and ask, your *abstraction* from the existence of nature and man has no meaning. Or are you such an egotist that you conceive everything as nothing, and yet want yourself to exist?

You can reply: I do not want to postulate the nothingness of nature, etc. I ask you about its *genesis*, just as I ask the anatomist about the formation of bones, etc.

But since for the socialist man the *entire so-called history of the world* is nothing but the creation of man through human labor, nothing but the emergence of nature for man, so he has the visible, irrefutable proof of his *birth* through himself, of his *genesis*. Since the *real existence* of man and nature has become evident in practice, through sense experience, because man has thus become evident for man as the being of nature, and nature for man as the being of man, the question about an *alien* being, about a being above nature and man—a question which implies the admission of the unreality of nature and of man—has become impossible in practice. *Atheism*, as the denial of this unreality, has no longer any meaning, for atheism is a *negation of God*, and postulates the *existence of man* through this negation; but socialism as socialism no longer stands in any need of such a mediation. It proceeds from the *theoretically and practically sensuous consciousness* of man and of nature as the *essence*. Socialism is man's *positive self-consciousness*, no longer mediated through the abolition of religion, just as *real life* is man's positive reality, no longer mediated through the abolition of private property, through *communism*. Communism is the position as the negation of the negation, and is hence the *actual* phase necessary for the next stage of historical development in the process of human emancipation and rehabilitation. *Communism* is the necessary form and the dynamic principle of the immediate future, but communism as such is not the goal of human development, the form of human society.

Translated by Martin Mulligan and Dirk J. Struik

What Is the Proletariat?

Proletariat and wealth are opposites; as such they form a single whole. They are both creations of the world of private property. The question is exactly what place each occupies in the antithesis. It is not sufficient to declare them two sides of a single whole.

Private property as private property, as wealth, is compelled to maintain *itself,* and thereby its opposite, the proletariat, in *existence.* That is the *positive* side of the antithesis, self-satisfied private property.

The proletariat, on the contrary, is compelled as proletariat to abolish itself and thereby its opposite, private property, which determines its existence, and which makes it proletariat. It is the *negative* side of the antithesis, its restlessness within its very self, dissolved and self-dissolving private property.

The propertied class and the class of the proletariat present the same human self-estrangement. But the former class feels at ease and strengthened in this self-estrangement, it recognizes estrangement as *its own power* and has in it the *semblance* of a human existence. The latter feels annihilated in estrangement; it sees in it its own powerlessness and the reality of an inhuman existence. It is, to use an expression of Hegel, in its abasement the *indignation* at that abasement, an indignation to which it is necessarily driven by the contradiction between its human *nature* and its condition of life, which is the outright, resolute and comprehensive negation of that nature.

Within this antithesis the private property-owner is therefore the *conservative* side, the proletarian the *destructive* side. From the former arises the action of preserving the antithesis, from the latter the action of annihilating it.

Indeed private property drives itself in its economic movement toward its own dissolution, but only through a development which does not depend on it, which is unconscious and which takes place against the will of private property by the very nature of things, only inasmuch as it produces the proletariat *as* proletariat, poverty which is conscious of its spiritual and physical poverty, dehumanization which is conscious of its dehumanization, and therefore self-abolishing. The proletariat executes the sentence that private property pronounces on itself by producing the proletariat, just as it executes the sentence that wage-labor pronounces on itself by producing wealth for others and poverty for itself. When the proletariat is victorious, it by no means becomes the absolute side of society, for it is victorious only by abolishing itself and its opposite. Then the proletariat disappears as well as the opposite which determines it, private property.

When socialist writers ascribe this world-historic role to the proletariat, it is not at all, as Critical Criticism pretends to believe, because they regard the proletarians as *gods*. Rather the contrary. Since in the fully-formed proletariat the abstraction of all humanity, even of the *semblance* of humanity, is practically complete; since the conditions of life of the proletariat sum up all the conditions of life of society today in their most inhuman form; since man has lost himself in the proletariat, yet at the same time has not only gained theoretical consciousness of that loss, but through urgent, no longer removable, no longer disguisable, absolutely imperative *need*—the practical expression of *necessity*—is driven directly to revolt against this inhumanity, it follows that the proletariat can and must emancipate itself. But it cannot emancipate itself without abolishing the conditions of its own life. It cannot abolish the conditions of its own life without abolishing *all* the inhuman conditions of life of society today which are summed up in its own situation. Not in vain does it go through the stern but steeling school of *labor*. It is not a question of what this or that proletarian, or even the whole proletariat, at the moment *regards* as its aim. It is a question of *what the proletariat is,* and what, in accordance with this *being,* it will historically be compelled to do. Its aim and historical action is visibly and irrevocably foreshadowed in its own life situation as well as in the whole organization of bourgeois society today. There is no need to explain here that a large part of the English and French proletariat is already *conscious* of its historic task and is constantly working to develop that consciousness into complete clarity.

Translated   Richard Dixon and Clemens Dutt

Letter to Joseph Weydemeyer in New York

London, 5 March 1852
If I were you, I should tell the democratic gents *en général* that they would do better to acquaint themselves with bourgeois literature before they venture to yap at its opponents. For instance they should study the historical works of Thierry, Guizot, John Wade and so forth, in order to enlighten themselves as to the past "history of the classes." They should acquaint themselves with the fundamentals of political economy before attempting to criticise the critique of political economy. For example, one need only open Ricardo's magnum opus to find, on the first page, the words with which he begins his preface:

> The produce of the earth—all that is derived from its surface by the united application of labor, machinery, and capital, is divided among *three classes* of the community; namely the proprietor of the land, the owner of the stock or capital necessary for its cultivation, and the laborers by whose industry it is cultivated.*

Now, in the United States bourgeois society is still far too immature for the class struggle to be made perceptible and comprehensible; striking proof of this is provided by *C. H. Carey* (of Philadelphia), the only North American economist of any note. He attacks *Ricardo,* the most classic representative of the bourgeoisie

---

*D. Ricardo, *On the Principles of Political Economy and Taxation,* third edition, London, 1821, p. V.

and the most stoical opponent of the proletariat, as a man whose works are an arsenal for anarchists and socialists, for all enemies of the bourgeois order. He accuses not only him, but also Malthus, Mill, Say, Torrens, Wakefield, MacCulloch, Senior, Whately, R. Jones, etc.—those who lead the economic dance in Europe—of tearing society apart, and of paving the way for civil war by showing that the economic bases of the various classes are such that they will inevitably give rise to a necessary and ever-growing antagonism between the latter. He tries to refute them, not by relating the existence of classes to the existence of *political* privileges and *monopolies,* but by seeking to demonstrate that *economic* conditions: rent (landed property), *profit* (capital), and wages (wage labor), rather than being conditions of struggle and antagonism, are conditions of association and harmony. All he proves, of course, is that the "undeveloped" relations in the United States are, to him, "normal relations."

Now as for myself, I do not claim to have discovered either the existence of classes in modern society or the struggle between them. Long before me, bourgeois historians had described the historical development of this struggle between the classes, as had bourgeois economists their economic anatomy. My own contribution was (1) to show that the *existence of classes* is merely bound up with *certain historical phases in the development of production;* (2) that the class struggle necessarily leads to the *dictatorship of the proletariat;* (3) that this dictatorship itself constitutes no more than a transition to the *abolition of all classes* and to a *classless society.* Ignorant louts, who deny not only the struggle but the very existence of classes, only demonstrate that, for all their bloodthirsty, mock-humanist yelping, they regard the social conditions in which the bourgeoisie is dominant as the final product, the *non plus ultra* of history, and that they themselves are simply the servants of the bourgeoisie, a servitude which is the more revolting, the less capable are the louts of grasping the very greatness and transient necessity of the bourgeois regime itself.

Translated by Peter and Betty Ross

The Future Results of British Rule in India

Modern industry, resulting from the railway system, will dissolve the hereditary divisions of labor, upon which rest the Indian castes, those decisive impediments to Indian progress and Indian power.

All the English bourgeoisie may be forced to do will neither emancipate nor materially mend the social condition of the mass of the people, depending not only on the development of the productive powers, but on their appropriation by the people. But what they will not fail to do is to lay down the material premises for both. Has the bourgeoisie ever done more? Has it ever effected a progress without dragging individuals and people through blood and dirt, through misery and degradation?

The Indians will not reap the fruits of the new elements of society scattered among them by the British bourgeoisie, till in Great Britain itself the now ruling classes shall have been supplanted by the industrial proletariat, or till the Hindus themselves shall have grown strong enough to throw off the English yoke altogether. At all events, we may safely expect to see, at a more or less remote period, the regeneration of that great and interesting country, whose gentle natives are, to use the expression of Prince Soltykov, even in the most inferior classes, *"plus fins et plus adroits que les Italiens,"** whose submission even is counterbalanced by a certain calm nobility, who, notwithstanding their natural langor, have astonished the British officers by their bravery, whose country has been the source of our languages, our religions, and who represent

---

*"More subtle and adroit than the Italians."

the type of the ancient German in the Jat, and the type of the ancient Greek in the Brahmin.

I cannot part with the subject of India without some concluding remarks.

The profound hypocrisy and inherent barbarism of bourgeois civilization lies unveiled before our eyes, turning from its home, where it assumes respectable forms, to the colonies, where it goes naked. They are the defenders of property, but did any revolutionary party ever originate agrarian revolutions like those in Bengal, in Madras, and in Bombay? Did they not, in India, to borrow an expression of that great robber, Lord Clive himself, resort to atrocious extortion, when simple corruption could not keep pace with their rapacity? While they prated in Europe about the inviolable sanctity of the national debt, did they not confiscate in India the dividends of the rajahs, who had invested their private savings in the Company's own funds? While they combatted the French revolution under the pretext of defending "our holy religion," did they not forbid, at the same time, Christianity to be propagated in India, and did they not, in order to make money out of the pilgrims streaming to the temples of Orissa and Bengal, take up the trade in the murder and prostitution perpetrated in the temple of Juggernaut? These are the men of "Property, Order, Family, and Religion."

The devastating effects of English industry, when contemplated with regard to India, a country as vast as Europe, and containing one-hundred-fifty-million acres, are palpable and confounding. But we must not forget that they are only the organic results of the whole system of production as it is now constituted. That production rests on the supreme rule of capital. The centralization of capital is essential to the existence of capital as an independent power. The destructive influence of that centralization upon the markets of the world does but reveal, in the most gigantic dimensions, the inherent organic laws of political economy now at work in every civilized town. The bourgeois period of history has to create the material basis of the new world—on the one hand universal intercourse founded upon the mutual dependency of mankind, and the means of that intercourse; on the other hand the development of the productive powers of man and the transformation of material production into a scientific domination of natural agencies. Bourgeois industry and commerce create these material conditions of a new world in the same way as geological revolutions have created the surface of the earth. When a great social revolution shall have mastered the results of the bourgeois epoch, the market of the world and the modern powers of production, and subjected them to the common control of the most advanced peoples, then only will human progress cease to resemble that hideous, pagan idol, who would not drink the nectar but from the skulls of the slain.

Published in the *New York Daily Tribune*, August 8, 1853.

III. POLITICAL ECONOMY OF CAPITALISM

Value, Price, and Profit

What then is the relation between *value* and *market prices,* or between *natural prices* and *market prices?* You all know that the *market price* is the *same* for all commodities of the same kind, however the conditions of production may differ for the individual producers. The market price expresses only the *average amount of social labor* necessary, under the average conditions of production, to supply the market with a certain mass of a certain article. It is calculated upon the whole lot of a commodity of a certain description.

So far the *market price* of a commodity coincides with its *value.* On the other hand, the oscillations of market prices, rising now over, sinking now under, the value or natural price, depend upon the fluctuations of supply and demand. The deviations of market prices from values are continual, but as *Adam Smith* says:

> "The natural price . . . is [. . .] the central price, to which the prices of all commodities are continually gravitating. Different accidents may sometimes keep them suspended a good deal above it, and sometimes force them down even somewhat below it. But whatever may be the obstacles which hinder them from settling in this centre of repose and continuance, they are constantly tending towards it."*

I cannot now sift this matter. It suffices to say that *if* supply and demand equilibrate each other, the market prices of commodities

---

*A. Smith, *An Inquiry into the Nature and Causes of the Wealth of Nations,* vol. 1, Edinburgh, 1814, p. 93.

will correspond to their natural prices, that is to say, to their values, as determined by the respective quantities of labor required for their production. But supply and demand *must* constantly tend to equilibrate each other, although they do so only by compensating one fluctuation by another, a rise by a fall, and vice versa. If instead of considering only the daily fluctuations you analyze the movement of market prices for longer periods, as Mr. Tooke, for example, has done in his *History of Prices,* you will find that the fluctuations of market prices, their deviations from values, their ups and downs, paralyze and compensate each other; so that, apart from the effect of monopolies and some other modifications I must now pass by, all descriptions of commodities are, on the average, sold at their respective *values* or natural prices. The average periods during which the fluctuations of market prices compensate each other are different for different kinds of commodities, because with one kind it is easier to adapt supply to demand than with the other.

If then, speaking broadly, and embracing somewhat longer periods, all descriptions of commodities sell at their respective values, it is nonsense to suppose that profit, not in individual cases, but that the constant and usual profits of different trades, spring from *surcharging* the prices of commodities, or selling them at a price over and above their *value.* The absurdity of this notion becomes evident if it is generalized. What a man would constantly win as a seller he would as constantly lose as a purchaser. It would not do to say that there are men who are buyers without being sellers, or consumers without being producers. What these people pay to the producers, they must first get from them for nothing. If a man first takes your money and afterwards returns that money in buying your commodities, you will never enrich yourselves by selling your commodities too dear to that same man. This sort of transaction might diminish a loss, but would never help in realizing a profit.

To explain, therefore, the *general nature of profits,* you must start from the theorem that, on an average, commodities are *sold at their real value,* and that *profits are derived from selling them at their values,* that is, in proportion to the quantity of labor realised in them. If you cannot explain profit upon this supposition, you cannot explain it at all. This seems a paradox and contrary to everyday observation. It is also a paradox that the earth moves round the sun, and that water consists of two highly inflammable gases. Scientific truth is always a paradox, if judged by everyday experience, which catches only the delusive appearance of things.

Laboring Power

Having now, as far as it could be done in such cursory manner, analyzed the nature of *Value*, of the *Value of any commodity whatever*, we must turn our attention to the specific *Value of Labor*. And here, again, I must startle you by a seeming paradox. All of you feel sure that what they daily sell is their Labor; that, therefore, Labor has a Price, and that, the price of a commodity being only the monetary expression of its value, there must certainly exist such a thing as the *Value of Labor*. However, there exists no such thing as the *Value of Labor* in the common acceptance of the word. We have seen that the amount of necessary labor crystallized in a commodity constitutes its value. Now, applying this notion of value, how could we define, say, the value of a ten hours' working day? How much labor is contained in that day? Ten hours' labor. To say that the value of a ten hours' working day is equal to ten hours' labor, or the quantity of labor contained in it, would be a tautological and, moreover, a nonsensical expression. Of course, having once found out the true but hidden sense of the expression *"Value of Labor,"* we shall be able to interpret this irrational, and seemingly impossible application of value, in the same way that, having once made sure of the real movement of the celestial bodies, we shall be able to explain their apparent or merely phenomenal movements.

What the working man sells is not directly his *Labor*, but his *Laboring Power*, the temporary disposal of which he makes over to the capitalist. This is so much the case that I do not know whether by the English Laws, but certainly by some Continental Laws, the *maximum time* is fixed for which a man is allowed to sell his laboring power. If allowed to do so for any indefinite period whatever, slavery would be immediately restored. Such a sale, if it comprised his lifetime, for example, would make him at once the lifelong slave of his employer.

One of the oldest economists and most original philosophers of England—Thomas Hobbes—has already, in his *Leviathan*, instinctively hit upon this point overlooked by all his successors. He says:

> The *value* or *worth of a man* is, as in all other things, his *price*: that is, so much as would be given for the *Use of his Power*.*

The English Works of Thomas Hobbes, vol. 3, London, 1839, p. 76.

Proceeding from this basis, we shall be able to determine the *Value of Labor* as that of all other commodities.

But before doing so, we might ask, how does this strange phenomenon arise, that we find on the market a set of buyers, possessed of land, machinery, raw material, and the means of subsistence, all of them, save land in its crude state, the *products of labor*, and on the other hand, a set of sellers who have nothing to sell except their laboring power, their working arms and brains? That the one set buys continually in order to make a profit and enrich themselves, while the other set continually sells in order to earn their livelihood? The inquiry into this question would be an inquiry into what the economists call "*Previous*, or *Original Accumulation*," but which ought to be called *Original Expropriation*. We should find that this so-called *Original Accumulation* means nothing but a series of historical processes, resulting in a *Decomposition of the Original Union* existing between the Laboring Man and his Instruments of Labor. Such an inquiry, however, lies beyond the pale of my present subject. The *Separation* between the Man of Labor and the Instruments of Labor once established, such a state of things will maintain itself and reproduce itself upon a constantly increasing scale, until a new and fundamental revolution in the mode of production should again overturn it, and restore the original union in a new historical form.

What, then, is the *Value of Laboring Power*?

Like that of every other commodity, its value is determined by the quantity of labor necessary to produce it. The laboring power of a man exists only in his living individuality. A certain mass of necessaries must be consumed by a man to grow up and maintain his life. But the man, like the machine, will wear out, and must be replaced by another man. Beside the mass of necessaries required for *his own* maintenance, he wants another amount of necessaries to bring up a certain quota of children that are to replace him on the labor market and to perpetuate the race of laborers. Moreover, to develop his laboring power, and acquire a given skill, another amount of values must be spent. For our purpose it suffices to consider only *average* labor, the costs of whose education and development are vanishing magnitudes. Still I must seize upon this occasion to state that, as the costs of producing laboring powers of different quality differ, so must differ the values of the laboring powers employed in different trades. The cry for an *equality of wages* rests, therefore, upon a mistake, an *insane* wish never to be fulfilled. It is an offspring of that false and superficial radicalism that accepts premises and tries to evade conclusions. Upon the basis of the wages system the value of laboring power is settled like that of every other commodity; and as different kinds of laboring power have different values, or require different quantities of labor for their production, they *must* fetch different prices in the labor market. To clamor for *equal or even equitable retribution* on the basis of the wages system is the same as to clamor for *freedom* on the basis of the slavery system. What you think just or equitable is out of the question. The question is: What is necessary and unavoidable with a given system of production?

After what has been said, it will be seen that the *value of laboring power* is determined by the *value of the necessaries* required to produce, develop, maintain, and perpetuate the laboring power.

Production of Surplus-Value

Now suppose that the average amount of the daily necessaries of a laboring man require *six hours of average labor* for their production. Suppose, moreover, six hours of average labor to be also realized in a quantity of gold equal to three shillings. Then three shillings would be the *Price,* or the monetary expression of the *Daily Value* of that man's *Laboring Power.* If he worked daily six hours he would daily produce a value sufficient to buy the average amount of his daily necessaries, or to maintain himself as a laboring man.

But our man is a wages laborer. He must, therefore, sell his laboring power to a capitalist. If he sells it at three shillings daily, or eighteen shillings weekly, he sells it at its value. Suppose him to be a spinner. If he works six hours daily he will add to the cotton a value of three shillings daily. This value, daily added by him, would be an exact equivalent for the wages, or the price of his laboring power, received daily. But in that case *no surplus-value* or *surplus-produce* whatever would go to the capitalist. Here, then, we come to the rub.

In buying the laboring power of the workman, and paying its value, the capitalist, like every other purchaser, has acquired the right to consume or use the commodity bought. You consume or use the laboring power of a man by making him work as you consume or use a machine by making it run. By paying the daily

or weekly value of the laboring power of the workman, the capitalist has, therefore, acquired the right to use or make that laboring
power work during the *whole day or week*. The working day or
the working week has, of course, certain limits, but those we shall
afterward look at more closely.

For the present I want to turn your attention to one decisive
point.

The *value* of the laboring power is determined by the quantity
of labor necessary to maintain or reproduce it, but the *use* of that
laboring power is only limited by the active energies and physical
strength of the laborer. The daily or weekly *value* of the laboring
power is quite distinct from the daily or weekly *exercise* of that
power, the same as the food a horse wants and the time it can
carry the horseman are quite distinct. The quantity of labor by
which the *value* of the workman's laboring power is limited forms
by no means a limit to the quantity of labor which his laboring
power is apt to perform. Take the example of our spinner. We have
seen that, to daily reproduce his laboring power, he must daily
reproduce a value of three shillings, which he will do by working
six hours daily. But this does not disable him from working ten or
twelve or more hours a day. But by paying the daily or weekly
value of the spinner's laboring power, the capitalist has acquired
the right of using that laboring power during the *whole day or
week*. He will, therefore, make him work daily, say, *twelve* hours.
Over and above the six hours required to replace his wages, or the
value of his laboring power, he will, therefore, have to work *six
other hours,* which I shall call hours of *surplus-labor,* which surplus labor will realize itself in a *surplus-value* and a *surplus-
produce.* If our spinner, for example, by his daily labor of six hours,
added three shillings' value to the cotton, a value forming an exact
equivalent to his wages, he will, in twelve hours, add six shillings'
worth to the cotton, and produce *a proportional surplus of yarn.*
As he has sold his laboring power to the capitalist, the whole value
or produce created by him belongs to the capitalist, the owner *pro
tempore* of his laboring power. By advancing three shillings, the
capitalist will, therefore, realize a value of six shillings, because,
advancing a value in which six hours of labor are crystallized, he
will receive in return a value in which twelve hours of labor are
crystallized. By repeating this same process daily, the capitalist will
daily advance three shillings and daily pocket six shillings, one-half
of which will go to pay wages anew, and the other half of which

will form *surplus-value,* for which the capitalist pays no equivalent. It is *this sort of exchange between capital and labor* upon which capitalistic production, or the wages system, is founded, and which must constantly result in reproducing the working man as a working man, and the capitalist as a capitalist.

The rate of surplus-value, all other circumstances remaining the same, will depend on the proportion between that part of the working day necessary to reproduce the value of the laboring power and the *surplus-time* or *surplus-labor* performed for the capitalist. It will, therefore, depend on the *ratio in which the working day is prolonged over and above that extent,* by working which the working man would only reproduce the value of his laboring power, or replace his wages.

Value of Labor

We must now return to the expression, *"Value, or Price of Labor."*

We have seen that, in fact, it is only the value of the laboring power, measured by the values of commodities necessary for its maintenance. But since the workman receives his wages *after* his labor is performed, and knows, moreover, that what he actually gives to the capitalist is his labor, the value or price of his laboring power necessarily appears to him as the *price* or *value of his labor itself.* If the price of his laboring power is three shillings, in which six hours of labor are realized, and if he works twelve hours, he necessarily considers these three shillings as the value or price of twelve hours of labor, although these twelve hours of labor realize themselves in a value of six shillings. A double consequence flows from this.

Firstly. The *value or price of the laboring power* takes the semblance of the *price or value of labor itself,* although, strictly speaking, value and price of labor are senseless terms.

Secondly. Although one part only of the workman's daily labor is *paid,* while the other part is *unpaid,* and while that unpaid or surplus-labor constitutes exactly the fund out of which *surplus-value* or *profit* is formed, it seems as if the aggregate labor was paid labor.

This false appearance distinguishes *wages labor* from other *historical* forms of labor. On the basis of the wages system even the *unpaid* labor seems to be *paid* labor. With the *slave,* on the contrary, even that part of his labor which is paid appears to be unpaid. Of course, in order to work the slave must live, and one part of his working day goes to replace the value of his own maintenance. But since no bargain is struck between him and his master, and no acts of selling and buying are going on between the two parties, all his labor seems to be given away for nothing.

Take, on the other hand, the peasant serf, such as he, I might say, until yesterday existed in the whole East of Europe. This peasant worked, for example, three days for himself on his own field or the field allotted to him, and the three subsequent days he performed compulsory and gratuitous labor on the estate of his lord. Here, then, the paid and unpaid parts of labor were visibly separated, separated in time and space; and our Liberals overflowed with moral indignation at the preposterous notion of making a man work for nothing.

In point of fact, however, whether a man works three days of the week for himself on his own field and three days for nothing on the estate of his lord, or whether he works in the factory or the workshop six hours daily for himself and six for his employer, comes to the same, although in the latter case the paid and unpaid portions of labor are inseparably mixed up with each other, and the nature of the whole transaction is completely masked by the *intervention of a contract* and the *pay* received at the end of the week. The gratuitous labor appears to be voluntarily given in the one instance, and to be compulsory in the other. That makes all the difference.

In using the expression *"value of labor,"* I shall only use it as a popular slang term for *"value of laboring power."*

Profit Is Made by Selling a Commodity *at* Its Value

Suppose an average hour of labor to be realized in a value equal to sixpence, or twelve average hours of labor to be realised in six shillings. Suppose, further, the value of labor to be three shillings or the produce of six hours' labor. If, then, in the raw material, machinery, and so forth, used up in a commodity, twenty-four hours of average labor were realized, its value would amount to twelve shillings. If, moreover, the workman employed by the capitalist added twelve hours of labor to those means of production, these twelve hours would be realized in an additional value of six shillings. The *total value of the product* would, therefore, amount to thirty-six hours of realized labor, and be equal to eighteen shillings. But as the value of labor, or the wages paid to the workman, would be three shillings only, no equivalent would have been paid by the capitalist for the six hours of surplus-labor worked by the workman, and realized in the value of the commodity. By selling this commodity at its value for eighteen shillings, the capitalist would, therefore, realize a value of three shillings, for which he had paid no equivalent. These three shillings would constitute the surplus-value or profit pocketed by him. The capitalist would consequently realize the profit of three shillings, not by selling his commodity at a price *over and above* its value, but by selling it *at its real value.*

The value of a commodity is determined by the *total quantity of labor* contained in it. But part of that quantity of labor is realized in a value for which an equivalent has been paid in the form of wages; part of it is realized in a value for which *no* equivalent has been paid. Part of the labor contained in the commodity is *paid* labor; part is *unpaid* labor. By selling, therefore, the commodity *at its value,* that is, as the crystallization of the *total quantity of labor* bestowed upon it, the capitalist must necessarily sell it at a profit. He sells not only what has cost him an equivalent, but he sells also what has cost him nothing, although it has cost his workman labor. The cost of the commodity to the capitalist and its real cost are different things. I repeat, therefore, that normal and average profits are made by selling commodities not *above* but *at their real values.*

The Different Parts into which Surplus-Value Is Decomposed

The *surplus-value,* or that part of the total value of the commodity in which the *surplus-labor* or *unpaid labor* of the working man is realized, I call *Profit.* The whole of that profit is not pocketed by the employing capitalist. The monopoly of land enables the landlord to take one part of that *surplus-value,* under the name of *rent,* whether the land is used for agriculture, buildings or railways, or for any other productive purpose. On the other hand, the very fact that the possession of the *means of labor* enables the employing capitalist to produce a *surplus-value,* or, what comes to the same, to *appropriate to himself a certain amount of unpaid labor,* enables the owner of the means of labor, which he lends wholly or partly to the employing capitalist—enables, in one word, the *money-lending capitalist* to claim for himself under the name of *interest* another part of that surplus-value, so that there remains to the employing capitalist *as such* only what is called *industrial* or *commercial* profit.

By what laws this division of the total amount of surplus-value among the three categories of people is regulated is a question quite foreign to our subject. This much, however, results from what has been stated.

Rent, Interest, and Industrial Profit are only *different names for different parts* of the *surplus-value* of the commodity, or the *unpaid labor enclosed in it,* and they are *equally derived from this source, and from this source alone.* They are not derived from *land* as such or from *capital* as such, but land and capital enable their owners to get their respective shares out of the surplus-value extracted by the employing capitalist from the laborer.

The Struggle between Capital and Labor and Its Results

(1) Having shown that the periodical resistance on the part of the working men against a reduction of wages, and their periodical attempts at getting a rise of wages, are inseparable from the wages system, and dictated by the very fact of labor being assimilated to commodities, and therefore subject to the laws regulating the general movement of prices; having, furthermore, shown that a general rise of wages would result in a fall in the general rate of profit, but not affect the average prices of commodities, or their values, the question now ultimately arises, how far, in this incessant struggle between capital and labor, the latter is likely to prove successful.

I might answer by a generalization, and say that, as with all other commodities, so with labor, its *market price* will, in the long run, adapt itself to its *value;* that, therefore, despite all the ups and downs, and do what he may, the working man will, on an average, only receive the value of his labor, which resolves into the value of his laboring power, which is determined by the value of the necessaries required for its maintenance and reproduction, which value of necessaries finally is regulated by the quantity of labor wanted to produce them.

But there are some peculiar features which distinguish the *value of the laboring power,* or *the value of labor,* from the values of all other commodities. The value of the laboring power is formed by two elements—the one merely physical, the other historical or social. Its *ultimate limit* is determined by the *physical* element, that is to say, to maintain and reproduce itself, to perpetuate its physical existence, the working class must receive the necessaries absolutely indispensable for living and multiplying. The *value* of those indispensable necessaries forms, therefore, the ultimate limit of the *value of labor.* On the other hand, the length of the working day is also limited by ultimate, although very elastic boundaries. Its ultimate limit is given by the physical force of the laboring man. If the daily exhaustion of his vital forces exceeds a certain degree, it cannot be exerted anew, day by day. However, as I said, this limit is very elastic. A quick succession of unhealthy and short-lived generations will keep the labor market as well supplied as a series of vigorous and long-lived generations.

Besides this mere physical element, the value of labor is in every country determined by a *traditional standard of life.* It is not mere physical life, but it is the satisfaction of certain wants springing from the social conditions in which people are placed and reared up. The English standard of life may be reduced to the Irish standard; the standard of life of a German peasant to that of a Livonian peasant. The important part which historical tradition and social habitude play in this respect, you may learn from Mr. Thornton's work on overpopulation, where he shows that the average wages in different agricultural districts of England still nowadays differ more or less according to the more or less favorable circumstances under which the districts have emerged from the state of serfdom.

This historical or social element, entering into the value of labor, may be expanded, or contracted, or altogether extinguished, so that nothing remains but the *physical limit.* During the time of the *anti-Jacobin war,* undertaken, as the incorrigible tax-eater and sinecurist, old George Rose, used to say, to save the comforts of our holy religion from the inroads of the French infidels, the honest English farmers, so tenderly handled in a former chapter of ours, depressed the wages of the agricultural laborers even beneath that *mere physical minimum,* but made up by *Poor Laws* the remainder necessary for the physical perpetuation of the race. This was a glorious way to convert the wages laborer into a slave, and Shakespeare's proud yeoman into a pauper.

By comparing the standard wages or values of labor in different countries, and by comparing them in different historical epochs of the same country, you will find that the *value of labor* itself is not a fixed but a variable magnitude, even supposing the values of all other commodities to remain constant.

A similar comparison would prove that not only the *market rates of profit* change but its *average rates.*

But as to *profits,* there exists no law which determines their *minimum.* We cannot say what is the ultimate limit of their decrease. And why cannot we fix that limit? Because, although we can fix the *minimum* of wages, we cannot fix their *maximum.* We can only say that, the limits of the working day being given, the *maximum of profit* corresponds to the *physical minimum of wages;* and that wages being given, the *maximum of profit* corresponds to such a prolongation of the working day as is compatible with the physical forces of the laborer. The maximum of profit is, therefore, limited by the physical minimum of wages and the physical maximum of the working day. It is evident that between the two limits of this *maximum rate of profit* an immense scale of variations is possible. The fixation of its actual degree is only settled by the continuous struggle between capital and labor, the capitalist constantly tending to reduce wages to their physical minimum, and to extend the working day to its physical maximum, while the working man constantly presses in the opposite direction.

The matter resolves itself into a question of the respective powers of the combatants.

(2) As to the *limitation of the working day* in England, as in all other countries, it has never been settled except by *legislative interference.* Without the working men's continuous pressure from without, that interference would never have taken place. But at all events, the result was not to be attained by private settlement between the working men and the capitalists. This very necessity of *general political action* affords the proof that in its merely economic action capital is the stronger side.

As to the *limits* of the *value of labor,* its actual settlement always depends upon supply and demand. I mean the demand for labor on the part of capital, and the supply of labor by the working men. In colonial countries the law of supply and demand favors the working man. Hence the relatively high standard of wages in the United States. Capital may there try its utmost. It cannot prevent the labor market from being continuously emptied by the continuous conversion of wages laborers into independent, self-sustaining peasants. The position of a wages laborer is for a very large part of the American people but a probational state, which they are sure to leave within a longer or shorter term. To mend this colonial state of things, the paternal British Government accepted for some time what is called the modern colonization theory, which consists in putting an artificial high price upon colonial land, in order to prevent the too quick conversion of the wages laborer into the independent peasant.

But let us now come to old civilized countries, in which capital domineers over the whole process of production. Take, for example, the rise in England of agricultural wages from 1849 to 1859. What was its consequence? The farmers could not, as our friend Weston would have advised them, raise the value of wheat, nor even its market prices. They had, on the contrary, to submit to their fall. But during these eleven years they introduced machinery of all sorts, adopted more scientific methods, converted part of arable land into pasture, increased the size of farms, and with this the scale of production, and by these and other processes, diminishing the demand for labor by increasing its productive power, made the agricultural population again relatively redundant. This is the general method in which a reaction, quicker or slower, of capital against a rise of wages takes place in old, settled countries. Ricardo has justly remarked that machinery is in constant competition with labor, and can often be only introduced when the price of labor has reached a certain height, but the appliance of machinery is but one of the many methods for increasing the productive powers of labor.* This very same development which makes common labor relatively redundant simplifies on the other hand skilled labor, and thus depreciates it.

The same law obtains in another form. With the development of the productive powers of labor the accumulation of capital will be accelerated, even despite a relatively high rate of wages. Hence, one might infer, as *Adam Smith*, in whose days modern industry was still in its infancy, did infer, that the accelerated accumulation

---

*D. Ricardo, *On the Principles of Political Economy, and Taxation*, London, 1821, p. 479.

of capital must turn the balance in favor of the working man, by securing a growing demand for his labor. From this same stand-point many contemporary writers have wondered that English capital having grown in the last twenty years so much quicker than English population, wages should not have been more enhanced. But simultaneously with the progress of accumulation there takes place a *progressive change* in the *composition of capital*. That part of the aggregate capital which consists of fixed capital, machinery, raw materials, means of production in all possible forms, progres-sively increases as compared with the other part of capital, which is laid out in wages or in the purchase of labor. This law has been stated in a more or less accurate manner by Mr. Barton, Ricardo, Sismondi, Professor Richard Jones, Professor Ramsay, Cherbuliez, and others.

If the proportion of these two elements of capital was originally one to one, it will, in the progress of industry, become five to one, and so forth. If of a total capital of six hundred, three hundred is laid out in instruments, raw materials, and so forth, and three hundred in wages, the total capital wants only to be doubled to create a demand for six hundred working men instead of for three hundred. But if of a capital of six hundred, five hundred is laid out in machinery, materials, and so forth, and one hundred only in wages, the same capital must increase from six hundred to three thousand six hundred in order to create a demand for six hundred workmen instead of three hundred. In the progress of industry the demand for labor keeps, therefore, no pace with accumulation of capital. It will still increase, but increase in a constantly diminishing ratio as compared with the increase of capital.

These few hints will suffice to show that the very development of modern industry must progressively turn the scale in favor of the capitalist against the working man, and that consequently the general tendency of capitalistic production is not to raise, but to sink the average standard of wages, or to push the *value of labor* more or less to its *minimum limit*. Such being the tendency of *things* in this system, is this saying that the working class ought to renounce their resistance against the encroachments of capital, and abandon their attempts at making the best of the occasional chances for their temporary improvement? If they did, they would be degraded to one level mass of broken wretches past salvation. I think I have shown that their struggles for the standard of wages are incidents inseparable from the whole wages system, that in ninety-nine cases out of one hundred their efforts at raising wages are only efforts at maintaining the given value of labor, and that the necessity of debating their price with the capitalist is inherent in their condition of having to sell themselves as commodities. By cowardly giving way in their everyday conflict with capital, they would certainly disqualify themselves for the initiating of any larger movement.

At the same time, and quite apart from the general servitude involved in the wages system, the working class ought not to exaggerate to themselves the ultimate working of these everyday struggles. They ought not to forget that they are fighting with effects, but not with the causes of those effects; that they are retarding the downward movement, but not changing its direction; that they are applying palliatives, not curing the malady. They ought, therefore, not to be exclusively absorbed in these unavoidable guerilla fights incessantly springing up from the never-ceasing encroachments of capital or changes of the market. They ought to understand that, with all the miseries it imposes upon them, the present system simultaneously engenders the *material conditions* and the *social forms* necessary for an economical reconstruction of society. Instead of the *conservative* motto, "*A fair day's wage for a fair day's work!*" they ought to inscribe on their banner the *revolutionary* watchword, "*Abolition of the wages system!*"

After this very long and, I fear, tedious exposition which I was obliged to enter into to do some justice to the subject-matter, I shall conclude by proposing the following resolutions:

Firstly. A general rise in the rate of wages would result in a fall of the general rate of profit, but, broadly speaking, not affect the prices of commodities.

Secondly. The general tendency of capitalist production is not to raise, but to sink the average standard of wages.

Thirdly. Trades Unions work well as centers of resistance against the encroachments of capital. They fail partially from an injudicious use of their power. They fail generally from limiting themselves to a guerilla war against the effects of the existing system, instead of simultaneously trying to change it, instead of using their organized forces as a lever for the final emancipation of the working class, that is to say, the ultimate abolition of the wages system.

The Process of
Capitalistic Production

We have seen that the capitalist process of production is a historically determined form of the social process of production in general. The latter is as much a production process of material conditions of human life as a process taking place under specific historical and economic production relations, producing and reproducing these production relations themselves, and thereby also the bearers of this process, their material conditions of existence and their mutual relations, i.e., their particular socio-economic form. For the aggregate of these relations, in which the agents of this production stand with respect to Nature and to one another, and in which they produce, is precisely society, considered from the standpoint of its economic structure. Like all its predecessors, the capitalist process of production proceeds under definite material conditions, which are, however, simultaneously the bearers of definite social relations entered into by individuals in the process of reproducing their life. Those conditions, like these relations, are on the one hand prerequisites, on the other hand results and creations of the capitalist process of production; they are produced and reproduced by it. We saw also that capital—and the capitalist is merely capital personified and functions in the process of production solely as the agent of capital—in its corresponding social process of production, pumps a definite quantity of surplus-labor out of the direct producers, or laborers; capital obtains this surplus-labor without an equivalent, and in essence it always remains forced labor—no matter how much it may seem to result from free contractual agreement. This surplus-labor appears as surplus-value, and this surplus-value exists as a surplus-product. Surplus-labor in general, as labor performed over and above the given requirements, must always remain. In the capitalist as well as in the slave system, it merely assumes an antagonistic form and is supplemented by complete idleness of a stratum of society. A definite quantity of surplus-labor is required as insurance against accidents, and by the necessary and progressive expansion of the process of reproduction in keeping with the development of the needs and the growth of population, which is called accumulation from the viewpoint of the capitalist. It is one of the civilizing aspects of capital that it enforces this surplus-labor in a manner and under conditions which are more advantageous to the development of the productive forces, social relations, and the creation of the elements for a new and higher form than under the preceding forms of slavery, serfdom, and so on. Thus it gives rise to a stage, on the one hand, in which coercion and monopolization of social development (including its material and intellectual advantages) by one portion of society at the expense of the other are eliminated; on the other hand, it creates the material means and embryonic conditions, making it possible in a higher form of society to combine this surplus-labor with a greater reduction of time devoted to material labor in general. For, depending on the development of labor productivity, surplus-labor may be large in a small total working-day, and relatively small in a large total working-day. If the necessary labor-time = 3 and the surplus-labor = 3, then the total working-day = 6 and the rate of surplus-labor = 100 percent. If the necessary labor = 9 and the surplus-labor = 3, then the total working-day = 12 and the rate of surplus-labor only = 33.3 percent. In that case, it depends upon the labor productivity how much use-value shall be produced in a definite time, hence also in a definite surplus labor-time. The actual wealth of society, and the possibility of constantly expanding its reproduction process, therefore, do not depend upon the duration of surplus-labor, but upon its productivity and the more or less copious conditions of production under which it is performed. In fact, the realm of freedom actually begins only where labor which is determined by necessity and mundane considerations ceases; thus in the very nature of things it lies beyond the sphere of actual material production. Just as the savage must wrestle with Nature to satisfy his wants, to maintain and reproduce life, so must civilized man, and he must do so in all social formations and under all possible modes of production. With his development this realm of physical necessity expands as a result of his wants; but, at the same time, the forces of production which satisfy these wants also increase. Freedom in this field can only consist in socialized man, the associated producers, rationally regulating their interchange with Nature, bringing it under their common control, instead of being ruled by it as by the blind forces of Nature; and achieving this with the least expenditure of energy and under conditions most favorable to, and worthy of, their human nature. But it nonetheless still remains a realm of necessity. Beyond it begins that development of human energy which is an end in itself, the true realm of freedom, which, however, can blossom forth only with this realm of necessity as its basis. The shortening of the working day is its basic prerequisite.

In a capitalist society, this surplus-value, or this surplus-product (leaving aside chance fluctuations in its distribution and considering only its regulating law, its standardizing limits), is divided among capitalists as dividends proportionate to the share of the social capital each holds. In this form surplus-value appears as average profit which falls to the share of capital, an average profit which in turn divides into profit of enterprise and interest, and which under these two categories may fall into the laps of different kinds of capitalists. This appropriation and distribution of surplus-value, or surplus-product, on the part of capital, however, has its barrier in landed property. Just as the operating capitalist pumps surplus-labor, and thereby surplus-value and surplus-product in the form of profit, out of the laborer, so the landlord in turn pumps a portion of this surplus-value, or surplus-product, out of the capitalist in the form of rent in accordance with the laws already elaborated.

Hence, when speaking here of profit as that portion of surplus-value falling to the share of capital, we mean average profit (equal to profit of enterprise plus interest) which is already limited by the deduction of rent from the aggregate profit (identical in mass with aggregate surplus-value); the deduction of rent is assumed. Profit of capital (profit of enterprise plus interest) and ground-rent are thus no more than particular components of surplus-value, categories by which surplus-value is differentiated depending on whether it falls to the share of capital or landed property, headings which in no whit however alter its nature. Added together, these form the sum of social surplus-value. Capital pumps the surplus-labor, which is represented by surplus-value and surplus-product, directly out of the laborers. Thus, in this sense, it may be regarded as the producer of surplus-value. Landed property has nothing to do with the actual process of production. Its role is confined to transferring a portion of the produced surplus-value from the pockets of capital to its own. However, the landlord plays a role in the capitalist process of production not merely through the pressure he exerts upon capital, nor merely because large landed property is a prerequisite and condition of capitalist production since it is a prerequisite and condition of the expropriation of the laborer from the means of production, but particularly because he appears as the personification of one of the most essential conditions of production.

Finally, the laborer in the capacity of owner and seller of his individual labor-power receives a portion of the product under the label of wages, in which that portion of his labor appears which we call necessary labor, i.e., that required for the maintenance and reproduction of this labor-power, be the conditions of this maintenance and reproduction scanty or bountiful, favorable or unfavorable.

Whatever may be the disparity of these relations in other respects, they all have this in common: Capital yields a profit year after year to the capitalist, land a ground-rent to the landlord, and labor-power, under normal conditions and so long as it remains useful labor-power, a wage to the laborer. These three portions of total value annually produced, and the corresponding portions of the annually created total product (leaving aside for the present any consideration of accumulation), may be annually consumed by their respective owners, without exhausting the source of their reproduction. . . .

In the case of the simplest categories of the capitalist mode of production, and even of commodity-production, in the case of commodities and money, we have already pointed out the mystifying character that transforms the social relations, for which the material elements of wealth serve as bearers in production, into properties of these things themselves (commodities) and still more pronouncedly transforms the production relation itself into a thing (money). All forms of society, in so far as they reach the stage of commodity-production and money circulation, take part in this perversion. But under the capitalist mode of production and in the case of capital, which forms its dominant category, its determining production relation, this enchanted and perverted world develops still more. If one considers capital, to begin with, in the actual process of production as a means of extracting surplus-labor, then this relationship is still very simple, and the actual connection impresses itself upon the bearers of this process, the capitalists themselves, and remains in their consciousness. The violent struggle over the limits of the working-day demonstrates this strikingly. But even within this nonmediated sphere, the sphere of direct action between labor and capital, matters do not rest in this simplicity. With the development of relative surplus-value in the actual specifically capitalist mode of production, whereby the productive powers of social labor are developed, these productive powers and the social interrelations of labor in the direct labor-process seem transferred from labor to capital. Capital thus becomes a very mystic being since all of labor's social productive forces appear to be due to capital, rather than labor as such, and seem to issue from the womb of capital itself. Then the process of circulation intervenes, with its changes of substance and form, on which all parts of capital, even agricultural capital, devolve to the same degree that the specifically capitalist mode of production develops. This is a sphere where the relations under which value is originally produced are pushed completely into the background. In the direct process of production the capitalist already acts simultaneously as producer of commodities and manager of commodity-production. Hence this process of production appears to him by no means simply as a process of producing surplus-value. But whatever may be the surplus-value extorted by capital in the actual production process and appearing in commodities, the value and surplus-value contained in the commodities must first be realized in the circulation process. And both the restitution of the values advanced in production and, particularly, the surplus-value contained in the commodities seem not merely to be realized in the circulation, but actually to arise from it; an appearance which is especially reinforced by two circumstances: first, the profit made in selling depends on cheating, deceit, inside knowledge, skill and a thousand favorable market opportunities; and then by the circumstance that added here to labor-time is a second determining element—time of circulation. This acts, in fact, only as a negative barrier against the formation of value and surplus-value, but it has the appearance of being as definite a basis as labor itself and of introducing a determining element that is independent of labor and resulting from the nature of capital. In book 2 we naturally had to present this sphere of circulation merely with reference to the form determinations which it created and to demonstrate the further development of the structure of capital taking place in this sphere. But in reality this sphere is the sphere of competition, which considered in each individual case, is dominated by chance; where, then, the inner law, which prevails in these accidents and regulates them, is only visible when these accidents are grouped together in large numbers, where it remains, therefore, invisible and unintelligible to the individual agents in production. But furthermore: the actual process of production, as a unity of the direct production process and the circulation process, gives rise to new formations, in which the vein of internal connections is increasingly lost, the production relations are rendered independent of one another, and the component values become ossified into forms independent of one another.

The conversion of surplus-value into profit, as we have seen, is determined as much by the process of circulation as by the process of production. Surplus-value, in the form of profit, is no longer related back to that portion of capital invested in labor from which it arises, but to the total capital. The rate of profit is regulated by laws of its own, which permit, or even require, it to change while the rate of surplus-value remains unaltered. All this obscures more and more the true nature of surplus-value and thus the actual mechanism of capital. Still more is this achieved through the transformation of profit into average profit and of values into prices of production, into the regulating averages of market-prices. A complicated social process intervenes here, the equalization process of capitals, which divorces the relative average prices of the commodities from their values, as well as the average profits in the various spheres of production (quite aside from the individual investments of capital in each particular sphere of production) from the actual exploitation of labor by the particular capitals. Not only does it appear so, but it is true in fact that the average price of commodities differs from their value, thus from the labor realized in them, and the average profit of a particular capital differs from the surplus-value which this capital has extracted from the laborers employed by it. The value of commodities appears, directly, solely in the influence of fluctuating productivity of labor upon the rise and fall of the prices of production, upon their movement and not upon their ultimate limits. Profit seems to be determined only secondarily by direct exploitation of labor, in so far as the latter permits the capitalist to realize a profit deviating from the average profit at the regulating market-prices, which apparently prevail independent of such exploitation. Normal average profits themselves seem immanent in capital and independent of exploitation; abnormal exploitation, or even average exploitation under favorable exceptional conditions, seems to determine only the deviations from average profit, not this profit itself. The division of profit into profit of enterprise and interest (not to mention the intervention of commercial profit and profit from money-dealing, which are founded upon circulation and appear to arise completely from it, and not from the process of production itself) consummates the individualization of the form of surplus-value, the ossification of its form as opposed to its substance, its essence. One portion of profit, as opposed to the other, separates itself entirely from the relationship of capital as such and appears as arising not out of the function of exploiting wage-labor, but out of the wage-labor of the capitalist himself. In contrast, thereto, interest then seems to be independent both of the laborer's wage-labor and the capitalist's own labor, and to arise from capital as its own independent source. If capital originally appeared on the surface of circulation as a fetishism of capital, as a value-creating value, so it now appears again in the form of interest-bearing capital, as in its most estranged and characteristic form. Wherefore also the formula capital—interest, as the third to land—rent and labor—wages, is much more consistent than capital—profit, since in profit there still remains a recollection of its origin, which is not only extinguished in interest, but is also placed in a form thoroughly antithetical to this origin.

Finally, capital as an independent source of surplus-value is joined by landed property, which acts as a barrier to average profit and transfers a portion of surplus-value to a class that neither works itself, nor directly exploits labor, nor can find morally edifying rationalizations, as in the case of interest-bearing capital, e.g., risk and sacrifice of lending capital to others. Since here a part of the surplus-value seems to be bound up directly with a natural element, the land, rather than with social relations, the form of mutual estrangement and ossification of the various parts of surplus-value is completed, the inner connection completely disrupted, and its source entirely buried, precisely because the relations of production, which are bound to the various material elements of the production process, have been rendered mutually independent.

In capital—profit, or still better capital—interest, land—rent, labor—wages, in this economic trinity represented as the connection between the component parts of value and wealth in general and its sources, we have the complete mystification of the capitalist mode of production, the conversion of social relations into things, the direct coalescence of the material production relations with their historical and social determination. It is an enchanted, perverted, topsy-turvy world, in which Monsieur le Capital and Madame la Terre do their ghost-walking as social characters and at the same time directly as mere things. It is the great merit of classical economy to have destroyed this false appearance and illusion, this mutual independence and ossification of the various social elements of wealth, this personification of things and conversion of production relations into entities, this religion of everyday life. It did so by reducing interest to a portion of profit, and rent to the surplus above average profit, so that both of them converge in surplus-value; and by representing the process of circulation as a mere metamorphosis of forms, and finally reducing value and surplus-value of commodities to labor in the direct production process. Nevertheless even the best spokesmen of classical economy remain more or less in the grip of the world of illusion which their criticism had dissolved, as cannot be otherwise from a bourgeois standpoint, and thus they all fall more or less into inconsistencies, half-truths and unsolved contradictions. On the other hand, it is just as natural for the actual agents of production to feel completely at home in these estranged and irrational forms of capital—interest, land—rent, labor—wages, since these are precisely the forms of illusion in which they move about and find their daily occupation. It is therefore just as natural that vulgar economy, which is no more than a didactic, more or less dogmatic, translation of everyday conceptions of the actual agents of production, and which arranges them in a certain rational order, should see precisely in this trinity, which is devoid of all inner connection, the natural and indubitable lofty basis for its shallow pompousness. This formula simultaneously corresponds to the interests of the ruling classes by proclaiming the physical necessity and eternal justification of their sources of revenue and elevating them to a dogma.

In our description of how production relations are converted into entities and rendered independent in relation to the agents of production, we leave aside the manner in which the interrelations, due to the world-market, its conjunctures, movements of market-

prices, periods of credit, industrial and commercial cycles, alterna-
tions of prosperity and crisis, appear to them as overwhelming
natural laws that irresistibly enforce their will over them, and confront them as blind necessity. We leave this aside because the actual
movement of competition belongs beyond our scope, and we need
present only the inner organization of the capitalist mode of production, in its ideal average, as it were.

In preceding forms of society this economic mystification arose
principally with respect to money and interest-bearing capital. In
the nature of things it is excluded, in the first place, where production for the use-value, for immediate personal requirements, pre-
dominates; and, secondly, where slavery or serfdom form the broad
foundation of social production, as in antiquity and during the
Middle Ages. Here, the domination of the producers by the conditions of production is concealed by the relations of dominion and
servitude, which appear and are evident as the direct motive power
of the process of production. In early communal societies in which
primitive communism prevailed, and even in the ancient communal
towns, it was this communal society itself with its conditions which
appeared as the basis of production, and its reproduction appeared
as its ultimate purpose. Even in the medieval guild system neither
capital nor labor appear untrammelled, but their relations are
rather defined by the corporate rules, and by the same associated
relations, and corresponding conceptions of professional duty,
craftsmanship, etc.

* * *

The new value added by the annual newly added labor—and thus
also that portion of the annual product in which this value is represented and which may be drawn out of the total output and separated from it—is thus split into three parts, which assume three
different forms of revenue, into forms which express one portion
of this value as belonging or falling to the share of the owner of
labor-power, another portion to the owner of capital, and a third
portion to the owner of landed property. These, then, are relations,
or forms of distribution, for they express the relations under which
the newly produced total value is distributed among the owners of
the various production factors.

From the common viewpoint these distribution relations appear
as natural relations, as relations arising directly from the nature of
all social production, from the laws of human production in gen-

eral. It cannot, indeed, be denied that precapitalist societies disclose other modes of distribution, but the latter are interpreted as undeveloped, unperfected and disguised, not reduced to their purest expression and their highest form and differently shaded modes of the natural distribution relations.

The only correct aspect of this conception is: Assuming some form of social production to exist (e.g., primitive Indian communities, or the more ingeniously developed communism of the Peruvians), a distinction can always be made between that portion of labor whose product is directly consumed individually by the producers and their families and—aside from the part which is productively consumed—that portion of labor which is invariably surplus-labor, whose product serves constantly to satisfy the general social needs, no matter how this surplus-product may be divided, and no matter who may function as representative of these social needs. Thus, the identity of the various modes of distribution amounts merely to this: they are identical if we abstract from their differences and specific forms and keep in mind only their unity as distinct from their dissimilarity.

A more advanced, more critical mind, however, admits the historically developed character of distribution relations,* but nevertheless clings all the more tenaciously to the unchanging character of production relations themselves, arising from human nature and thus independent of all historical development.

On the other hand, scientific analysis of the capitalist mode of production demonstrates the contrary, that it is a mode of production of a special kind, with specific historical features; that, like any other specific mode of production, it presupposes a given level of the social productive forces and their forms of development as its historical precondition: a precondition which is itself the historical result and product of a preceding process, and from which the new mode of production proceeds as its given basis; that the production relations corresponding to this specific, historically determined mode of production—relations which human beings enter into during the process of social life, in the creation of their social life—possess a specific, historical and transitory character; and, finally, that the distribution relations essentially coincident with these production relations are their opposite side, so that both share the same historically transitory character.

---

*J. Stuart Mill, *Some Unsettled Questions in Political Economy*, London, 1844.

In the study of distribution relations, the initial point of departure is the alleged fact that the annual product is apportioned among wages, profit and rent. But if so expressed, it is a misstatement. The product is apportioned on one side to capital, on the other to revenue. One of these revenues, wages, never itself assumes the form of revenue, revenue of the laborer, until after it has first confronted this laborer in the *form of capital*. The confrontation of produced conditions of labor and of the products of labor generally, as capital, with the direct producers implies from the outset a definite social character of the material conditions of labor in relation to the laborers, and thereby a definite relationship into which they enter with the owners of the means of production and among themselves during production itself. The transformation of these conditions of labor into capital implies in turn the expropriation of the direct producers from the land, and thus a definite form of landed property.

If one portion of the product were not transformed into capital, the other would not assume the forms of wages, profit and rent.

On the other hand, if the capitalist mode of production presupposes this definite social form of the conditions of production, so does it reproduce it continually. It produces not merely the material products, but reproduces continually the production relations in which the former are produced, and thereby also the corresponding distribution relations.

It may be said, of course, that capital itself (and landed property which it includes as its antithesis) already presupposes a distribution: the expropriation of the laborer from the conditions of labor, the concentration of these conditions in the hands of a minority of individuals, the exclusive ownership of land by other individuals, in short, all the relations which have been described in the part dealing with primitive accumulation. But this distribution differs altogether from what is understood by distribution relations when the latter are endowed with a historical character in contradistinction to production relations. What is meant thereby are the various titles to that portion of the product which goes into individual consumption. The aforementioned distribution relations, on the contrary, are the basis of special social functions performed within the production relations by certain of their agents, as opposed to the direct producers. They imbue the conditions of production themselves and their representatives with a specific social quality.

They determine the entire character and the entire movement of production.

Capitalist production is distinguished from the outset by two characteristic features.

First. It produces its products as commodities. The fact that it produces commodities does not differentiate it from other modes of production; but rather the fact that being a commodity is the dominant and determining characteristic of its products. This implies, first and foremost, that the laborer himself comes forward merely as a seller of commodities, and thus as a free wage-laborer, so that labor appears in general as wage-labor. In view of what has already been said, it is superfluous to demonstrate anew that the relation between capital and wage-labor determines the entire character of the mode of production. The principal agents of this mode of production itself, the capitalist and the wage-laborer, are as such merely embodiments, personifications of capital and wage-labor; definite social characteristics stamped upon individuals by the process of social production; the products of these definite social production relations.

The characteristic (1) of the product as a commodity, and (2) of the commodity as a product of capital, already implies all circulation relations, i.e., a definite social process through which the products must pass and in which they assume definite social characteristics; it likewise implies definite relations of the production agents, by which the value-expansion of their product and its reconversion, either into means of subsistence or into means of production, are determined. But even apart from this, the entire determination of value and the regulation of the total production by value results from the above two characteristics of the product as a commodity, or of the commodity as a capitalisatically produced commodity. In this entirely specific form of value, labor prevails on the one hand solely as social labor; on the other hand, the distribution of this social labor and the mutual supplementing and interchanging of its products, the subordination under, and introduction into, the social mechanism, are left to the accidental and mutually nullifying motives of individual capitalists. Since these latter confront one another only as commodity-owners, and everyone seeks to sell his commodity as dearly as possible (apparently even guided in the regulation of production itself solely by his own free will), the inner law enforces itself only through their competition, their mutual pressure upon each other, whereby the deviations are mutually canceled. Only as an inner law, vis-à-vis the individual agents, as a blind law of Nature, does the law of value exert its influence here and maintain the social equilibrium of production amidst its accidental fluctuations.

Furthermore, already implicit in the commodity, and even more so in the commodity as a product of capital, is the materialization of the social features of production and the personification of the material foundations of production, which characterize the entire capitalist mode of production.

The *second* distinctive feature of the capitalist mode of production is the production of surplus-value as the direct aim and determining motive of production. Capital produces essentially capital, and does so only to the extent that it produces surplus-value. We have seen in our discussion of relative surplus-value, and further in considering the transformation of surplus-value into profit, how a mode of production peculiar to the capitalist period is founded hereon—a special form of development of the social productive powers of labor, but confronting the laborer as powers of capital rendered independent, and standing in direct opposition therefore to the laborer's own development. Production for value and surplus-value implies, as has been shown in the course of our analysis, the constantly operating tendency to reduce the labor-time necessary for the production of a commodity, i.e., its value, below the actually prevailing social average. The pressure to reduce cost-price to its minimum becomes the strongest lever for raising the social productiveness of labor, which, however, appears here only as a continual increase in the productiveness of capital.

The authority assumed by the capitalist as the personification of capital in the direct process of production, the social function performed by him in his capacity as manager and ruler of production, is essentially different from the authority exercised on the basis of production by means of slaves, serfs, and so on.

Whereas, on the basis of capitalist production, the mass of direct producers is confronted by the social character of their production in the form of strictly regulating authority and a social mechanism of the labor-process organized as a complete hierarchy—this authority reaching its bearers, however, only as the personification of the conditions of labor in contrast to labor, and not as political or theocratic rulers as under earlier modes of production—among the bearers of this authority, the capitalists themselves, who confront one another only as commodity-owners, there reigns complete anarchy within which the social interrelations of production assert themselves only as an overwhelming natural law in relation to individual free will.

Only because labor preexists in the form of wage-laborer, and the means of production in the form of capital—i.e., solely because of this specific social form of these essential production factors—does a part of the value (product) appear as surplus-value and this surplus-value as profit (rent), as the gain of the capitalist, as additional available wealth belonging to him. But only because this surplus-value thus appears as *his profit* do the additional means of production, which are intended for the expansion of reproduction, and which constitute a part of this profit, present themselves as new additional capital, and the expansion of the process of reproduction in general as a process of capitalist accumulation.

Although the form of labor as wage-labor is decisive for the form of the entire process and the specific mode of production itself, it is not wage-labor which determines value. In the determination of value, it is a question of social labor-time in general, the quantity of labor which society generally has at its disposal, and whose relative absorption by the various products determines, as it were, their respective social importance. The definite form in which the social labor-time prevails as decisive in the determination of the value of commodities is of course connected with the form of labor as wage-labor and with the corresponding form of the means of production as capital, insofar as solely on this basis does commodity-production become the general form of production.

Let us moreover consider the so-called distribution relations themselves. The wage presupposes wage-labor, and profit—capital. These definite forms of distribution thus presuppose definite social characteristics of production conditions, and definite social relations of production agents. The specific distribution relations are thus merely the expression of the specific historical production relations.

And now let us consider profit. This specific form of surplus-value is the precondition for the fact that the new creation of means of production takes place in the form of capitalist production; thus, a relation dominating reproduction, although it seems to the individual capitalist as if he could in reality consume his entire profit as revenue. However, he thereby meets barriers even in the form of insurance and reserve funds laws of competition, etc., which hamper him and prove to him in practice that profit is not a mere distribution category of the individually consumable product. The entire process of capitalist production is furthermore regulated by the prices of the products. But the regulating prices of production are themselves in turn regulated by the equalization of the rate of profit and its corresponding distribution of capital among the various social spheres of production. Profit, then, appears here as the main factor, not of the distribution of products, but of their production itself, as a factor in the distribution of capital and labor itself among the various spheres of production. The division of profit into profit of enterprise and interest appears as the distribution of the same revenue. But it arises, to begin with, from the development of capital as a self-expanding value, a creator of surplus-value, i.e., from this specific social form of the prevailing process of production. It evolves credit and credit institutions out of itself, and thereby the form of production. As interest, etc., the ostensible distribution forms enter into the price as determining production factors.

Ground-rent might seem to be a mere form of distribution, because landed property as such does not perform any, or at least any normal, function in the process of production itself. But the circumstance that (1) rent is limited to the excess above the average profit, and that (2) the landlord is reduced from the manager and master of the process of production and of the entire process of social life to the position of mere lessor of land, usurer in land and mere collector of rent, is a specific historical result of the capitalist mode of production. The fact that the earth received the form of landed property is a historical precondition for this. The fact that landed property assumes forms which permit the capitalist mode of operation in agriculture is a product of the specific character of this mode of production. The income of the landlord may be called rent, even under other forms of society. But it differs essentially from rent as it appears in this mode of production.

The so-called distribution relations, then, correspond to and arise from historically determined specific social forms of the process of production and mutual relations entered into by men in the reproduction process of human life. The historical character of these distribution relations is the historical character of production relations, of which they express merely one aspect. Capitalist distribution differs from those forms of distribution which arise from other modes of production, and every form of distribution disappears with the specific form of production from which it is descended and to which it corresponds.

The view that regards only distribution relations as historical, but not production relations, is, on the one hand, solely the view of the initial, but still handicapped, criticism of bourgeois economy. On the other hand, it rests on the confusion and identification of the process of social production with the simple labor-process, such as might even be performed by an abnormally isolated human being without any social assistance. To the extent that the labor-process is solely a process between man and Nature, its simple elements remain common to all social forms of development. But each specific historical form of this process further develops its material foundations and social forms. Whenever a certain stage of maturity has been reached, the specific historical form is discarded and makes way for a higher one. The moment of arrival of such a crisis is disclosed by the depth and breadth attained by the contradictions and antagonisms between the distribution relations, and thus the specific historical form of their corresponding production relations, on the one hand, and the productive forces, the production powers and the development of their agencies, on the other hand. A conflict then ensues between the material development of production and its social form.

Translated by Samuel Moore and Edward Aveling

FRIEDRICH ENGELS

Feuerbach and the End of Classical German Philosophy

The work* before us takes us back to a period which, although in time no more than a good generation behind us, has become as foreign to the present generation in Germany as if it were already a full century old. Yet it was the period of Germany's preparation for the Revolution of 1848; and all that has happened since then in our country has been merely a continuation of 1848, merely the execution of the testament of the revolution.

Just as in France in the eighteenth century, so in Germany in the nineteenth, a philosophical revolution ushered in the political collapse. But how different the two looked! The French were in open combat against all official science, against the Church and often also against the State; their writings were printed across the frontier, in Holland or England, while they themselves were often in jeopardy of imprisonment in the Bastille. On the other hand, the Germans were professors, State-appointed instructors of youth; their writings were recognized textbooks, and the system that rounded off the whole development—the Hegelian system—was even raised, as it were, to the rank of a royal Prussian philosophy of State! Was it possible that a revolution could hide behind these professors, behind their obscure, pedantic phrases, their ponderous, wearisome periods? Were not precisely those people who were then regarded as the representatives of the revolution, the liberals, the bitterest opponents of this befuddling philosophy? But what neither governments nor liberals saw was seen at least by one man as early as 1833, and this man was none other than Heinrich Heine.

Ludwig Feuerbach, by C. N. Starcke, Ph.D., Stuttgart, Ferd. Encke, 1885.

Let us take an example. No philosophical proposition has earned more gratitude from narrow-minded governments and wrath from equally narrow-minded liberals than Hegel's famous statement: "All that is real is rational; and all that is rational is real."

That was blatantly a sanctification of the existing order of things, the philosophical benediction upon despotism, the police state, arbitrary justice, and censorship. And so it was understood by Frederick William III, and by his subjects. But according to Hegel certainly not everything that exists is also real, without further qualification. For Hegel the attribute of reality belongs only to that which is at the same time necessary: "In the course of its development reality proves to be necessity."

Any particular governmental measure—Hegel himself cites the example of "a certain tax regulation"—is therefore for him by no means real without qualification. That which is necessary, however, proves in the last resort to be also rational; and, applied to the Prussian state of that time, the Hegelian proposition, therefore, merely means: this state is rational, corresponds to reason, in so far as it [the state] is necessary; and if it nevertheless appears evil to us, but still, in spite of its evilness, continues to exist, then the evilness of the government is justified and explained by the corresponding evilness of the subjects. The Prussians of that day had the government that they deserved.

Now, according to Hegel, reality is, however, in no way an attribute predicable of any given state of affairs, social or political, in all circumstances and at all times. On the contrary: the Roman Republic was real, but so was the Roman Empire which superseded it. In 1789 the French monarchy had become so unreal, that is to say, so robbed of all necessity, so irrational, that it had to be destroyed by the Great Revolution, of which Hegel always speaks with the greatest enthusiasm. In this case, therefore, the monarchy was the unreal and the revolution the real. And so, in the course of development, all that was previously real becomes unreal, loses its necessity, its right of existence, its rationality. And in the place of moribund reality comes a new, viable reality—peacefully if the old has enough common sense to go to its death without a struggle; forcibly if it resists this necessity. Thus the Hegelian proposition turns into its opposite through Hegelian dialectics itself: All that is real in the sphere of human history becomes irrational in the course of time, is therefore irrational by its very destination, is encumbered with irrationality from the outset; and everything which is rational in the minds of men is destined to become real, however much it may contradict existing apparent reality. In accordance with all the rules of the Hegelian method of thought, the proposition of the rationality of everything which is real is dissolved to become the other proposition: All that exists deserves to perish.*

But precisely therein lay the true significance and the revolutionary character of Hegelian philosophy (to which, as the termination of the whole movement since Kant, we must here confine ourselves), that it once and for all dealt the death blow to the finality of all products of human thought and action. Truth, the cognition of which was the business of philosophy, was in the hands of Hegel no longer a collection of ready-made dogmatic statements, which, once discovered, had merely to be learned by heart. Truth now lay in the process of cognition itself, in the long historical development of science, which ascends from lower to ever higher levels of knowledge without ever reaching, by discovering so-called absolute truth, a point at which it can proceed no further, where it has nothing more to do than to sit back and gaze in wonder at the absolute truth to which it had attained. And what holds good for the realm of philosophical cognition holds good also for that of every other kind of cognition and also for practical action. Just as cognition is unable to reach a definitive conclusion in a perfect, ideal condition of humanity, so is history; a perfect society, a perfect "State," are things which can only exist in the imagination. On the contrary, all successive historical states are only transitory stages in the endless course of development of human society from the lower to the higher. Each stage is necessary, and therefore justified for the time and conditions to which it owes its origin. But in the face of new, higher conditions which gradually develop in its own womb, it loses its validity and justification. It must give way to a higher stage, which will also in its turn decay and perish. Just as the bourgeoisie by large-scale industry, competition and the world market dissolves in practice all stable time-honored institutions, so this dialectical philosophy dissolves all conceptions of final, absolute truth and of absolute states of humanity corresponding to it. Against it [dialectical philosophy] nothing is final, absolute, sacred. It reveals the transitory character of everything and in everything;

---

*A paraphrase of Mephistopheles' words from Goethe's *Faust*, act 1, scene 3 ("Faust's Study").

nothing can endure against it except the uninterrupted process of becoming and passing away, of ascending without end from the lower to the higher. And dialectical philosophy itself is nothing more than the mere reflection of this process in the thinking brain. It has, however, also a conservative side: it recognises that definite stages of cognition and society are justified for their time and circumstances; but only so far. The conservatism of this outlook is relative; its revolutionary character is absolute—the only absolute dialectical philosophy admits.

It is not necessary, here, to go into the question of whether this outlook is thoroughly in accord with the present state of natural science, which predicts a possible end for the earth itself and for its habitability a fairly certain one; which therefore recognizes that for the history of mankind, too, there is not only an ascending but also a descending branch. At any rate we are still a considerable distance from the turning point at which the historical course of society becomes one of descent, and we cannot expect Hegelian philosophy to be concerned with a subject which, in its time, natural science had not yet placed on the agenda at all.

But what really must be said here is this: that in Hegel the views developed above are not so sharply defined. They are a necessary conclusion from his method, but one which he himself never drew with such explicitness. And this, indeed, for the simple reason that he was compelled to make a system and, in accordance with traditional requirements, a system of philosophy must conclude with some sort of absolute truth. Therefore, however much Hegel, especially in his *Logik,* emphasises that this eternal truth is nothing but the logical, or, the historical, process itself, he nevertheless finds himself compelled to supply this process with an end, just because he has to bring his system to a termination at some point or other. In his *Logik* he can make this end a beginning again, since here the point of conclusion, the absolute idea—which is only absolute in so far as he has absolutely nothing to say about it—"alienates," that is, transforms itself into nature and comes to itself again later in the mind, that is, in thought and in history. But at the end of the whole philosophy a similar return to the beginning is possible only in one way. Namely, by conceiving the end of history as follows: mankind arrives at the cognition of this selfsame absolute idea, and declares that this cognition of the absolute idea is attained in Hegelian philosophy. In this way, however, the whole dogmatic content of the Hegelian system is declared to be absolute truth, in contradiction to his dialectical method, which dissolves all that is dogmatic. Thus the revolutionary side is smothered beneath the overgrowth of the conservative side. And what applies to philosophical cognition applies also to historical practice. Having, in the person of Hegel, reached the point of working out the absolute idea, mankind must also in practice have advanced so far that it can carry out this absolute idea in reality. Hence the practical political demands of the absolute idea on contemporaries should not be pitched too high. And so we find at the conclusion of the *Rechtsphilosophie* that the absolute idea is to be implemented in that monarchy based on social estates which Frederick William III so persistently promised his subjects to no avail, that is, in a limited and moderate, indirect rule of the possessing classes suited to the petty-bourgeois German conditions of that time; and, moreover, the necessity of the nobility is demonstrated to us in a speculative fashion.

The inner necessities of the system are, therefore, of themselves sufficient to explain why a thoroughly revolutionary method of thinking produced an extremely tame political conclusion. As a matter of fact, the specific form of this conclusion derives from the fact that Hegel was a German, and like his contemporary Goethe, had a bit of the philistine's tail dangling behind. Each of them was an Olympian Zeus in his own sphere, yet neither of them ever quite freed himself from German philistinism.

But all this did not prevent the Hegelian system from covering an incomparably greater domain than any earlier system, nor from developing in this domain a wealth of thought which is astounding even today. The phenomenology of the mind (which one may call a parallel to the embryology and palaeontology of the mind, a development of individual consciousness through its different stages, set in the form of an abbreviated reproduction of the stages through which the consciousness of man has passed in the course of history), logic, philosophy of nature, philosophy of the mind, and the latter in turn elaborated in its separate, historical subdivisions: philosophy of history, of law, of religion, history of philosophy, aesthetics, etc.—in all these different historical fields Hegel worked to discover and demonstrate the pervading thread of development. And as he was not only a creative genius but also a man of encyclopaedic erudition, he played an epoch-making role in every sphere. It is self-evident that owing to the needs of the "system" he very often had to resort to those forced constructions about which his pygmean opponents make such a terrible fuss even today. But these constructions are only the frame and scaffolding of his work. If one does not loiter here needlessly, but presses on farther into the huge edifice, one finds innumerable treasures which still today retain their full value. With all philosophers it is precisely the "system" which is perishable; and for the simple reason that it springs from an imperishable need of the human mind—the need to overcome all contradictions. But if all contradictions are once for all disposed of, we shall have arrived at so-called absolute truth—world history will be at an end. And yet it has to continue, although there is nothing left for it to do—hence, a new, insoluble contradiction. Once we have realized—and in the long run no one has helped us to realize it more than Hegel himself—that the task of philosophy thus stated means nothing but the task that a single philosopher should accomplish that which can only be accomplished by the entire human race in its ongoing development—as soon as we realize that, it is the end of all philosophy in the hitherto accepted sense of the word. One leaves alone "absolute truth," which is unattainable along this path or by any single individual; instead, one pursues attainable relative truths along the path of the positive sciences, and the summation of their results by means of dialectical thinking. With Hegel philosophy comes to an end altogether: on the one hand, because in his system he sums up its whole development in the most splendid fashion; and on the other hand, because, even if unconsciously, he shows us the way out of the labyrinth of systems to real positive cognition of the world.

One can imagine what a tremendous effect this Hegelian system must have produced in the philosophy-tinged atmosphere of Germany. It was a triumphal procession which lasted for decades and which by no means came to a standstill on the death of Hegel. On the contrary, it was precisely from 1830 to 1840 that "Hegelianism" reigned most exclusively, and to a greater or lesser extent infected even its opponents. It was precisely in this period that Hegelian views, consciously or unconsciously, most extensively penetrated the most diversified sciences and leavened even popular literature and the daily press, from which the average "educated consciousness" derives its mental pabulum. But this victory along the whole front was only the prelude to an internal struggle.

As we have seen, Hegel's doctrine, taken as a whole, left plenty of room to accommodate the most diverse practical party views. And in the theoretical Germany of that time, two things were practical above all; religion and politics. Whoever placed the emphasis on the Hegelian *system* could be fairly conservative in both spheres; whoever regarded the dialectical *method* as the main thing could belong to the most extreme opposition, both in religion and politics. Hegel himself, despite the fairly frequent outbursts of revolutionary wrath in his works, seemed on the whole to be more inclined to the conservative side. Indeed, his system had cost him much more "hard mental plugging" than his method. Toward the end of the thirties, the cleavage in the school became more and more apparent. The Left wing, the so-called Young Hegelians, in their fight with the pietist orthodox and the feudal reactionaries, abandoned bit by bit that philosophical-genteel reserve in regard to the burning questions of the day which up to that time had secured state toleration and even protection for their teachings. And when, in 1840, orthodox sanctimony and absolutist feudal reaction ascended the throne with Frederick William IV, open partisanship became unavoidable. The fight was still carried on with philosophical weapons, but no longer for abstract philosophical aids. It turned directly on the destruction of traditional religion and the existing state. And while in the *Deutsche Jahrbücher* the practical ends were still predominantly put forward in philosophical disguise, in the *Rheinische Zeitung* of 1842 the Young Hegelian school revealed itself directly as the philosophy of the aspiring radical bourgeoisie and used the meager cloak of philosophy only to deceive the censors.

At that time, however, politics was a very thorny field, and hence the main fight came to be directed against religion; this fight, particularly since 1840, was indirectly also political. Strauss's *Leben Jesu,* published in 1835, had provided the initial impetus. The theory therein developed of the formation of the gospel myths was combated later by Bruno Bauer with proof that a whole series of evangelical stories had been invented by the authors themselves. The controversy between these two was carried on in the philosophical disguise of a battle between "self-consciousness" and "substance." The question whether the miracle stories of the gospels came into being through unconscious traditional myth-creation within the bosom of the community or whether they were invented by the evangelists themselves was blown up into the question whether, in world history, "substance" or "self-consciousness" was the decisive operative force. Finally came Stirner, the prophet of contemporary anarchism—Bakunin has taken a great deal from him—and surpassed the sovereign "self-consciousness" by his sovereign "ego."

We shall not go further into this aspect of the decomposition process of the Hegelian school. More important for us is the following: the bulk of the most determined Young Hegelians were, by the practical necessities of their fight against positive religion, driven back to Anglo-French materialism. This brought them into conflict with their school system. While materialism conceives nature as the sole reality, nature in the Hegelian system represents merely the "alienation" of the absolute idea, so to say, a degradation of the idea. At all events, thinking and its thought-product, the idea, is here the primary, nature the derivative, which only exists at all by the condescension of the idea. And in this contradiction they floundered as well or as ill as they could.

Then came Feuerbach's *Wesen des Christenthums*. With *one* blow it pulverized the contradiction, by plainly placing materialism on the throne again. Nature exists independently of all philosophy. It is the foundation upon which we human beings, ourselves products of nature, have grown up. Nothing exists outside nature and man, and the higher beings our religious fantasies have created are only the fantastic reflection of our own essence. The spell was broken; the "system" was exploded and cast aside, and the contradiction, shown to exist only in our imagination, was dissolved. One must have experienced the liberating effect of this book for oneself to get an idea of it. Enthusiasm was universal; we were all Feuerbachians for a moment. How enthusiastically Marx greeted the new conception and how much—in spite of all critical reservations—he was influenced by it, one may read in *The Holy Family*.

Even the shortcomings of the book contributed to its immediate effect. Its literary, sometimes even bombastic, style secured for it a large public and was at any rate refreshing after long years of abstract and abstruse Hegelianizing. The same is true of is extravagant deification of love, which, coming after the now intolerable sovereign rule of "pure reason," had its excuse, if not justification. But what we must not forget is that it was precisely these two weaknesses of Feuerbach that "true socialism," which had been spreading like a plague in "educated" Germany since 1844, took as its starting-point, putting literary phrases in the place of scientific knowledge, the liberation of mankind by means of "love" in place of the emancipation of the proletariat through the economic transformation of production—in short, losing itself in the nauseous fine writing and ecstasies of love typified by Herr Karl Grün.

Another thing we must not forget is this: the Hegelian school had disintegrated, but Hegelian philosophy had not been overcome through criticism; Strauss and Bauer each took one of its sides and set it polemically against the other. Feuerbach broke through the system and simply discarded it. But a philosophy is not disposed of by the mere assertion that it is false. And so mighty a work as Hegelian philosophy, which had exercised so enormous an influence on the intellectual development of the nation, could not be disposed of by simply being ignored. It had to be "transcended" in its own sense, that is, in the sense that while its form had to be annihilated through criticism, the new content which had been won through it had to be saved. How this was brought about we shall see below.

But in the meantime the Revolution of 1848 thrust the whole of philosophy aside as unceremoniously as Feuerbach had thrust aside Hegel. And in the process Feuerbach himself was also pushed into the background.

Strauss, Bauer, Stirner, Feuerbach—these were the offshoots of Hegelian philosophy, insofar as they did not abandon the field of philosophy. Strauss, after his *Leben Jesu* and *Dogmatik*, produced only literary studies in philosophy and ecclesiastical history *à la* Renan. Bauer worked only in the field of the history of the origin of Christianity, though what he did here was important. Stirner remained an oddity, even after Bakunin blended him with Proudhon and labelled the blend "anarchism." Feuerbach alone was of significance as a philosopher. But not only did philosophy— claimed to soar above all individual sciences and to be the science of sciences, connecting them—remain to him an impassable barrier, an inviolable sacrament, but as a philosopher, too, he stopped halfway, was a materialist below and an idealist above. He could not cope with Hegel through criticism; he simply cast him aside as useless, while he himself, compared with the encyclopaedic wealth of the Hegelian system, achieved nothing positive beyond a bombastic religion of love and a meager, impotent morality.

Out of the dissolution of the Hegelian school, however, there emerged still another tendency, the only one which has borne real fruit. And this tendency is essentially connected with the name of Marx.*

The departure from Hegelian philosophy was here too the result of a return to the materialist standpoint. That means it was resolved to comprehend the real world—nature and history—just as it presents itself to everyone who approaches it free from preconceived idealist quirks. It was decided mercilessly to sacrifice every idealist quirk which could not be brought into harmony with the facts conceived in their own, and not in a fantastic, interconnection. And materialism means nothing more than this. But here the materialistic world outlook was taken really seriously for the first time and was carried through consistently—at least in its basic features—in all relevant domains of knowledge.

Hegel was not simply put aside. On the contrary, his revolutionary side, described above, the dialectical method was taken up. But in its Hegelian form this method was no use. According to Hegel, dialectics is the self-development of the concept. The absolute concept does not only exist—unknown where—from eternity, it is also the actual living soul of the whole existing world. It develops into itself through all the preliminary stages which are treated at length in *Logik* and which are all included in it. Then it "alienates" itself by changing itself into nature, where, without consciousness of itself, disguised as the necessity of nature, it goes through a new development and finally comes again to self-consciousness in man. This self-consciousness then elaborates itself again in history from the crude form until finally the absolute concept again comes to itself completely in Hegelian philosophy. According to Hegel, therefore, the dialectical development apparent in nature and history, that is, the causal interconnection of the progressive movement from the lower to the higher, which asserts itself through all

---

*Here I may be permitted to make a personal explanation. Lately repeated reference has been made to my share in this theory, and so I can hardly avoid saying a few words here to settle this point. I cannot deny that both before and during my forty years' collaboration with Marx I had a certain independent share in laying the foundations of the theory, and more particularly in its elaboration. But the greater part of its leading basic principles, especially in the realm of economics and history, and, above all, their final trenchant formulation, belongs to Marx. What I contributed—at any rate with the exception of my work in a few special fields—Marx could very well have done without me. What Marx accomplished I would not have achieved. Marx stood higher, saw further, and took a wider and quicker view than all the rest of us. Marx was a genius; we others were at best talented. Without him the theory would not be by far what it is today. It therefore rightly bears his name.

zigzag movements and temporary retrogressions, is only a copy of the self-movement of the concept going on from eternity, no one knows where, but at all events independently of any thinking human brain. This ideological perversion had to be done away with. We comprehended the concepts in our heads once more materialistically—as images of real things instead of regarding the real things as images of some or other stage of the absolute concept. Thus dialectics reduced itself to the science of the general laws of motion, both of the external world and of human thinking—two sets of laws which are identical in substance, but differ in their expression insofar as the human mind can apply them consciously, while in nature and also up to now for the most part in human history, these laws assert themselves unconsciously, in the form of external necessity, in the midst of an endless series of apparent accidents. Thereby the dialectic of concepts itself became merely the conscious reflection of the dialectical motion of the real world and thus the Hegelian dialectic was placed upon its head; or rather, turned off its head, on which it was standing, and placed upon its feet. And this materialist dialectic, which for years was our best means of labor and our sharpest weapon, was, remarkably enough, rediscovered not only by us but also, independently of us and even of Hegel, by a German worker, Joseph Dietzgen.*

In his way, however, the revolutionary side of Hegelian philosophy was again taken up and at the same time freed from the idealist trimmings which with Hegel had prevented its consistent execution. The great basic thought that the world is not to be comprehended as a complex of ready-made *things,* but as a complex of *processes,* in which the apparently stable things, no less than their mental images in our heads, the concepts, go through uninterrupted change of coming into being and passing away, in which, for all apparent accidentality and despite all temporary retrogression, a progressive development asserts itself in the end—this great fundamental thought has, especially since the time of Hegel, so thoroughly permeated ordinary consciousness that in this generality it is now scarcely ever contradicted. But to acknowledge this fundamental thought in words and to apply it in reality in detail to each domain of investigation are two different things. If, however, investigation always proceeds from this standpoint, the demand for final solutions and eternal truth ceases once and for all; one is

---

*See *Das Wesen der Kopfarbeit, von einem Handarbeiter.* Hamburg, Meißner.

always conscious of the necessary limitation of all acquired knowledge, of the fact that it is conditioned by the circumstances in which it was acquired. On the other hand, one no longer permits oneself to be impressed by the antitheses, unsuperable for the still common old metaphysics, between true and false, good and bad, identical and different, necessary and accidental. One knows that these antitheses have only a relative validity; that that which is now recognized as true has also its hidden false side which will later manifest itself, just as that which is now recognized as false has also its true side by virtue of which it was previously regarded as true. One knows that what is maintained to be necessary is composed of sheer accidents and that the allegedly accidental is the form behind which necessity hides itself—and so on.

The old method of investigation and thinking which Hegel calls "metaphysical," which preferred to investigate *things* as given, as fixed and stable, a method the relics of which still strongly haunt people's minds, had a great deal of historical justification in its day. It was necessary first to examine things before it was possible to examine processes. One had first to know what any particular thing was before one could observe the changes it was undergoing. And such was the case with natural science. The old metaphysics, which accepted things as *faits accomplis,* arose from a natural science which investigated dead and living things as *faits accomplis.* But when this investigation had progressed so far that it became possible to take the decisive step forward, that is, to pass on to the systematic investigation of the changes which these things undergo in nature itself, then the death knell of the old metaphysics struck in the realm of philosophy too. And in fact, while natural science up to the end of the last century was predominantly a *collecting* science, a science of *faits accomplis,* in our century it is essentially a *systematizing* science, a science of the processes, of the origin and development of these things and of the interconnection which binds all these natural processes into one great whole. Physiology, which investigates the processes occurring in plant and animal organisms; embryology, which deals with the development of individual organisms from germ to maturity; geology, which traces the gradual formation of the earth's surface—all these are the offspring of our century.

But, above all, there are three great discoveries which have advanced our knowledge of the interconnection of natural processes by leaps and bounds:

First, the discovery of the cell as the unit from whose multiplication and differentiation the whole plant and animal body develops, so that not only is the development and growth of all higher organisms recognized to proceed according to a single general law, but also, in the capacity of the cell to change, the way is pointed out by which organisms can change their species and thus go through a more than individual development.

Second, the transformation of energy, which has demonstrated to us that all the so-called forces operative in the first instance in inorganic nature—mechanical force and its complement, so-called potential energy, heat, radiation (light, or radiant heat), electricity, magnetism and chemical energy—are different forms of manifestation of universal motion; which pass into one another in definite proportions so that in place of a certain quantity of one which disappears, a certain quantity of another makes its appearance and thus the whole motion of nature is reduced to this incessant process of transformation from one form into another. Finally, the proof which Darwin first developed in coherent form that the stock of organic products of nature surrounding us today, including man, is the product of a long process of evolution from a few originally unicellular germs, and that these in turn arose from protoplasm or albumen, which came into existence by chemical means.

Thanks to these three great discoveries and the other immense advances in natural science, we have now arrived at the point where we can demonstrate the interconnection between the processes in nature not only in particular spheres but also the interconnection of these particular spheres as a whole, and so can present in an approximately systematic form a clear picture of the coherence in nature by means of the facts provided by empirical natural science itself. To furnish this overall picture was formerly the task of so-called philosophy of nature. It could do this only by putting in place of the real but as yet unknown interconnections ideational, fancied ones, filling in the missing facts by mental images and bridging the actual gaps merely in imagination. In the course of this procedure it conceived many brilliant ideas and foreshadowed many later discoveries, but it also produced a considerable amount of nonsense, which indeed could not have been otherwise. Today, when one needs to comprehend the results of natural science only dialectically, that is, in the sense of their own interconnection, in order to arrive at a "system of nature" sufficient for our time; when the dialectical character of this interconnection is forcing itself against their will even into the metaphysically trained minds of the natural scientists, today the philosophy of nature is definitively discarded. Every attempt at resurrecting it would be not only superfluous but a *step backward*.

But what is true of nature, which is hereby recognized also as a historical process of development, is likewise true of the history of society in all its branches and of the totality of all sciences which occupy themselves with things human (and divine). Here, too, the philosophy of history, of law, of religion, etc., has consisted in the substitution of an interconnection fabricated in the mind of the philosopher for the real interconnection demonstrable in events; has consisted in the comprehension of history as a whole, as well as in its separate parts, as the gradual implementation of ideas—and naturally always only the pet ideas of the philosopher himself. According to this, history worked unconsciously but of necessity towards a certain ideal goal set in advance—as, for example, in Hegel, towards the implementation of his absolute idea—and the unshakeable trend towards this absolute idea formed the inner interconnection of the events in history. A new mysterious providence—unconscious or gradually coming into consciousness—was thus put in the place of the real, still unknown interconnection. Here, therefore, just as in the realm of nature, it was necessary to do away with these fabricated, artificial interconnections by the discovery of the real ones—a task that ultimately amounts to the discovery of the general laws of motion which assert themselves as the ruling ones in the history of human society.

In one point, however, the history of the development of society turns out to be essentially different from that of nature. In nature—insofar as we ignore man's reverse action upon nature—there are only blind, unconscious agencies acting upon one another, out of whose interplay the general law comes into operation. Of all that happens—whether in the innumerable apparent accidents observable upon the surface, or in the ultimate results that confirm the regularity inherent in these accidents—nothing happens as a consciously desired aim. In the history of society, on the contrary, the actors are all endowed with consciousness, are men acting with deliberation or passion, working towards definite goals; nothing happens without a deliberate intention, without a desired aim. But this distinction, important as it is for historical investigation, particularly of individual epochs and events, cannot alter the fact that the course of history is governed by innate general laws. For here, too, on the whole, in spite of the consciously desired aims of all individuals, accident apparently reigns on the surface. What is desired happens but rarely; in the majority of instances the numerous desired ends cross and conflict with one another, or these ends themselves are from the outset impracticable or the means of attaining them are insufficient. Thus the conflicts of innumerable individual wills and individual actions in the domain of history lead to a state of affairs quite similar to that prevailing in the realm of unconscious nature. The ends of the actions are desired, but the results which actually follow from these actions are not desired; or when they do seem to correspond to the desired end, they ultimately have consequences quite other than those desired. Historical events thus appear on the whole to be likewise governed by chance. But wherever on the surface chance holds sway, it is always governed by inner, hidden laws and these laws only have to be discovered.

Men make their own history, whatever its outcome may be, in that each person follows his own consciously desired end, and it is precisely the result of these many wills operating in different directions and of their manifold effects upon the world outside that constitutes history. Thus it is also a question of what the many individuals desire. The will is determined by passion or deliberation. But the levers which immediately determine passion or deliberation are of very different kinds. In part they may be external objects, in part ideal motives, ambition, "enthusiasm for truth and justice," personal hatred or even purely individual whims of all kinds. But, on the one hand, we have seen that the many individual wills active in history for the most part produce results quite other than those desired—often quite the opposite; that their motives, therefore, in relation to the total result are likewise of only secondary importance. On the other hand, the question also arises: What driving forces in turn stand behind these motives? What are the historical causes which transform themselves into these motives in the minds of the actors?

The old materialism never asked itself this question. Its conception of history, as far as it has one at all, is therefore essentially pragmatic; it judges everything according to the motives of the action; it divides men who act in history into noble and ignoble and then finds that as a rule the noble are defrauded and the ignoble are victorious. Hence, it follows for the old materialism that nothing very edifying is to be got from the study of history, and for us that in the realm of history the old materialism becomes untrue to itself because it takes the ideal driving forces which operate there as ultimate causes, instead of investigating what is behind them, what are the driving forces of these driving forces. The inconsistency does not lie in the fact that *ideal* driving forces are recognized, but in the investigation not being carried further back from these into their motive causes. On the other hand, the philosophy of history, particularly as represented by Hegel, recognizes that the ostensible and also the actually operating motives of men who act in history are by no means the ultimate causes of historical events; that behind these motives are other motive powers, which have to be explored. But it does not seek these powers in history itself, it imports them rather from outside, from philosophical ideology, into history. Hegel, for example, instead of explaining the history of Ancient Greece out of its own inner coherence, simply maintains that it is nothing more than the bringing out of "forms of beautiful individuality," more the realization of a "work of art" as such. He says much in this connection about the Ancient Greeks that is fine and profound, but that does not prevent us today from refusing to be palmed off with such an explanation, which is mere empty talk.

When, therefore, it is a question of investigating the driving powers which—consciously or unconsciously, and indeed very often unconsciously—lie behind the motives of men who act in history and which constitute the real ultimate driving forces of history, then it is not a question so much of the motives of single individuals, however eminent, as of those motives which set in motion great masses, whole peoples, and again whole classes of the people in each people; and even this, not momentarily, giving rise to the transient flaring up of a straw-fire which quickly dies down, but to lasting action resulting in a great historical transformation. Ascertaining the driving causes which in this context, in the minds of the acting masses and their leaders—the so-called great men—are reflected as conscious motives, clearly or unclearly, directly or in ideological, even sanctified form—that is the only way which can put us on the track of the laws holding sway in history as a whole, as well as in particular periods and in particular countries. Everything which sets men in motion must pass through their minds; but what form it takes in the mind depends very much upon the circumstances. The workers have by no means become reconciled to capitalist machine industry now that they no longer simply break the machines to pieces, as they did as recently as 1848 on the Rhine.

But while in all earlier periods the investigation of these driving causes of history was almost impossible—on account of the complicated and concealed interconnections with their effects—our present period has so far simplified these interconnections that it has been possible to solve the riddle. Since the establishment of large-scale industry, that is, at least since the European peace of 1815, it has been no longer a secret to any man in England that the whole political struggle there turned on the claims to supremacy of two classes: the LANDED ARISTOCRACY and the bourgeoisie (MIDDLE CLASS). In France, with the return of the Bourbons, the same fact was perceived, the historians of the Restoration period, from Thierry to Guizot, Mignet and Thiers, speak of it everywhere as the key to the understanding of French history since the Middle Ages. And since 1830 the working class, the proletariat, has been recognized in both countries as a third competitor for power. Conditions had become so simplified that one would have had to close one's eyes deliberately not to see in the fight of these three great classes and in the conflict of their interests the driving force of modern history—at least in the two most advanced countries.

But how had these classes come into existence? If it was possible at first glance still to ascribe the origin of the large, formerly feudal landed property—at least in the first instance—to political causes, to seizure by force, this could not be done in regard to the bourgeoisie and the proletariat. Here the origin and development of two great classes was seen to lie clearly and palpably in purely economic causes. And it was just as clear that in the struggle between landed proprietors and the bourgeoisie, no less than in the struggle between the bourgeoisie and the proletariat, the matter at issue was, first and foremost, economic interests, which were to be secured using political power merely as a means. Bourgeoisie and proletariat both arose in consequence of a change in the economic conditions, more precisely, in the mode of production. The transition, first from guild handicrafts to manufacture, and then from manufacture to large-scale industry with steam and mechanical power, had caused the development of these two classes. At a certain stage the new forces of production set in motion by the bourgeoisie—in the first place the division of labor and the combination of many workers performing individual operations in one manufactory handling all stages of production—and the conditions and requirements of exchange, developed through these forces of production, became incompatible with the existing order of production handed down through history and sanctified by law, that is to say, incompatible with the privileges of the guild and the numerous other personal and local privileges (which were just as numerous fetters for the unprivileged estates) of the feudal order of society. The forces of production represented by the bourgeoisie rebelled against the order of production represented by the feudal landlords and the guild-masters. The result is well known: the feudal fetters were smashed, gradually in England, at one blow in France. In Germany the process is not yet finished. But just as, at a definite stage of its development, manufacture came into conflict with the feudal order of production, so large-scale industry has even now come into conflict with the bourgeois order of production established in its place. Tied down by this order, by the narrow limits of the capitalist mode of production, this industry produces, on the one hand, an ever-increasing proletarianization of the great mass of the people, and on the other hand, an ever greater volume of unsalable products. Overproduction and mass destitution, each the cause of the other—that is the absurd contradiction which is its outcome, and which of necessity calls for the productive forces to be unfettered by means of a change in the mode of production.

In modern history at least it is, therefore, proved that all political struggles are class struggles, and all struggles by classes for emancipation, despite their necessarily political form—for every class struggle is a political struggle—turn ultimately on the question of *economic* emancipation. Therefore, here at least, the state—the political order—is the subordinate factor and civil society—the realm of economic relations—the decisive element. The traditional conception, to which Hegel, too, pays homage, saw in the state the determining element, and in civil society the element determined by it. Appearances correspond to this. As all the driving forces of the actions of any individual person must pass through his brain, and transform themselves into motives of his will in order to set him into action, so also all the needs of civil society—no matter which class happens to be the ruling one—must pass through the will of the state in order to attain general validity in the form of laws. That is the formal aspect of the matter which is self-evident. The question arises, however, as to the content of this merely formal will—of the individual as well as of the state—and whence this content is derived. Why is just this willed and not something else? If we inquire into this, we discover that in modern history the will of the state is, on the whole, determined by the changing needs of civil society, by the supremacy of this or that class, in the last resort, by the development of the productive forces and relations of exchange.

But if even in our modern era, with its gigantic means of production and communication, the state is not an independent domain with independent development, but one whose existence as well as development is to be explained in the last resort by the economic conditions of life of society, then this must be still more true of all earlier times when the production of the material life of man was not yet carried on with these abundant auxiliary aids, and when, therefore, the necessity of such production must have exercised a still greater rule over men. If the state even today, in the era of large-scale industry and railways, is on the whole only the reflection, in concentrated form, of the economic needs of the class controlling production, then this must have been much more the case in an epoch when each generation of men had to spend a far greater part of its aggregate lifetime satisfying its material needs, and was therefore much more dependent on them than we are today. An examination of the history of earlier periods, as soon as it deals seriously with this aspect, most abundantly confirms this. But, of course, this cannot be gone into here.

If the state and public law are determined by economic relations, so, too, of course is private law, which indeed in essence only sanctions the existing economic relations between individuals which are normal in the given circumstances. The form in which this occurs can, however, vary considerably. It is possible, as happened in England, in harmony with the whole of national development, to retain to a large extent the forms of the old feudal laws and give them a bourgeois content; in fact, directly reading a bourgeois meaning into the feudal name. But, also, as happened in continental Western Europe, Roman Law, the first world law of a commodity-producing society, with its unsurpassably fine elaboration of all the essential legal relations of simple commodity owners (of buyers and sellers, creditors and debtors, contracts, obligations, etc.), can be taken as the foundation. In which case, for the benefit of a still petty-bourgeois and semi-feudal society it can either be reduced to the level of such a society simply through judicial practice (common law) or else, with the help of allegedly enlightened, moralizing jurists, it can be worked into a special code of law to correspond with such a social level—a code which in these circumstances will be a bad one even from the legal standpoint (for instance, Prussian common law). In which case, however, after a great bourgeois revolution, it is also possible to work out upon the basis of this same Roman Law such a classic legal code of bourgeois society as the French *Code civile*. If, therefore, bourgeois legal rules merely express the economic conditions of life in society in legal form, then they can do so well or badly according to circumstances.

The state presents itself to us as the first ideological power over man. Society creates for itself an organ for the safeguarding of its common interests against internal and external attacks. This organ is the state power. Hardly come into being, this organ makes itself independent vis-à-vis society; and, indeed, all the more so, the more it becomes the organ of a particular class, the more it directly enforces the rule of that class. The fight of the oppressed class against the ruling class necessarily becomes a political fight, a fight first of all against the political rule of this class. Consciousness of the connection between this political struggle and its economic foundation becomes dulled and can be lost altogether. While this is not wholly the case with the participants, it almost always happens with the historians. Of the ancient sources on the struggles within the Roman Republic only Appian tells us clearly and distinctly what was ultimately at issue—namely, landed property.

But once the state has become an independent power vis-à-vis society, it immediately produces a further ideology. It is among professional politicians, theorists of public law and jurists of private law that the connection with economic facts gets well and truly lost. Since in each particular case the economic facts must assume the form of juristic motives in order to receive legal sanction; and since, in so doing, consideration has, of course, to be given to the whole legal system already in operation, the juristic form is, in consequence, made everything and the economic content nothing. Public law and private law are treated as separate spheres, each having its own independent historical development, each being capable of, and needing, a systematic presentation by the consistent elimination of all innate contradictions.

Still higher ideologies, that is, such as are still further removed from the material, economic basis, take the form of philosophy and religion. Here the connection between conceptions and their material conditions of existence becomes more and more complicated, more and more obscured by intermediate links. But the connection exists. Just as the whole Renaissance period, from the middle of the fifteenth century, was an essential product of the towns and, therefore, of the burghers, so also was the subsequently newly awakened philosophy. Its content was in essence only the philosophical expression of the thoughts corresponding to the development of the small and middle burghers into a big bourgeoisie. Among the last century's Englishmen and Frenchmen who in many cases were just as much political economists as philosophers, this is clearly evident; and we have proved it above in regard to the Hegelian school.

Let us now in addition deal only briefly with religion, since this stands furthest away from material life and seems to be most alien to it. Religion arose in very primitive times from erroneous, primitive conceptions by men about their own nature and external nature surrounding them. Every ideology, however, once it has arisen, develops in connection with the given concept-material, and develops this material further; otherwise it would not be an ideology, that is, occupation with thoughts as with independent entities, developing independently and subject only to their own laws. That the material conditions of life of the persons inside whose heads this thought process goes on in the last resort determine the course of this process remains of necessity unknown to these persons, for otherwise all ideology would be finished. These original religious notions, therefore, which in the main are common to each group of kindred peoples, develop, after the group separates, in a manner peculiar to each people, according to the conditions of life falling to their lot. For a number of groups of peoples, and particularly for the Aryans (so-called Indo-Europeans), this process has been demonstrated in detail by comparative mythology. The gods thus fashioned among each people were national gods, whose domain extended no farther than the national territory which they were to protect; on the other side of its frontiers other gods held undisputed sway. They could continue to exist, in the imagination, only as long as the nation existed; they fell with its fall. The Roman world empire, the economic conditions of whose origin we do not need to examine here, brought about this downfall of the old nationalities. The old national gods declined, even those of the Romans, which also were geared to suit only the narrow confines of the city of Rome. The need to complement the world empire by means of a world religion was clearly revealed in the attempts made to provide in Rome recognition and altars for all the foreign gods that were to the slightest degree respectable, alongside the indigenous ones. But a new world religion is not to be made in this fashion, by imperial decrees. The new world religion, Christianity, had already quietly come into being, out of a mixture of generalized Oriental, particularly Jewish, theology, and vulgarized Greek, particularly Stoic, philosophy. What it originally looked like has yet to be laboriously discovered, since its official form, as it has been handed down to us, is merely that in which it became the state religion, to which purpose it was adapted by the Council of Nicaea. The fact that it became the state religion in as little as two hundred fifty years suffices to show that it was the religion corresponding to the conditions of the time. In the Middle Ages, in the same measure as feudalism developed, Christianity grew into its religious counterpart, with a corresponding feudal hierarchy. And when the burghers began to thrive, there developed, in opposition to feudal Catholicism, the Protestant heresy, which first appeared in Southern France, among the Albigenses, at the time the cities there were in their heyday. The Middle Ages had attached to theology all the other forms of ideology—philosophy, politics, jurisprudence—and made them subdivisions of theology. It thereby constrained every social and political movement to take on a theological form. The sentiments of the masses, fed exclusively on religion, had to have their own interests presented to them in a religious guise in order to create a great turbulence. And just as the burghers from the beginning produced an appendage of propertyless urban plebeians, day laborers and servants of all kinds, belonging to no recognized social estate, precursors of the later proletariat, so likewise heresy soon become divided into a moderate burgher heresy and a revolutionary plebeian one, the latter an abomination even to the burgher heretics.

The ineradicableness of the Protestant heresy corresponded to the invincibility of the rising burghers. When these burghers had become sufficiently strengthened, their struggle against the feudal nobility, which till then had been predominantly local, began to assume national dimensions. The first great campaign occurred in Germany—the so-called Reformation. The burghers were neither powerful enough nor sufficiently developed to be able to unite under their banner the remaining rebellious estates—the plebeians of the towns, the lower nobility and the peasants in the countryside. The nobles were the first to be defeated; the peasants rose in a revolt which formed the climax of the whole revolutionary movement; the cities left them in the lurch, and thus the revolution succumbed to the armies of the sovereigns, who swept the board.

Thenceforward Germany disappears for three centuries from among the countries playing an independent active part in history. But beside the German Luther there had appeared the Frenchman Calvin. With true French acuity he put the bourgeois character of the Reformation in the forefront, republicanized and democratized the Church. While the Lutheran Reformation in Germany degenerated and reduced the country to rack and ruin, the Calvinist Reformation served as a banner for the republicans in Geneva, in Holland and in Scotland, freed Holland from Spain and from the German Empire and provided the ideological costume for the second act of the bourgeois revolution, which was taking place in England. Here Calvinism stood the test as the true religious disguise of the interests of the contemporary bourgeoisie and on this account did not attain full recognition when the revolution ended in 1689 in a compromise between part of the nobility and the bourgeoisie. The English Established Church was reconstituted; but not in its earlier form, as a Catholicism with the king for its pope, being, instead, strongly Calvinised. The old Established Church had celebrated the merry Catholic Sunday and had fought against the dull Calvinist one. The new, bourgeois Church introduced the latter, which adorns England to this day.

In France, the Calvinist minority was suppressed in 1685 and either Catholicised or driven out of the country. But what was the good? Already at that time the freethinker Pierre Bayle was hard at work, and in 1694 Voltaire was born. The forcible measures of Louis XIV only made it easier for the French bourgeoisie to carry through its revolution in the irreligious, exclusively political form which alone was suited to a developed bourgeoisie. Instead of Protestants, freethinkers took their seats in the national assemblies. Christianity had thus entered into its final stage. It had become incapable of continuing to serve any progressive class as the ideological garb of its aspirations. It became more and more the exclusive possession of the ruling classes and they use it as a mere means of government, to keep the lower classes within certain bounds. Moreover, each of the different classes uses its own appropriate religion: the landed Junkers—Catholic Jesuitism or Protestant orthodoxy; the liberal and radical bourgeoisie—rationalism; and it makes no difference whether these gentlemen themselves believe in their respective religions or not.

We see, therefore: religion, once formed, always contains traditional material, just as in all ideological domains tradition constitutes a great conservative force. But the changes which this material undergoes spring from class relations, that is to say, from the economic relations of the people who carry out these changes. And here that is sufficient.

In the above it could only be a question of giving a general outline of the Marxian conception of history, at most with a few illustrations as well. The proof must be derived from history itself; and in this regard I may be permitted to say that it has been sufficiently provided in other writings. This conception, however, puts an end to philosophy in the realm of history, just as the dialectical conception of nature makes all philosophy of nature as unnecessary as it is impossible. It is no longer a question anywhere of inventing interconnections from out of our brains, but of discovering them in the facts. For philosophy, having been expelled from nature and history, there remains only the realm of pure thought, so far as anything is left of it: the theory of the laws of the thought process itself, logic and dialectics.

With the revolution of 1848, "educated" Germany said farewell to theory and went over to the field of practice. Small-scale production and manufacture, based upon manual labor, were superseded by real large-scale industry. Germany again appeared on the world market. The new little German Empire abolished at least the most flagrant of the abuses with which this development had been obstructed by the system of petty states, the relics of feudalism, and bureaucratic management. But to the same degree that speculation abandoned the philosopher's study in order to erect its temple in the Stock Exchange, educated Germany lost the great aptitude for theory which had been the glory of Germany in the days of its deepest political humiliation—the aptitude for purely scientific investigation, irrespective of whether the result obtained was applicable in practice or not, adverse to the police or not. Official German natural science, it is true, kept abreast of the times, particularly in the field of specialized research. But even the American journal *Science* rightly remarks that the decisive advances in the sphere of the comprehensive correlation of particular facts and their generalization into laws are now being made much more in England, instead of in Germany, as used to be the case. And in the sphere of the historical sciences, philosophy included, the old reckless zeal for theory has now well and truly disappeared along with classical philosophy. Inane eclecticism and an obsessive concern for career and income, down to the most vulgar tuft-hunting, have taken its place. The official representatives of these sciences have become the undisguised ideologists of the bourgeoisie and the existing state—but at a time when both stand in open antagonism to the working class.

Only among the working class does the German aptitude for theory remain unimpaired. Here it cannot be exterminated. Here there is no concern for careers, for profiteering, or for gracious patronage from above. On the contrary, the more ruthlessly and disinterestedly science proceeds the more it finds itself in harmony with the interests and aspirations of the workers. The new tendency, which recognized that the key to the understanding of the whole history of society lies in the history of the development of labor, from the outset addressed itself preferentially to the working class and here found the response which it neither sought nor expected from official science. The German working-class movement is the heir to German classical philosophy.

Translator unknown

The Dialectics of Nature: Introduction

Modern research into nature, which alone has achieved a scientific, systematic, all-round development, in contrast to the brilliant natural-philosophical intuitions of antiquity and the extremely important but sporadic discoveries of the Arabs, which for the most part vanished without results—this modern research into nature dates, like all more recent history, from that mighty epoch which we Germans term the Reformation, from the national misfortune that overtook us at that time, and which the French term the Renaissance and the Italians the *Cinquecento*,* although it is not fully expressed by any of these names. It is the epoch which had its rise in the latter half of the fifteenth century. Royalty, with the support of the burghers of the towns, broke the power of the feudal nobility and established the great monarchies, based essentially on nationality, within which the modern European nations and modern bourgeois society came to development. And while the burghers and nobles were still fighting one another, the German Peasant War pointed prophetically to future class struggles, by bringing on to the stage not only the peasants in revolt—that was no longer anything new—but behind them the beginnings of the modern proletariat, with the red flag in their hands and the demand for common ownership of goods on their lips. In the manuscripts saved from the fall of Byzantium, in the antique statues dug out of the ruins of Rome, a new world was revealed to the astonished West, that of ancient Greece; the ghosts of the Middle Ages vanished before

---

*Short for *milcinquecento*, 1500, used for the period A.D. 1500–1599.

its shining forms; Italy rose to an undreamed-of flowering of art, which was like a reflection of classical antiquity and was never attained again. In Italy, France, and Germany a new literature arose, the first modern literature; shortly afterward came the classical epochs of English and Spanish literature. The bounds of the old *orbis terrarum** were pierced, only now for the first time was the world really discovered and the basis laid for subsequent world trade and the transition from handicraft to manufacture, which in its turn formed the starting-point for modern large-scale industry. The dictatorship of the Church over men's minds was shattered; it was directly cast off by the majority of the Germanic peoples, who adopted Protestantism, while among the Latins a cheerful spirit of free thought, taken over from the Arabs and nourished by the newly-discovered Greek philosophy, took root more and more and prepared the way for the materialism of the eighteenth century.

It was the greatest progressive revolution that mankind had so far experienced, a time which called for giants and produced giants—giants in power of thought, passion and character, in universality and learning. The men who founded the modern rule of the bourgeoisie had anything but bourgeois limitations. On the contrary, the adventurous character of the time inspired them to a greater or lesser degree. There was hardly any man of importance then living who had not traveled extensively, who did not speak four or five languages, who did not shine in a number of fields. Leonardo da Vinci was not only a great painter but also a great mathematician, mechanician, and engineer, to whom the most diverse branches of physics are indebted for important discoveries. Albrecht Dürer was painter, engraver, sculptor, and architect, and in addition invented a system of fortification embodying many of the ideas that much later were again taken up by Montalembert and the modern German science of fortification. Machiavelli was statesman, historian, poet, and at the same time the first notable military author of modern times. Luther not only cleaned the Augean stable of the Church but also that of the German language; he created modern German prose and composed the text and melody of that triumphal hymn imbued with confidence in victory which became the Marseillaise of the sixteenth century. The heroes of that time were not yet in thrall to the division of labor, the restricting effects of which, with its production of one-sidedness,

---

*Orbis terrarum—the circle of lands, the whole world.

we so often notice in their successors. But what is especially characteristic of them is that they almost all live and pursue their activities in the midst of the contemporary movements, in the practical struggle; they take sides and join in the fight, one by speaking and writing, another with the sword, many with both. Hence the fullness and force of character that makes them complete men. Men of the study are the exception—either persons of second or third rank or cautious philistines who do not want to burn their fingers.

At that time natural science also developed in the midst of the general revolution and was itself thoroughly revolutionary; it had indeed to win in struggle its right of existence. Side by side with the great Italians from whom modern philosophy dates, it provided its martyrs for the stake and the dungeons of the Inquisition. And it is characteristic that Protestants outdid Catholics in persecuting the free investigation of nature. Calvin had Servetus burnt at the stake when the latter was on the point of discovering the circulation of the blood, and indeed he kept him roasting alive during two hours; for the Inquisition at least it sufficed to have Giordano Bruno simply burned alive.

The revolutionary act by which natural science declared its independence and, as it were, repeated Luther's burning of the Papal Bull was the publication of the immortal work by which Copernicus, though timidly and, so to speak, only from his death-bed, threw down the gauntlet to ecclesiastical authority in the affairs of nature. The emancipation of natural science from theology dates from this, although the fighting out of particular mutual claims has dragged on down to our day and in many minds is still far from completion. After that time, however, the development of the sciences proceeded with giant strides, and, it might be said, gained in force in proportion to the square of the distance (in time) from its point of departure. It was as if the world were to be shown that henceforth for the highest product of organic matter, the human mind, the law of motion holds good that is the reverse of that for inorganic matter.

The main work in the first period of natural science that now opened lay in mastering the material immediately at hand. In most fields a start had to be made from the very beginning. Antiquity had bequeathed Euclid and the Ptolemaic solar system; the Arabs had left behind the decimal notation, the beginnings of algebra, the modern numerals, and alchemy; the Christian Middle Ages nothing at all. Of necessity, in this situation the most fundamental natural science, the mechanics of terrestrial and heavenly bodies, occupied first place, and alongside of it, as handmaiden to it, the discovery and perfecting of mathematical methods. Great things were achieved here. At the end of the period characterized by Newton and Linnaeus we find these branches of science brought to a certain perfection. The basic features of the most essential mathematical methods were established; analytical geometry by Descartes especially, logarithms by Napier, and the differential and integral calculus by Leibniz and perhaps Newton. The same holds good of the mechanics of rigid bodies, the main laws of which were made clear once for all. Finally in the astronomy of the solar system Kepler discovered the laws of planetary movement and Newton formulated them from the point of view of the general laws of motion of matter. The other branches of natural science were far removed even from this preliminary perfection. Only toward the end of the period did the mechanics of fluid and gaseous bodies receive further treatment. Physics had still not gone beyond its first beginnings, with the exception of optics, the exceptional progress of which was due to the practical needs of astronomy. By the phlogistic theory, chemistry for the first time emancipated itself from alchemy. Geology had not yet gone beyond the embryonic stage of mineralogy; hence palaeontology could not yet exist at all. Finally, in the field of biology the essential preoccupation was still with the collection and first sifting of the immense material, not only botanical and zoological but also anatomical and properly physiological. There could as yet be hardly any talk of the comparison of the various forms of life, of the investigation of their geographical distribution and their climatic, etc., conditions of existence. Here only botany and zoology arrived at an approximate completion owing to Linnaeus.

But what especially characterizes this period is the elaboration of a peculiar general outlook, the central point of which is the view *of the absolute immutability of nature.* In whatever way nature itself might have come into being, once present it remained as it was as long as it continued to exist. The planets and their satellites, once set in motion by the mysterious "first impulse," circled on and on in their predestined ellipses for all eternity, or at any rate until the end of all things. The stars remained forever fixed and immovable in their places, keeping one another therein by "universal gravitation." The earth had remained the same without alteration from all eternity or, alternatively, from the first day of its creation. The "five continents" of the present day had always existed, and they had always had the same mountains, valleys, and rivers, the same climate, and the same flora and fauna, except in so far as change or transplantation had taken place at the hand of man. The species of plants and animals had been established once for all when they came into existence; like continually produced like, and it was already a good deal for Linnaeus to have conceded that possibly here and there new species could have arisen by crossing. In contrast to the history of mankind, which develops in time, there was ascribed to the history of nature only an unfolding in space. All change, all development in nature, was denied. Natural science, so revolutionary at the outset, suddenly found itself confronted by an out-and-out conservative nature, in which even today everything was as it had been from the beginning and in which—to the end of the world or for all eternity—everything would remain as it had been since the beginning.

High as the natural science of the first half of the eighteenth century stood above Greek antiquity in knowledge and even in the sifting of its material, it stood just as deeply below Greek antiquity in the theoretical mastery of this material, in the general outlook on nature. For the Greek philosophers the world was essentially something that had emerged from chaos, something that had developed, that had come into being. For the natural scientists of the period that we are dealing with it was something ossified, something immutable, and for most of them something that had been created at one stroke. Science was still deeply enmeshed in theology. Everywhere it sought and found the ultimate cause in an impulse from outside that was not to be explained from nature itself. Even if attraction, by Newton pompously baptised as "universal gravitation," was conceived as an essential property of matter, whence comes the unexplained tangential force which first gives rise to the orbits of the planets? How did the innumerable species of plants and animals arise? And how, above all, did man arise, since after all it was certain that he was not present from all eternity? To such questions natural science only too frequently answered by making the creator of all things responsible. Copernicus, at the beginning of the period, shows theology the door; Newton closes the period with the postulate of a divine first impulse. The highest general idea to which this natural science attained was that of the purposiveness of the arrangements of nature, the shallow teleology of Wolff, according to which cats were created to eat mice, mice to be eaten by cats, and the whole of nature to testify to the wisdom of the creator. It is to the highest credit of the philosophy of the time that it did not let itself be led astray by the restricted state of contemporary natural knowledge, and that— from Spinoza down to the great French materialists—it insisted on explaining the world from the world itself and left the justification in detail to the natural sciences of the future.

I include the materialists of the eighteenth century in this period because no natural-scientific material was available to them other than that above described. Kant's epoch-making work remained a secret to them, and Laplace came long after them. We should not forget that this obsolete outlook on nature, although riddled through and through by the progress of science, dominated the entire first half of the nineteenth century,* and in substance is even now still taught in all schools.

The first breach in this petrified outlook on nature was made not by a natural scientist but by a philosopher. In 1755 appeared Kant's *Allgemeine Naturgeschichte und Theorie des Himmels.* The question of the first impulse was done away with; the earth and the whole solar system appeared as something that had *come into being* in the course of time. If the great majority of the natural scientists had had a little less of the repugnance to thinking that Newton expressed in the warning: Physics, beware of metaphysics! they would have been compelled from this single brilliant discovery of Kant's to draw conclusions that would have spared them endless deviations and immeasurable amounts of time and labor wasted in false directions. For Kant's discovery contained the point of departure for all further progress. If the earth was something that had come into being, then its present geological, geographical, and climatic state, and its plants and animals likewise, must be something that had come into being; it must have had a history not only of coexistence in space but also of succession in time. If at once further investigations had been resolutely pursued in this direction, natural science would now be considerably further advanced than it is. But what good could come of philosophy? Kant's work remained without immediate results, until many years later Laplace

---

*The rigidity of the old outlook on nature provided the basis for the general comprehension of all natural science as a single whole. The French encyclopedists, still purely mechanically—alongside of one another; and then simultaneously St. Simon and German philosophy of nature, perfected by Hegel.

and Herschel expounded its contents and gave them a deeper foundation, thereby gradually bringing the "nebular hypothesis" into favor. Further discoveries finally brought it victory; the most important of these were: the discovery of proper motion of the fixed stars, the demonstration of a resistant medium in universal space, the proof furnished by spectral analysis of the chemical identity of the matter of the universe and of the existence of such glowing nebular masses as Kant had postulated.

It is, however, permissible to doubt whether the majority of natural scientists would so soon have become conscious of the contradiction of a changing earth that bore immutable organisms, had not the dawning conception that nature does not just *exist,* but *comes into being* and *passes away,* derived support from another quarter. Geology arose and pointed out not only the terrestrial strata formed one after another and deposited one upon another, but also the shells and skeletons of extinct animals and the trunks, leaves, and fruits of no longer existing plants contained in these strata. The decision had to be taken to acknowledge that not only the earth as a whole but also its present surface and the plants and animals living on it possessed a history in time. At first the acknowledgment occurred reluctantly enough. Cuvier's theory of the revolutions of the earth was revolutionary in phrase and reactionary in substance. In place of a *single* divine creation, he put a whole series of repeated acts of creation, making the miracle an essential natural agent. Lyell first brought sense into geology by substituting for the sudden revolutions due to the moods of the creator the gradual effects of a slow transformation of the earth.

Lyell's theory* was even more incompatible than any of its predecessors with the assumption of constant organic species. Gradual transformation of the earth's surface and of all conditions of life led directly to gradual transformation of the organisms and their adaptation to the changing environment, to the mutability of species. But tradition is a power not only in the Catholic Church but also in natural science. For years, Lyell himself did not see the contradiction, and his pupils still less. This can only be explained by the division of labor that had meanwhile become dominant in natural science, which more or less restricted each person to his

---

*Ch. Lyell, *Principles of Geology, Being an Attempt to Explain the Former Changes of the Earth's Surface, by Reference to Causes Now in Operation,* vols. 1–3.

special sphere, there being only a few whom it did not rob of a comprehensive view.

Meanwhile physics had made mighty advances, the results of which were summed up almost simultaneously by three different persons in the year 1842, an epoch-making year for this branch of natural science. Mayer in Heilbronn and Joule in Manchester demonstrated the transformation of heat into mechanical force and of mechanical force into heat. The determination of the mechanical equivalent of heat put this result beyond question. Simultaneously, by simply working up the separate results of physics already arrived at, Grove—not a natural scientist by profession, but an English lawyer—proved that all so-called physical forces, mechanical force, heat, light, electricity, magnetism, indeed even so-called chemical force, become transformed into one another under definite conditions without any loss of force occurring, and so proved additionally along physical lines Descartes' principle that the quantity of motion present in the world is constant. With that the special physical forces, the as it were immutable "species" of physics, were resolved into variously differentiated forms of the motion of matter, passing into one another according to definite laws. The fortuitousness of the existence of such and such a number of physical forces was abolished from science by the proof of their interconnections and transitions. Physics, like astronomy before it, had arrived at a result that necessarily pointed to the eternal cycle of matter in motion as the ultimate conclusion.

The wonderfully rapid development of chemistry, since Lavoisier and especially since Dalton, attacked the old ideas about nature from another aspect. The preparation by inorganic means of compounds that hitherto had been produced only in the living organism proved that the laws of chemistry have the same validity for organic as for inorganic bodies, and to a large extent bridged the gulf between inorganic and organic nature, a gulf that even Kant regarded as for ever impassable.

Finally, in the sphere of biological research also the scientific journeys and expeditions that had been systematically organized since the middle of the previous [i.e., eighteenth] century, the more thorough exploration of the European colonies in all parts of the world by specialists living there, and further the progress of paleontology, anatomy, and physiology in general, particularly since the systematic use of the microscope and the discovery of the cell, had accumulated so much material that the application of the compara-

tive method became possible and at the same time indispensable. On the one hand the conditions of life of the various floras and faunas were established by means of comparative physical geography; on the other hand the various organisms were compared with one another according to their homologous organs, and this not only in the adult condition but at all stages of their development. The more deeply and exactly this research was carried on, the more did the rigid system of an immutably fixed organic nature crumble away at its touch. Not only did the separate species of plants and animals become more and more inextricably intermingled, but animals turned up, such as *Amphioxus* and *Lepidosiren*, that made a mockery of all previous classification, and finally organisms were encountered of which it was not possible to say whether they belonged to the plant or animal kingdom. More and more the gaps in the palaeontological record were filled up, compelling even the most reluctant to acknowledge the striking parallelism between the history of the development of the organic world as a whole and that of the individual organism, the Ariadne's thread that was to lead the way out of the labyrinth in which botany and zoology appeared to have become more and more deeply lost. It was characteristic that, almost simultaneously with Kant's attack on the eternity of the solar system, C. F. Wolff in 1759 launched the first attack on the fixity of species and proclaimed the theory of descent. But what in his case was still only a brilliant anticipation took firm shape in the hands of Oken, Lamarck, Baer, and was victoriously carried through by Darwin in 1859, exactly a hundred years later.*
Almost simultaneously it was established that protoplasm and the cell, which had already been shown to be the ultimate morphological constituents of all organisms, occurred independently, existing as the lowest forms of organic life. This not only reduced the gulf between inorganic and organic nature to a minimum but removed one of the most essential difficulties that had previously stood in the way of the theory of descent of organisms. The new outlook on nature was complete in its main features: all rigidity was dissolved, all fixity dissipated, all particularity that had been regarded as eternal became transient, the whole of nature was shown as moving in eternal flux and cyclical course.

---

*Ch. Darwin, *On the Origin of Species by Means of Natural Selection; or, the Preservation of Favoured Races in the Struggle for Life.*

Thus we have once again returned to the mode of outlook of the great founders of Greek philosophy, the view that the whole of nature, from the smallest element to the greatest, from grains of sand to suns, from Protista to man, has its existence in eternal coming into being and passing away, in ceaseless flux, in unresting motion and change. Only with the essential difference that what in the case of the Greeks was a brilliant intuition, is in our case the result of strictly scientific research in accordance with experience, and hence also it emerges in a much more definite and clear form. It is true that the empirical proof of this cyclical course is not wholly free from gaps, but these are insignificant in comparison with what has already been firmly established, and with each year they become more and more filled up. And how could the proof in detail be other than one containing gaps when one bears in mind that the most important branches of science—transplanetary astronomy, chemistry, geology—have a scientific existence of barely a century, and the comparative method in physiology, one of barely fifty years, and that the basic form of almost all organic development, the cell, is a discovery not yet forty years old?

The innumerable suns and solar systems of our island universe, bounded by the outermost stellar rings of the Milky Way, developed by contraction and cooling from swirling, glowing masses of vapor, the laws of motion of which will perhaps be disclosed after the observations of some centuries have given us an insight into the proper motion of the stars. Obviously, this development did not proceed everywhere at the same rate. Astronomy is more and more being forced to recognise the existence of dark bodies, not merely planetary in nature, hence extinct suns in our stellar system (Mädler); on the other hand (according to Secchi) a part of the vaporous nebular patches belong to our stellar system as suns not yet fully formed, which does not exclude the possibility that other nebulae are, as Mädler maintains, distant independent island universes, the relative stage of development of which must be determined by the spectroscope.

How a solar system develops from an individual nebular mass has been shown in detail by Laplace in a manner still unsurpassed; subsequent science has more and more confirmed him.

On the separate bodies so formed—suns as well as planets and satellites—the form of motion of matter at first prevailing is that which we call heat. There can be no question of chemical compounds of the elements even at a temperature like that still possessed by the sun; the extent to which heat is transformed into electricity or magnetism under such conditions, continued solar observations will show; it is already as good as proved that the mechanical motion taking place in the sun arises solely from the conflict of heat with gravity.

The smaller the individual bodies, the quicker they cool down, the satellites, asteroids, and meteors first of all, just as our moon has long been extinct. The planets cool more slowly, the central body slowest of all.

With progressive cooling the interplay of the physical forms of motion which become transformed into one another comes more and more to the forefront until finally a point is reached from when on chemical affinity begins to make itself felt, the previously chemically indifferent elements become differentiated chemically one after another, acquire chemical properties, and enter into combination with one another. These compounds change continually with the decreasing temperature, which affects differently not only each element but also each separate compound of the elements, changing also with the consequent passage of part of the gaseous matter first to the liquid and then the solid state, and with the new conditions thus created.

The time when the planet acquires a firm shell and accumulations of water on its surface coincides with that from when on its intrinsic heat diminishes more and more compared with the heat emitted to it from the central body. Its atmosphere becomes the arena of meteorological phenomena in the sense in which we now understand the term; its surface becomes the arena of geological changes in which the deposits resulting from atmospheric precipitation become of ever greater importance compared with the slowly decreasing external effects of the hot fluid interior.

If, finally, the temperature becomes so far equalized that over a considerable portion of the surface at least it no longer exceeds the limits within which protein is capable of life, then, if other chemical pre-conditions are favorable, living protoplasm is formed. What these preconditions are, we do not yet know, which is not to be wondered at since so far not even the chemical formula of protein has been established—we do not even know how many chemically different protein bodies there are—and since it is only about ten years ago that the fact became known that completely structureless protein exercises all the essential functions of life: digestion, excretion, movement, contraction, reaction to stimuli, and reproduction.

Thousands of years may have passed before the conditions arose in which the next advance could take place and this shapeless protein produced the first cell by formation of nucleus and cell membrane. But this first cell also provided the foundation for the morphological development of the whole organic world; the first to develop, as it is permissible to assume from the whole analogy of the paleontological record, were innumerable species of noncellular and cellular Protista, of which *Eozoon canadense* alone has come down to us, and of which some were gradually differentiated into the first plants and others into the first animals. And from the first animals were developed, essentially by further differentiation, the numerous classes, orders, families, genera, and species of animals; and finally vertebrates, the form in which the nervous system attains its fullest development; and among these again finally that vertebrate in which nature attains consciousness of itself—man.

Man, too, arises by differentiation. Not only individually—by development from a single egg-cell to the most complicated organism that nature produces—but also historically. When after thousands of years of struggle the differentiation of hand from foot, and erect gait, were finally established, man became distinct from the ape and the basis was laid for the development of articulate speech and the mighty development of the brain that has since made the gulf between man and the ape an unbridgeable one. The specialization of the hand—this implies the *tool,* and the tool implies specific human activity, the transforming reaction of man on nature, production. Animals in the narrower sense also have tools, but only as limbs of their bodies: the ant, the bee, the beaver; animals also produce, but their productive effect on surrounding nature, in relation to nature, amounts to nothing at all. Man alone has succeeded in impressing his stamp on nature, not only by shifting plant and animal species from one place to another, but also by so altering the aspect and climate of his dwelling-place, and even the plants and animals themselves, that the consequences of his activity can disappear only with the general extinction of the terrestrial globe. And he has accomplished this primarily and essentially by means of the *hand.* Even the steam-engine, so far his most powerful tool for the transformation of nature, depends, because it is a tool, in the last resort on the hand. But step by step with the development of the hand went that of the brain; first of all came consciousness of the conditions for separate practically useful actions, and later, among the more favored peoples and arising from that consciousness, insight into the natural laws governing them. And with the rapidly growing knowledge of the laws of nature the means for reacting on nature also grew; the hand alone would never have achieved the steam-engine if, along with and parallel to the hand, and partly owing to it, the brain of man had not correspondingly developed.

With man we enter *history*. Animals also have a history, that of their descent and gradual evolution to their present position. This history, however, is made for them, and in so far as they themselves take part in it, this occurs without their knowledge and desire. On the other hand, the more the human beings become removed from animals in the narrower sense of the word, the more they make their history themselves, consciously, the less becomes the influence of unforeseen effects and uncontrolled forces on this history, and the more accurately does the historical result correspond to the aim laid down in advance. If, however, we apply this measure to human history, to that of even the most developed peoples of the present day, we find that there still exists here a colossal disproportion between the proposed aims and the results arrived at, that unforeseen effects predominate, and that the uncontrolled forces are far more powerful than those set into motion according to plan. And this cannot be otherwise as long as the most essential historical activity of men, the one which has raised them from the animal to the human state and which forms the material foundation of all their other activities, namely the production of their requirements of life, i.e., in our day social production, is above all subject to the interplay of unintended effects from uncontrolled forces and achieves its desired end only by way of exception, but much more frequently the exact opposite. In the most advanced industrial countries we have subdued the forces of nature and pressed them into the service of mankind; we have thereby infinitely multiplied production, so that a child now produces more than a hundred adults previously did. And what is the result? Increasing overwork and increasing misery of the masses, and every ten years a great collapse. Darwin did not know what a bitter satire he wrote on mankind, and especially on his countrymen, when he showed that free competition, the struggle for existence, which the economists celebrate as the highest historical achievement, is the normal state of the *animal kingdom*. Only conscious

organization of social production, in which production and distribution are carried on in a planned way, can lift mankind above
the rest of the animal world as regards the social aspect, in the
same way that production in general has done this for mankind in
the specifically biological aspect. Historical development makes
such an organization daily more indispensable, but also with every
day more possible. From it will date a new epoch of history, in
which mankind itself, and with mankind all branches of its activity,
and particularly natural science, will experience an advance that
will put everything preceding it in the deepest shade.

Nevertheless, "all that comes into being deserves to perish."*
Millions of years may elapse, hundreds of thousands of generations
be born and die, but inexorably the time will come when the declin-
ing warmth of the sun will no longer suffice to melt the ice thrusting
itself forward from the poles; when the human race, crowding
more and more about the equator, will finally no longer find even
there enough heat for life; when gradually even the last trace of
organic life will vanish; and the earth, an extinct frozen globe like
the moon, will circle in deepest darkness and in an ever narrower
orbit about the equally extinct sun, and at last fall into it. Other
planets will have preceded it, others will follow it; instead of the
bright, warm solar system with its harmonious arrangement of
members, only a cold, dead sphere will still pursue its lonely path
through universal space. And what will happen to our solar system
will happen sooner or later to all the other systems of our island
universe; it will happen to all the other innumerable island universes, even to those the light of which will never reach the earth
while there is a living human eye to receive it.

And when such a solar system has completed its life history and
succumbs to the fate of all that is finite, death, what then? Will
the sun's corpse roll on for all eternity through infinite space, and
all the once infinitely diversely differentiated natural forces pass
for ever into one single form of motion, attraction?

> "Or"—as Secchi asks—"are there forces in nature which can
> reconvert the dead system into its original state of glowing neb-
> ula and re-awaken it to new life? We do not know."

Of course, we do not know it in the sense that we know that
$2 \times 2 = 4$, or that the attraction of matter increases and decreases

---

*Mephistopheles' words in Goethe's *Faust,* act 1, scene 3 ("Faust's Study").

according to the square of the distance. In theoretical natural science, however, which as far as possible builds up its outlook on nature into a harmonious whole, and without which nowadays even the most unthinking empiricist cannot get anywhere, we have very often to calculate with incompletely known magnitudes, and consistency of thought must at all times help to get over defective knowledge. Modern natural science has had to take over from philosophy the principle of indestructibility of motion; it cannot any longer exist without this principle. But the motion of matter is not merely crude mechanical motion, mere change of place, it is heat and light, electric and magnetic tension, chemical combination and dissociation, life and, finally, consciousness. To say that matter during the whole unlimited time of its existence has only once, and for what is an infinitesimally short period in comparison to its eternity, found itself able to differentiate its motion and thereby to unfold the whole wealth of this motion, and that before and after this it remains restricted for eternity to mere change of place— this is equivalent to maintaining that matter is mortal and motion transient. The indestructibility of motion cannot be conceived merely quantitatively; it must also be conceived qualitatively; matter whose purely mechanical change of place includes indeed the possibility under favorable conditions of being transformed into heat, electricity, chemical action, life, but which is not capable of producing these conditions from out of itself, such matter has *forfeited motion;* motion which has lost the capacity of being transformed into the various forms appropriate to it may indeed still have *dynamis* but no longer *energeia,* and so has become partially destroyed. Both, however, are unthinkable.

This much is certain: there was a time when the matter of our island universe had transformed into heat such an amount of motion—of what kind we do not yet know—that there could be developed from it the solar systems appertaining to (according to Mädler) at least twenty million stars, the gradual extinction of which is likewise certain. How did this transformation take place? We know just as little as Father Secchi knows whether the future *caput mortuum** of our solar system will once again be converted into the raw material of new solar systems. But here either we must have recourse to a creator, or we are forced to the conclusion that the incandescent raw material for the solar systems of our universe

---

*Literally: "dead head"; figuratively, waste remaining after a chemical reaction.

was produced in a natural way by transformations of motion which are *by nature inherent* in moving matter, and the conditions for which, therefore, must also be reproduced by matter, even if only after millions and millions of years and more or less by chance, but with the necessity that is also inherent in chance.

The possibility of such a transformation is more and more being conceded. The view is being arrived at that the heavenly bodies are ultimately destined to fall into one another, and calculations are even made of the amount of heat which must be developed on such collisions. The sudden flaring up of new stars, and the equally sudden increase in brightness of familiar ones, of which we are informed by astronomy, are most easily explained by such collisions. Moreover, not only does our group of planets move about the sun, and our sun within our island universe, but our whole island universe also moves in space in temporary, relative equilibrium with the other island universes, for even the relative equilibrium of freely floating bodies can only exist where the motion is reciprocally determined; and it is assumed by many that the temperature in space is not everywhere the same. Finally, we know that, with the exception of an infinitesimal portion, the heat of the innumerable suns of our island universe vanishes into space and fails to raise the temperature of space even by a millionth of a degree Centigrade. What becomes of all this enormous quantity of heat? Is it for ever dissipated in the attempt to heat universal space, has it ceased to exist practically, and does it only continue to exist theoretically, in the fact that universal space has become warmer by a decimal fraction of a degree beginning with ten or more noughts? Such an assumption denies the indestructibility of motion; it concedes the possibility that by the successive falling into one another of the heavenly bodies all existing mechanical motion will be converted into heat and the latter radiated into space, so that in spite of all "indestructibility of force" all motion in general would have ceased. (Incidentally, it is seen here how inaccurate is the term "indestructibility of force" instead of "indestructibility of motion"). Hence we arrive at the conclusion that in some way, which it will later be the task of scientific research to demonstrate, it must be possible for the heat radiated into space to be transformed into another form of motion, in which it can once more be stored up and become active. Thereby the chief difficulty in the way of the reconversion of extinct suns into incandescent vapor disappears.

For the rest, the eternally repeated succession of worlds in infinite time is only the logical complement to the coexistence of innumerable worlds in infinite space—a principle the necessity of which has forced itself even on the anti-theoretical Yankee brain of Draper.*

It is an eternal cycle in which matter moves, a cycle that certainly only completes its orbit in periods of time for which our terrestrial year is no adequate measure, a cycle in which the time of highest development, the time of organic life and still more that of the life of beings conscious of nature and of themselves, is just as narrowly restricted as the space in which life and self-consciousness come into operation; a cycle in which every finite mode of existence of matter, whether it be sun or nebular vapour, single animal or genus of animals, chemical combination or dissociation, is equally transient, and wherein nothing is eternal but eternally changing, eternally moving matter and the laws according to which it moves and changes. But however often, and however relentlessly, this cycle is completed in time and space; however many millions of suns and earths may arise and pass away; however long it may last before, in one solar system and only on *one* planet, the conditions for organic life develop; however innumerable the organic beings, too, that have to arise and to pass away before animals with a brain capable of thought are developed from their midst, and for a short span of time find conditions suitable for life, only to be exterminated later without mercy—we have the certainty that matter remains eternally the same in all its transformations, that none of its attributes can ever be lost, and therefore, also, that with the same iron necessity that it will exterminate on the earth its highest creation, the thinking mind, it must somewhere else and at another time again produce it.

Translated by Clemens Dutt

---

* "The multiplicity of worlds in infinite space leads to the conception of a succession of worlds in infinite time." (J. W. Draper, *History of the Intellectual Development of Europe,* vol. 2 [p. 325].)

The Part Played by Labor
in the Transition
from Ape to Man

Labor is the source of all wealth, the political economists assert. And it really is the source—next to nature, which supplies it with the material that it converts into wealth. But it is even infinitely more than this. It is the prime basic condition for all human existence, and this to such an extent that, in a sense, we have to say that labor created man himself.

Many hundreds of thousands of years ago, during an epoch, not yet definitely determinable, of that period of the earth's history known to geologists as the Tertiary period, most likely toward the end of it, a particularly highly-developed race of anthropoid apes lived somewhere in the tropical zone—probably on a great continent that has now sunk to the bottom of the Indian Ocean. Darwin has given us an approximate description of these ancestors of ours. They were completely covered with hair, they had beards and pointed ears, and they lived in bands in the trees.*

First, owing to their way of living which meant that the hands had different functions than the feet when climbing, these apes began to lose the habit of using their hands to walk and adopted a more and more erect posture. This was *the decisive step in the transition from ape to man.*

All extant anthropoid apes can stand erect and move about on their feet alone, but only in case of urgent need and in a very clumsy

---

*See Ch. Darwin, *The Descent of Man, and Selection in Relation to Sex,* vol. 1, ch. 6.

way. Their natural gait is in a half-erect posture and includes the use of the hands. The majority rest the knuckles of the fist on the ground and, with legs drawn up, swing the body through their long arms, much as a cripple moves on crutches. In general, all the transition stages from walking on all fours to walking on two legs are still to be observed among the apes today. The latter gait, however, has never become more than a makeshift for any of them.

It stands to reason that if erect gait among our hairy ancestors became first the rule and then, in time, a necessity, other diverse functions must, in the meantime, have devolved upon the hands. Already among the apes there is some difference in the way the hands and the feet are employed. In climbing, as mentioned above, the hands and feet have different uses. The hands are used mainly for gathering and holding food in the same way as the forepaws of the lower mammals are used. Many apes use their hands to build themselves nests in the trees or even to construct roofs between the branches to protect themselves against the weather, as the chimpanzee, for example, does. With their hands they grasp sticks to defend themselves against enemies, or bombard their enemies with fruits and stones. In captivity they use their hands for a number of simple operations copied from human beings. It is in this that one sees the great gulf between the undeveloped hand of even the most manlike apes and the human hand that has been highly perfected by hundreds of thousands of years of labor. The number and general arrangement of the bones and muscles are the same in both hands, but the hand of the lowest savage can perform hundreds of operations that no simian hand can imitate—no simian hand has ever fashioned even the crudest stone knife.

The first operations for which our ancestors gradually learned to adapt their hands during the many thousands of years of transition from ape to man could have been only very simple ones. The lowest savages, even those in whom regression to a more animallike condition with a simultaneous physical degeneration can be assumed, are nevertheless far superior to these transitional beings. Before the first flint could be fashioned into a knife by human hands, a period of time probably elapsed in comparison with which the historical period known to us appears insignificant. But the decisive step had been taken, *the hand had become free* and could henceforth attain ever greater dexterity; the greater flexibility thus acquired was inherited and increased from generation to generation.

Thus the hand is not only the organ of labor, *it is also the product of labor.* Only by labor, by adaptation to ever new operations, through the inheritance of muscles, ligaments, and, over longer periods of time, bones that had undergone special development and the ever-renewed employment of this inherited finesse in new, more and more complicated operations, have given the human hand the high degree of perfection required to conjure into being the pictures of a Raphael, the statues of a Thorwaldsen, the music of a Paganini.

But the hand did not exist alone, it was only one member of an integral, highly complex organism. And what benefited the hand, benefited also the whole body it served; and this in two ways.

In the first place, the body benefited from the law of correlation of growth, as Darwin called it. This law states that the specialized forms of separate parts of an organic being are always bound up with certain forms of other parts that apparently have no connection with them. Thus all animals that have red blood cells without cell nuclei, and in which the head is attached to the first vertebra by means of a double articulation (condyles), also without exception possess lacteal glands for suckling their young. Similarly, cloven hoofs in mammals are regularly associated with the possession of a multiple stomach for rumination. Changes in certain forms involve changes in the form of other parts of the body, although we cannot explain the connection. Perfectly white cats with blue eyes are always, or almost always, deaf. The gradually increasing perfection of the human hand, and the commensurate adaptation of the feet for erect gait, have undoubtedly, by virtue of such correlation, reacted on other parts of the organism. However, this action has not as yet been sufficiently investigated for us to be able to do more here than to state the fact in general terms.

Much more important is the direct, demonstrable influence of the development of the hand on the rest of the organism. It has already been noted that our simian ancestors were gregarious; it is obviously impossible to seek the derivation of man, the most social of all animals, from nongregarious immediate ancestors. Mastery over nature began with the development of the hand, with labor, and widened man's horizon at every new advance. He was continually discovering new, hitherto unknown properties in natural objects. On the other hand, the development of labor necessarily helped to bring the members of society closer together by increasing cases of mutual support and joint activity, and by making clear the advantage of this joint activity to each individual. In short, men in the making arrived at the point where *they had something to say* to each other. Necessity created the organ; the undeveloped larynx of the ape was slowly but surely transformed by modulation to produce constantly more developed modulation, and the organs of the mouth gradually learned to pronounce one articulate sound after another.

Comparison with animals proves that this explanation of the origin of language from and in the process of labor is the only correct one. The little that even the most highly-developed animals need to communicate to each other does not require articulate speech. In its natural state, no animal feels handicapped by its inability to speak or to understand human speech. It is quite different when it has been tamed by man. The dog and the horse, by association with man, have developed such a good ear for articulate speech that they easily learn to understand any language within their range of concept. Moreover they have acquired the capacity for feelings such as affection for man, gratitude, and so forth, which were previously foreign to them. Anyone who has had much to do with such animals will hardly be able to escape the conviction that in many cases they *now* feel their inability to speak as a defect, although, unfortunately, it is one that can no longer be remedied because their vocal organs are too specialized in a definite direction. However, where vocal organs exist, within certain limits even this inability disappears. The buccal organs of birds are as different from those of man as they can be, yet birds are the only animals that can learn to speak; and it is the bird with the most hideous voice, the parrot, that speaks best of all. Let no one object that the parrot does not understand what it says. It is true that for the sheer pleasure of talking and associating with human beings, the parrot will chatter for hours at a stretch, continually repeating its whole vocabulary. But within the limits of its range of concepts it can also learn to understand what it is saying. Teach a parrot swear words in such a way that it gets an idea of their meaning (one of the great amusements of sailors returning from the tropics); tease it and you will soon discover that it knows how to use its swear words just as correctly as a Berlin peddlar. The same is true of begging for titbits.

First labor, after it and then with it speech—these were the two most essential stimuli under the influence of which the brain of the ape gradually changed into that of man, which for all its similarity is far larger and more perfect. Hand in hand with the development of the brain went the development of its most immediate instruments—the senses. Just as the gradual development of speech is inevitably accompanied by a corresponding refinement of the organ of hearing, so the development of the brain as a whole is accompanied by a refinement of all the senses. The eagle sees much farther than man, but the human eye discerns considerably more in things than does the eye of the eagle. The dog has a far keener sense of smell than man, but it does not distinguish a hundredth part of the odors that for man are definite signs denoting different things. And the sense of touch, which the ape hardly possesses in its crudest initial form, has been developed only side by side with the development of the human hand itself, through the medium of labor.

The reaction on labor and speech of the development of the brain and its attendant senses, of the increasing clarity of consciousness, power of abstraction and of conclusion, gave both labor and speech an ever-renewed impulse to further development. This development did not reach its conclusion when man finally became distinct from the ape, but on the whole made further powerful progress, its degree and direction varying among different peoples and at different times, and here and there even being interrupted by local or temporary regression. This further development has been strongly urged forward, on the one hand, and guided along more definite directions, on the other, by a new element which came into play with the appearance of fully-fledged man, namely, *society*.

Hundreds of thousands of years—of no greater significance in the history of the earth than one second in the life of man*—certainly elapsed before human society arose out of a troupe of tree-climbing monkeys. Yet it did finally appear. And what do we find once more as the characteristic difference between the troupe of monkeys and human society? *Labor*. The ape herd was satisfied to browse over the feeding area determined for it by geographical conditions or the resistance of neighboring herds; it undertook migrations and struggles to win new feeding grounds, but it was incapable of extracting from them more than they offered in their natural state, except that it unconsciously fertilized the soil with its own excrement. As soon as all possible feeding grounds were

---

*A leading authority in this respect, Sir William Thomson, has calculated that *little more than a hundred million years* could have elapsed since the time when the earth had cooled sufficiently for plants and animals to be able to live on it.

occupied, there could be no further increase in the ape population; the number of animals could at best remain stationary. But all animals waste a great deal of food, and, in addition, destroy in the germ the next generation of the food supply. Unlike the hunter, the wolf does not spare the doe which would provide it with the young the next year; the goats in Greece, that eat away the young bushes before they grow to maturity, have eaten bare all the mountains of the country. This "predatory economy" of animals plays an important part in the gradual transformation of species by forcing them to adapt themselves to other than the usual food, thanks to which their blood acquires a different chemical composition and the whole physical constitution gradually alters, while species that have remained unadapted die out. There is no doubt that this predatory economy contributed powerfully to the transition of our ancestors from ape to man. In a race of apes that far surpassed all others in intelligence and adaptability, this predatory economy must have led to a continual increase in the number of plants used for food and the consumption of more and more edible parts of food plants. In short, food became more and more varied, as did also the substances entering the body with it, substances that were the chemical premises for the transition to man. But all that was not yet labor in the proper sense of the word. Labor begins with the making of tools. And what are the most ancient tools that we find—the most ancient judging by the heirlooms of prehistoric man that have been discovered, and by the mode of life of the earliest historical peoples and of the rawest of contemporary savages? They are hunting and fishing implements, the former at the same time serving as weapons. But hunting and fishing presuppose the transition from an exclusively vegetable diet to the concomitant use of meat, and this is another important step in the process of transition from ape to man. A *meat diet* contained in an almost ready state the most essential ingredients required by the organism for its metabolism. By shortening the time required for digestion, it also shortened the other vegetative bodily processes that correspond to those of plant life, and thus gained further time, material and desire for the active manifestation of animal life proper. And the farther man in the making moved from the vegetable kingdom the higher he rose above the animal. Just as becoming accustomed to a vegetable diet side by side with meat converted wild cats and dogs into the servants of man, so also adaptation to a meat diet, side by side with a vegetable diet, greatly contributed towards giving bodily strength and independence to man in the making. The meat diet, however, had its greatest effect on the brain, which now received a far richer flow of the materials necessary for its nourishment and development, and which, therefore, could develop more rapidly and perfectly from generation to generation. With all due respect to the vegetarians man did not come into existence without a meat diet, and if the latter, among all peoples known to us, has led to cannibalism at some time or other (the forefathers of the Berliners, the Weletabians or Wilzians, used to eat their parents as late as the tenth century), that is of no consequence to us today.

The meat diet led to two new advances of decisive importance—the harnessing of fire and the domestication of animals. The first still further shortened the digestive process, as it provided the mouth with food already, as it were, half-digested; the second made meat more copious by opening up a new, more regular source of supply in addition to hunting, and moreover provided, in milk and its products, a new article of food at least as valuable as meat in its composition. Thus both these advances were, in themselves, new means for the emancipation of man. It would lead us too far afield to dwell here in detail on their indirect effects notwithstanding the great importance they have had for the development of man and society.

Just as man learned to consume everything edible, he also learned to live in any climate. He spread over the whole of the habitable world, being the only animal fully able to do so of its own accord. The other animals that have become accustomed to all climates—domestic animals and vermin—did not become so independently, but only in the wake of man. And the transition from the uniformly hot climate of the original home of man to colder regions, where the year was divided into summer and winter, created new requirements—shelter and clothing as protection against cold and damp, and hence new spheres of labor, new forms of activity, which further and further separated man from the animal.

By the combined functioning of hand, speech organs and brain, not only in each individual but also in society, men became capable of executing more and more complicated operations, and were able to set themselves, and achieve, higher and higher aims. The work of each generation itself became different, more perfect and more diversified. Agriculture was added to hunting and cattle raising;

then came spinning, weaving, metalworking, pottery and navigation. Along with trade and industry, art and science finally appeared. Tribes developed into nations and states. Law and politics arose, and with them that fantastic reflection of human things in the human mind—religion. In the face of all these images, which appeared in the first place to be products of the mind and seemed to dominate human societies, the more modest productions of the working hand retreated into the background, the more so since the mind that planned the labor was able, at a very early stage in the development of society (for example, already in the primitive family), to have the labor that had been planned carried out by other hands than its own. All merit for the swift advance of civilization was ascribed to the mind, to the development and activity of the brain. Men became accustomed to explain their actions as arising out of thought instead of their needs (which in any case are reflected and perceived in the mind); and so in the course of time there emerged that idealistic world outlook which, especially since the fall of the world of antiquity, has dominated men's minds. It still rules them to such a degree that even the most materialistic natural scientists of the Darwinian school are still unable to form any clear idea of the origin of man, because under this ideological influence they do not recognize the part that has been played therein by labor.

Animals, as has already been pointed out, change the environment by their activities in the same way, even if not to the same extent, as man does, and these changes, as we have seen, in turn react upon and change those who made them. In nature nothing takes place in isolation. Everything affects and is affected by every other thing, and it is mostly because this manifold motion and interaction is forgotten that our natural scientists are prevented from gaining a clear insight into the simplest things. We have seen how goats have prevented the regeneration of forests in Greece; on the island of St. Helena, goats and pigs brought by the first arrivals have succeeded in exterminating its old vegetation almost completely, and so have prepared the ground for the spreading of plants brought by later sailors and colonists. But animals exert a lasting effect on their environment unintentionally and, as far as the animals themselves are concerned, accidentally. The further removed men are from animals, however, the more their effect on nature assumes the character of premeditated, planned action directed towards definite preconceived ends. The animal destroys the vegetation of a locality without realizing what it is doing. Man destroys it in order to sow field crops on the soil thus released, or to plant trees or vines which he knows will yield many times the amount planted. He transfers useful plants and domestic animals from one country to another and thus changes the flora and fauna of whole continents. More than this. Through artificial breeding both plants and animals are so changed by the hand of man that they become unrecognizable. The wild plants from which our grain varieties originated are still being sought in vain. There is still some dispute about the wild animals from which our very different breeds of dogs or our equally numerous breeds of horses are descended.

It goes without saying that it would not occur to us to dispute the ability of animals to act in a planned, premeditated fashion. On the contrary, a planned mode of action exists in embryo wherever protoplasm, living albumen, exists and reacts, that is, carries out definite, even if extremely simple, movements as a result of definite external stimuli. Such reaction takes place even where there is yet no cell at all, far less a nerve cell. There is something of the planned action in the way insect-eating plants capture their prey, although they do it quite unconsciously. In animals the capacity for conscious, planned action is proportional to the development of the nervous system, and among mammals it attains a fairly high level. While fox-hunting in England one can daily observe how unerringly the fox makes use of its excellent knowledge of the locality in order to elude its pursuers, and how well it knows and turns to account all favorable features of the ground that cause the scent to be lost. Among our domestic animals, more highly developed thanks to association with man, one can constantly observe acts of cunning on exactly the same level as those of children. For, just as the development history of the human embryo in the mother's womb is only an abbreviated repetition of the history, extending over millions of years, of the bodily development of our animal ancestors, starting from the worm, so the mental development of the human child is only a still more abbreviated repetition of the intellectual development of these same ancestors, at least of the later ones. But all the planned action of all animals has never succeeded in impressing the stamp of their will upon the earth. That was left for man.

In short, the animal merely *uses* its environment, and brings about changes in it simply by its presence; man by his changes makes it serve his ends, *masters* it. This is the final, essential distinction between man and other animals, and once again it is labor that brings about this distinction.

Let us not, however, flatter ourselves overmuch on account of our human victories over nature. For each such victory nature takes its revenge on us. Each victory, it is true, in the first place brings about the results we expected, but in the second and third places it has quite different, unforeseen effects which only too often cancel the first. The people who, in Mesopotamia, Greece, Asia Minor and elsewhere, destroyed the forests to obtain cultivable land, never dreamed that by removing along with the forests the collecting centers and reservoirs of moisture they were laying the basis for the present forlorn state of those countries. When the Italians of the Alps used up the pine forests on the southern slopes, so carefully cherished on the northern slopes, they had no inkling that by doing so they were cutting at the roots of the dairy industry in their region; they had still less inkling that they were thereby depriving their mountain springs of water for the greater part of the year, and making it possible for them to pour still more furious torrents on the plains during the rainy seasons. Those who spread the potato in Europe were not aware that with these farinaceous tubers they were at the same time spreading scrofula. Thus at every step we are reminded that we by no means rule over nature like a conqueror over a foreign people, like someone standing outside nature—but that we, with flesh, blood and brain, belong to nature, and exist in its midst, and that all our mastery of it consists in the fact that we have the advantage over all other creatures of being able to learn its laws and apply them correctly.

And, in fact, with every day that passes we are acquiring a better understanding of these laws and getting to perceive both the more immediate and the more remote consequences of our interference with the traditional course of nature. In particular, after the mighty advances made by the natural sciences in the present century, we are more than ever in a position to realize, and hence to control, also the more remote natural consequences of at least our day-to-day production activities. But the more this progresses the more will men not only feel but also know their oneness with nature, and the more impossible will become the senseless and unnatural idea of a contrast between mind and matter, man and nature, soul and body, such as arose after the decline of classical antiquity in Europe and obtained its highest elaboration in Christianity.

It required the labor of thousands of years for us to learn a little of how to calculate the more remote *natural* effects of our actions in the field of production, but it has been still more difficult in regard to the more remote *social* effects of these actions. We mentioned the potato and the resulting spread of scrofula. But what is scrofula compared to the effects which the reduction of the workers to a potato diet had on the living conditions of the popular masses in whole countries, or compared to the famine the potato blight brought to Ireland in 1847, which consigned to the grave a million Irishmen, nourished solely or almost exclusively on potatoes, and forced the emigration overseas of two million more? When the Arabs learned to distil spirits, it never entered their heads that by so doing they were creating one of the chief weapons for the annihilation of the aborigines of the then still undiscovered American continent. And when afterward Columbus discovered this America, he did not know that by doing so he was giving a new lease of life to slavery, which in Europe had long ago been done away with, and laying the basis for the African slave trade. The men who in the seventeenth and eighteenth centuries labored to create the steam engine had no idea that they were preparing the instrument which more than any other was to revolutionize social relations throughout the world. Especially in Europe, by concentrating wealth in the hands of a minority and dispossessing the huge majority, this instrument was destined at first to give social and political domination to the bourgeoisie, but later, to give rise to a class struggle between bourgeoisie and proletariat which can end only in the overthrow of the bourgeoisie and the abolition of all class antagonisms.—But in this sphere too, by long and often cruel experience and by collecting and analysing historical material, we are gradually learning to get a clear view of the indirect, more remote social effects of our production activity, and so are afforded an opportunity to control and regulate these effects as well.

This regulation, however, requires something more than mere knowledge. It requires a complete revolution in our hitherto existing mode of production, and simultaneously a revolution in our whole contemporary social order.

All hitherto existing modes of production have aimed merely at achieving the most immediately and directly useful effect of labor. The further consequences, which appear only later and become effective through gradual repetition and accumulation, were totally neglected. The original common ownership of land corresponded, on the one hand, to a level of development of human beings in which their horizon was restricted in general to what lay immediately available, and presupposed, on the other hand, a certain superfluity of land that would allow some latitude for correcting the possible bad results of this primeval type of economy. When this surplus land was exhausted, common ownership also declined. All higher forms of production, however, led to the division of the population into different classes and thereby to the antagonism of ruling and oppressed classes. Thus the interests of the ruling class became the driving factor of production, since production was no longer restricted to providing the barest means of subsistence for the oppressed people. This has been put into effect most completely in the capitalist mode of production prevailing today in Western Europe. The individual capitalists, who dominate production and exchange, are able to concern themselves only with the most immediate useful effect of their actions. Indeed, even this useful effect—inasmuch as it is a question of the usefulness of the article that is produced or exchanged—retreats far into the background, and the sole incentive becomes the profit to be made on selling.

Classical political economy, the social science of the bourgeoisie, in the main examines only social effects of human actions in the fields of production and exchange that are actually intended. This fully corresponds to the social organization of which it is the theoretical expression. As individual capitalists are engaged in production and exchange for the sake of the immediate profit, only the nearest, most immediate results must first be taken into account. As long as the individual manufacturer or merchant sells a manufactured or purchased commodity with the usual coveted profit, he is satisfied and does not concern himself with what afterward becomes of the commodity and its purchasers. The same thing applies to the natural effects of the same actions. What cared the Spanish planters in Cuba, who burned down forests on the slopes of the mountains and obtained from the ashes sufficient fertilizer for *one* generation of very highly profitable coffee trees—what cared they that the heavy tropical rainfall afterwards washed away the unprotected upper stratum of the soil, leaving behind only bare rock! In relation to nature, as to society, the present mode of production is predominantly concerned only about the immediate, the most tangible result; and then surprise is expressed that the more remote effects of actions directed to this end turn out to be quite different, are mostly quite the opposite in character; that the harmony of supply and demand is transformed into the very reverse opposite, as shown by the course of each ten years' industrial cycle—even Germany has had a little preliminary experience of it in the "crash"; that private ownership based on one's own labor must of necessity develop into the expropriation of the workers, while all wealth becomes more and more concentrated in the hands of nonworkers.

Translated by Clemens Dutt

Letters on Historical Materialism

To Conrad Schmidt in Berlin

London, August 5, 1890

... I saw a review of Paul Barth's book* by that bird of ill omen, Moritz Wirth, in the Vienna *Deutsche Worte,* and *this* criticism left on my mind an unfavorable impression of the book itself, as well. I will have a look at it, but I must say that if little Moritz is right when he quotes Barth as stating that the sole example of the dependence of philosophy, and so forth, on the material conditions of existence which he can find in all Marx's works is that Descartes declares animals to be machines, then I am sorry for the man who can write such a thing. And this man cannot possibly have understood the subject he is writing about if he has not yet discovered that although the material mode of existence is the *primum agens†* this does not prevent the ideological spheres from reacting upon it and influencing it in their turn, but this is a secondary effect. However, as I have said, all this is second-hand and little Moritz is a dangerous friend. The materialist conception of history has a lot of dangerous friends nowadays, who use it as an excuse for *not* studying history. Just as Marx, commenting on the French "Marxists" of the late 1870s used to say: "All I know is that I am not a Marxist."

There has also been a discussion in the *Volks-Tribüne* about the distribution of products in future society, whether this will take place according to the amount of work done or otherwise. The question has been approached very "materialistically" in opposi-

---

Hegel's Philosophy of History and the Hegelians up to Marx and Hartmann.
†Primary agent, prime cause.

tion to certain idealistic phraseology about justice. But strangely enough it has not struck anyone that, after all, the method of distribution essentially depends on *how much* there is to distribute, and that this must surely change with the progress of production and social organization, and that therefore the method of distribution will also change. But everyone who took part in the discussion, described "socialist society" not as something continuously changing and advancing but as something stable and fixed once and for all, which must, therefore, also have a method of distribution fixed once and for all. All one can reasonably do, however, is (1) to try and discover the method of distribution to be used *at the beginning,* and (2) to try and find the *general tendency* of the further development. But about this I do not find a single word in the whole debate.

In general, the word "materialist" serves many of the younger writers in Germany as a mere phrase with which anything and everything is labeled without further study, that is, they stick on this label and then consider the question disposed of. But our conception of history is above all a guide to study, not a lever for construction after the Hegelian manner. All history must be studied afresh, the conditions of existence of the different formations of society must be examined in detail before the attempt is made to deduce from them the political, civil-law, aesthetic, philosophic, religious, and so forth, views corresponding to them.

To Joseph Bloch in Königsberg

London, September 21[–22], 1890

... According to the materialist conception of history, the *ultimately* determining factor in history is the production and reproduction of real life. Neither Marx nor I have ever asserted more than this. Hence if somebody twists this into saying that the economic factor is the *only* determining one, he transforms that proposition into a meaningless, abstract, absurd phrase. The economic situation is the basis, but the various elements of the superstructure—political forms of the class struggle and its results, such as constitutions established by the victorious class after a successful battle, and so on, juridical forms, and especially the reflections of all these real struggles in the brains of the participants, political, legal, philosophical theories, religious views and their further development into systems of dogmas—also exercise their influence upon the course of the historical struggles and in many cases determine their *form* in particular. There is an interaction of all these elements in which, amid all the endless host of accidents (that is, of things and events whose inner interconnection is so remote or so impossible of proof that we can regard it as nonexistent and neglect it), the economic movement is finally bound to assert itself. Otherwise the application of the theory to any period of history would be easier than the solution of a simple equation of the first degree.

We make our history ourselves, but, in the first place, under very definite antecedents and conditions. Among these the economic ones are ultimately decisive. But the political ones, etc., and indeed even the traditions that haunt human minds also play a part, although not the decisive one. The Prussian state also arose and developed from historical, ultimately economic, causes. But it could scarcely be maintained without pedantry that among the many small states of North Germany, it was precisely Brandenburg that had to become the great power embodying the economic, linguistic, and, after the Reformation, also the religious differences between North and South, because of economic necessity and not also because of other factors (above all its entanglement with Poland, owing to the possession of Prussia, and hence with international political relations—which were indeed also decisive in the formation of the Austrian dynastic power). It is hardly possible, without making oneself ridiculous, to explain in terms of economics the existence of every small state in Germany, past and present, or the origin of the High German consonant shift, which widened the geographic partition formed by the mountain ranges, from the Sudetes to the Taunus, into a regular fissure running across Germany.

In the second place, however, history proceeds in such a way that the final result always arises from conflicts between many individual wills, and every one of them is in turn made into what it is by a host of particular conditions of life. Thus there are innumerable intersecting forces, an infinite series of parallelograms of forces which give rise to one resultant—the historical event. This may in its turn again be regarded as the product of a power which operates as a whole *unconsciously* and without volition. For what each individual wills is obstructed by everyone else, and what emerges is something that no one intended. Thus history has proceeded hitherto in the manner of a natural process and is essentially subject to the same laws of motion. But from the fact that the wills of individuals—each of whom desires what he is impelled to by his physical constitution and external, in the last resort economic, circumstances (either his own personal circumstances or those of society in general)—do not achieve what they want, but are merged into an aggregate mean, a common resultant, it must not be concluded that they are equal to zero. On the contrary, each contributes to the resultant and is to this extent included in it.

I would furthermore ask you to study this theory from its original sources and not at second-hand; it is really much easier. Marx hardly wrote anything in which it did not play a part. But especially *The Eighteenth Brumaire of Louis Bonaparte* is a most excellent example of its application. There are also many allusions to it in *Kapital.* Perhaps I may also refer you to my writings: *Herr Eugen Dühring's Revolution in Science* and *Ludwig Feuerbach and the End of Classical German Philosophy,* in which I have given the most detailed account of historical materialism which, as far as I know, exists.

Marx and I are ourselves partly to blame for the fact that the younger people sometimes lay more stress on the economic side than is due to it. We had to emphasise the main principle vis-à-vis our adversaries, who denied it, and we had not always the time, the place, or the opportunity to give their due to the other factors involved in the interaction. But when it came to presenting a section of history, that is, to applying the theory in practice, it was a different matter and there no error was permissible. Unfortunately, however, it happens only too often that people think they have fully understood a new theory and can apply it without more ado as soon as they have assimilated its main principles, and even those not always correctly. And I cannot exempt many of the more recent "Marxists" from this reproach, for the most amazing stuff has been produced in that quarter, too. . . .

To Conrad Schmidt in Berlin

London, October 27, 1890

Dear Schmidt,

I am taking advantage of the first free hour to reply to you. I think it would be wise to accept the post in Zurich. You could certainly learn a good deal about economics there, especially if you bear in mind that Zurich is after all only a third-rate money and speculative market, and that therefore the impressions felt there are weakened by twofold or threefold reflection or are deliberately distorted. But you will get a practical knowledge of the mechanism and be obliged to follow the stock exchange reports from London, New York, Paris, Berlin and Vienna at firsthand, and thus gain an insight into the world market, as it is reflected in the money and stock market. Economic, political and other reflections are just like those in the human eye: they pass through a convex lens and therefore appear upside down, standing on their heads. But the nervous apparatus to put them on their feet again in our imagination is lacking. The money market man sees the movement of industry and of the world market only in the inverted reflection of the money and stock market and thus effect becomes cause to him. I noticed that already in the forties in Manchester: the London stock exchange reports were utterly useless for understanding the course of industry and its periodical maxima and minima because these gentlemen tried to explain everything by crises on the money market, which were after all usually only symptoms. At that time the point was to prove that temporary over-production is not the cause of industrial crises, so that the thing had in addition its tendentious side, conducive to distortion. This point has now ceased to exist—for us, at any rate, once and for all—it is moreover a fact that the money market can also have its own crises, in which direct disturbances of industry play only a subordinate part or no part at all, and in this context a great deal has still to be ascertained and examined, especially in the history of the last twenty years.

Where there is division of labor on a social scale the separate labor processes become independent of each other. In the last instance production is the decisive factor. But as soon as trade in products becomes independent of production proper, it has a movement of its own, which, although by and large governed by that of production, nevertheless in particulars and within this general dependence again follows laws of its own inherent in the nature of this new factor; this movement has phases of its own and in its turn reacts on the movement of production. The discovery of America was due to the thirst for gold which had previously driven the Portuguese to Africa (cf. Soetbeer's *Production of Precious Metals*), because European industry and accordingly trade which had grown enormously in the fourteenth and fifteenth centuries required more means of exchange than Germany, the great silver country from 1450 to 1550, could provide. The conquest of India by the Portuguese, Dutch and English between 1500 and 1800 had *imports from* India as its object—nobody dreamed of exporting anything there. And yet what colossal repercussions upon industry had these discoveries and conquests, which were called forth solely by trade interests; it was only the need for *exports to* these countries that created and developed modern large-scale industry.

So it is, too, with the money market. As soon as trade in money becomes separate from trade in commodities it has—under definite conditions determined by production and commodity trade and within these limits—a development of its own, specific laws determined by its own nature and distinct phases. Add to this the fact that money trade, developing further, comes to include trade in securities and that these securities are not only government papers but also industrial and transport stocks, consequently money trade gains direct control over a portion of the production by which it is on the whole itself controlled, thus the repercussions of money trading on production become still stronger and more complicated. The money-dealers become owners of railways, mines, iron works, etc. These means of production take on a double aspect: their operation is governed sometimes by the interests of direct production, sometimes however also by the requirements of the shareholders, in so far as they are money-dealers. The most striking example of this is furnished by the North American railways, whose operation is entirely dependent on the daily stock exchange transactions of a Jay Gould or a Vanderbilt, which have nothing whatever to do with the particular railway and its interests as means of communication. And even here in England we have seen contests between different railway companies over the boundaries of their respective territories that last for decades—contests on which an enormous amount of money was thrown away, not in the interests of production and communication but simply because of a rivalry whose sole object usually was to facilitate the stock exchange transactions of the shareholding money dealers.

With these few indications of my conception of the relation of production to commodity trade and of both to money trade, I have generally answered your questions about "historical materialism." The thing is easiest to grasp from the point of view of the division of labor. Society gives rise to certain common functions which it cannot dispense with. The persons appointed for this purpose form a new branch of the division of labor *within society*. This gives them particular interests, distinct, too, from the interests of their mandators; they make themselves independent of the latter and—the state is in being. And now things proceed in a way similar to that in commodity trade and later in money trade: the new independent power, while having in the main to follow the movement of production, reacts in its turn, by virtue of its inherent relative independence—that is, the relative independence once transferred to it and gradually further developed—upon the conditions and course of production. It is the interaction of two unequal forces: on the one hand, the economic movement, on the other, the new political power, which strives for as much independence as possible, and which, having once been set up, is endowed with a movement of its own. On the whole, the economic movement prevails, but it has also to endure reactions from the political movement which it itself set up and endowed with relative independence, from the movement of the state power, on the one hand, and of the opposition simultaneously engendered, on the other. Just as the movement of the industrial market is, in the main and with the reservations already indicated, reflected in the money market and, of course, in *inverted* form, so the struggle between the classes already existing and fighting with one another is reflected in the struggle between government and opposition, but likewise in inverted form, no longer directly but indirectly, not as a class struggle but as a fight for political principles, and it is so distorted that it has taken us thousands of years to get to the bottom of it.

The retroaction of the state power upon economic development can be of three kinds: it can proceed in the same direction, and then things move more rapidly; it can move in the opposite direction, in which case nowadays it [the state] will go to pieces in the long run in every great people; or it can prevent the economic development from proceeding along certain lines, and prescribe other lines. This case ultimately reduces itself to one of the two previous ones. But it is obvious that in cases two and three the political power can do great damage to the economic development and cause extensive waste of energy and material.

Then there is also the case of the conquest and brutal destruction of economic resources, as a result of which, in certain circumstances, the entire economic development in a particular locality or in a country could be ruined in former times. Nowadays such a case usually has the opposite effect, at least with great peoples:

in the long run the vanquished often gains more economically, politically, and morally than the victor.

Similarly with law. As soon as the new division of labor which creates professional lawyers becomes necessary, another new and independent sphere is opened up which, for all its general dependence on production and trade, has also a specific capacity for reacting upon these spheres. In a modern state, law must not only correspond to the general economic condition and be its expression, but must also be an *internally coherent* expression which does not, owing to internal conflicts, contradict itself. And in order to achieve this, the faithful reflection of economic conditions suffers increasingly. All the more so the more rarely it happens that a code of law is the blunt, unmitigated, unadulterated expression of the domination of a class—this in itself would offend the "conception of right." Even in the *Code Napoléon* the pure, consistent conception of right held by the revolutionary bourgeoisie of 1792–96 is already adulterated in many ways, and, in so far as it is embodied in the Code, has daily to undergo all sorts of attenuations owing to the rising power of the proletariat. This does not prevent the *Code Napoléon* from being the statute book that serves as the basis of every new code of law in every part of the world. Thus to a great extent the course of the "development of law" simply consists in first attempting to eliminate contradictions which arise from the direct translation of economic relations into legal principles, and to establish a harmonious system of law, and then in the repeated breaches made in this system by the influence and compulsion of further economic development, which involves it in further contradictions. (I am speaking here for the moment only of civil law.)

The reflection of economic relations in the form of legal principles is likewise bound to be inverted: it goes on without the person who is acting being conscious of it; the jurist imagines he is operating with *a priori* propositions, whereas they are really only economic reflections; everything is therefore upside down. And it seems to me obvious that this inversion, which, so long as it remains unrecognised, forms what we call *ideological outlook,* influences in its turn the economic basis and may, within certain limits, modify it. The basis of the right of inheritance is an economic one, provided the level of development of the family is the same. It would, nevertheless, be difficult to prove, for instance, that the absolute liberty of the testator in England and the severe and very detailed restrictions imposed upon him in France are due to economic causes alone. But in their turn they exert a very considerable effect on the economic sphere, because they influence the distribution of property.

As to the realms of ideology which soar still higher in the air—religion, philosophy, etc.—these have a prehistoric stock, found already in existence by and taken over in the historical period, of what we should today call nonsense. These various false conceptions of nature, of man's own being, of spirits, magic forces, etc., have for the most part only a negative economic factor as their basis; the low economic development of the prehistoric period is supplemented and also partially conditioned and even caused by the false conceptions of nature. And even though economic necessity was the main driving force of the increasing knowledge of nature and has become ever more so, yet it would be pedantic to try and find economic causes for all this primitive nonsense. The history of science is the history of the gradual clearing away of this nonsense or rather of its replacement by fresh but less absurd nonsense. The people who attend to this belong in their turn to special spheres in the division of labor and they think that they are working in an independent field. And to the extent that they form an independent group within the social division of labor, their output, including their errors, exerts in its turn an effect upon the whole development of society, and even on its economic development. But all the same they themselves are in turn under the predominant influence of economic development. In philosophy, for instance, this can be most readily proved true for the bourgeois period. Hobbes was the first modern materialist (in the sense of the eighteenth century) but he was an absolutist at a time when absolute monarchy was in its heyday throughout Europe and began the battle against the people in England. Locke was in religion and in politics the child of the class compromise of 1688. The English deists and their consistent followers, the French materialists, were the true philosophers of the bourgeoisie, the French even of the bourgeois revolution. The German philistinism runs through German philosophy from Kant to Hegel, sometimes in a positive and sometimes negative way. But the precondition of the philosophy of each epoch regarded as a distinct sphere in the division of labor is a definite body of thought which is handed down to it by its predecessors, and which is also its starting point. And that is why economically backward countries can still play first fiddle in philosophy: France in the eighteenth century as compared with England, on whose philosophy the French based themselves, and later Germany as compared with both. But both in France and in Germany philosophy and the general blossoming of literature at that time were the result of an economic revival. The ultimate supremacy of economic development is for me an established fact in these spheres too, but it operates within the terms laid down by the particular sphere itself: in philosophy, for instance, by the action of economic influences (which in their turn generally operate only in their political, etc., make-up) upon the existing philosophic material which has been handed down by predecessors. Here economy creates nothing anew, but it determines the way in which the body of thought found in existence is altered and further developed, and that too for the most part indirectly, for it is the political, legal and moral reflexes that exert the greatest direct influence on philosophy.

Regarding religion, I have said everything necessary in the last section on Feuerbach.

Hence if Barth alleges that we altogether deny that the political, etc., reflections of the economic movement in their turn exert any effect upon the movement itself, he is simply tilting at windmills. He should only look at Marx's *Eighteenth Brumaire,* which deals almost exclusively with the *particular* part played by political struggles and events, of course within their *general* dependence upon economic conditions. Or *Kapital,* the section on the working day, for instance, where legislation, which is surely a political act, has such a drastic effect. Or the section on the history of the bourgeoisie. And why do we fight for the political dictatorship of the proletariat if political power is economically impotent? Force (that is, state power) is also an economic power!

What these gentlemen all lack is dialectics. They always see only cause here, effect there. That this is an empty abstraction, that such metaphysical polar opposites exist in the real world only during crises, and that the whole vast process goes on in the form of interaction—though of very unequal forces, the economic movement being by far the strongest, the primary and most decisive and that in this context everything is relative and nothing absolute— they cannot grasp at all. As far as they are concerned Hegel never existed. . . .

To Franz Mehring in Berlin

London, July 14, 1893

Dear Mr. Mehring,

Today is my first opportunity to thank you for the *Lessing-Legende* you were kind enough to send me. I did not want to reply with a bare formal acknowledgment of receipt of the book but intended at the same time to say something about it, about its contents. Hence the delay.

I shall begin at the end—the appendix "On Historical Materialism," in which you have summarized the main points excellently and for any unprejudiced person convincingly. If I find anything to object to it is that you give me more credit than I deserve, even if I count everything which I might perhaps have found out for myself—in time—but which Marx with his more rapid *coup d'oeil* and wider vision discovered much more quickly. When one had the good fortune to work for forty years with a man like Marx, one usually does not during his lifetime get the recognition one thinks one deserves. Then, when the greater man dies, the lesser easily gets overrated and this seems to me to be just my case at present; history will set all this right in the end and by that time one has managed to kick the bucket and does no longer know anything about anything.

Otherwise only one more point is lacking, which, however, Marx and I always failed to stress enough in our writings and in regard to which we are all equally guilty. That is to say, in the first instance we all laid, and *were bound to lay,* the main emphasis on the *derivation* of political, juridical and other ideological notions, and of actions arising through the medium of these notions, from basic economic facts. But at the same time we have on account of the content neglected the formal side—the manner in which these notions, etc., come about. This has given our adversaries a welcome opportunity for misunderstandings and distortions, of which Paul Barth is a striking example.

Ideology is a process which is indeed accomplished consciously by the so-called thinker, but it is the wrong kind of consciousness. The real motive forces impelling him remain unknown to the thinker; otherwise it simply would not be an ideological process. Hence he imagines false or illusory motive forces. Because it is a rational process he derives its form as well as its content from pure reasoning, either his own or that of his predecessors. He works exclusively with thought material, which he accepts without examination as something produced by reasoning, and does not investigate further for a more remote source independent of reason; indeed this is a matter of course to him, because, as all action is *mediated* by thought, it appears to him to be ultimately *based* upon thought.

The historical ideologist (historical is here simply a comprehensive term comprising political, juridical, philosophical, theological—in short, all the spheres belonging to *society* and not only to nature) thus possesses in every sphere of science material which has arisen independently out of the thought of previous generations and has gone through its own independent course of development in the brains of these successive generations. True, external facts belonging to one or another sphere may have exercised a co-determining influence on this development, but the tacit presupposition is that these facts themselves are also only the fruits of a process of thought, and so we still remain within that realm of mere thought, which apparently has successfully digested even the hardest facts.

It is above all this semblance of an independent history of state constitutions, of systems of law, of ideological conceptions in every separate domain that dazzles most people. If Luther and Calvin "overcome" the official Catholic religion, or Hegel "overcomes" Fichte and Kant, or Rousseau with his republican *Contrat social* indirectly "overcomes" the constitutional Montesquieu, this is a process which remains within theology, philosophy or political science, represents a stage in the history of these particular spheres of thought and never passes beyond the sphere of thought. And since the bourgeois illusion of the eternity and finality of capitalist production has been added to this, even the overcoming of the mercantilists by the physiocrats and Adam Smith is regarded as a sheer victory of thought; not as the reflection in thought of changed economic facts but as the finally achieved correct understanding of actual conditions subsisting always and everywhere—in fact, if Richard Coeur-de-Lion and Philip Augustus had introduced free trade instead of getting mixed up in the crusades we should have been spared five hundred years of misery and stupidity.

Connected with this is the fatuous notion of the ideologists that because we deny an independent historical development to the various ideological spheres which play a part in history we also deny them any *effect upon history*. The basis of this is the common undialectical conception of cause and effect as rigidly opposite poles, the total disregard of interaction. These gentlemen often almost deliberately forget that once an historic element has been brought into the world by other, ultimately economic causes, it reacts, and can react on its environment and even on the causes that have given rise to it.

In studying German history—the story of a continuous state of wretchedness—I have always found that only a comparison with the corresponding French periods produces a correct idea of proportions, because what happens there is the direct opposite of what happens in our country. There, they have the establishment of a national state from the scattered parts of the feudal state precisely at the time we pass through the period of our greatest decline. There, a rare objective logic during the whole course of the process; with us, increasingly dreary desultoriness. There, during the Middle Ages, the English conqueror, who intervenes in favor of the Provençal nationality against the Northern French nationality, represents foreign intervention, and the wars with England represent, in a way, the Thirty Years' War, which there, however, ends in the ejection of the foreign invaders and the subjugation of the South by the North. Then comes the struggle between the central power and Burgundy, the vassal, which relies on its foreign possessions, and plays the part of Brandenburg–Prussia, a struggle which ends, however, in the victory of the central power and conclusively establishes the national state. And precisely at that moment the national state completely collapses in our country (insofar as the "German kingdom" within the Holy Roman Empire can be called a national state) and the plundering of German territory on a large scale sets in. This comparison is most humiliating for Germans but for that very reason the more instructive; and since our workers have put Germany back again in the forefront of the historical movement it has become somewhat easier for us to swallow the ignominy of the past.

Another especially significant feature of the development of Germany is the fact that not one of the two member states which in the end partitioned Germany between them was purely German— both were colonies on conquered Slav territory: Austria a Bavarian and Brandenburg a Saxon colony—and that they acquired power *within* Germany only by relying upon the support of foreign, non-

German possessions: Austria upon that of Hungary (not to mention Bohemia) and Brandenburg that of Prussia. On the Western border, the one in greatest jeopardy, nothing of the kind took place; on the Northern border it was left to the Danes to protect Germany against the Danes; and in the South there was so little to protect that the frontier guard, the Swiss, even succeeded in tearing themselves loose from Germany!

To W. Borgius in Breslau

London, January 25, 1894

Dear Sir,

Here is the answer to your questions:

(1) By economic relations, which we regard as the determining basis of the history of society, we understand the manner in which men in a given society produce their means of subsistence and exchange the products (in so far as division of labor exists). They comprise therefore the *entire technique* of production and transport. According to our conception this technique also determines the mode of exchange and, further more, of the distribution of products and hence, after the dissolution of gentile society, also the division into classes, and consequently the relations of lordship and servitude and consequently the state, politics, law, etc. The economic relations comprise also the *geographical basis* on which they operate and those remnants of earlier stages of economic development which have been actually transmitted and have survived—often only as a result of tradition or inertia; and of course also the external environment which surrounds this form of society.

If, as you say, technique largely depends on the state of science, science depends far more still on the *state* and the *requirements* of technique. If society has a technical need, that advances science more than ten universities. The whole of hydrostatics (Torricelli, etc.) was called forth by the necessity for regulating the mountain streams of Italy in the sixteenth and seventeenth centuries. Only since the technical applicability of electricity was discovered do we know anything rational about it. But unfortunately it is customary in Germany to write the history of the sciences as if they had fallen from the skies.

(2) We regard economic conditions as that which ultimately determines historical development. But race is itself an economic factor. In this context, however, two points must not be overlooked:

(a) Political, legal, philosophical, religious, literary, artistic, etc., development is based on economic development. But all these react upon one another and also upon the economic basis. One must think that the economic situation is *cause, and solely active,* whereas everything else is only passive effect. On the contrary, interaction takes place on the basis of economic necessity, which *ultimately* always asserts itself. The state, for instance, exercises an influence by protective tariffs, free trade, good or bad fiscal system; and even the extreme debility and impotence of the German philistine, arising from the wretched economic condition of Germany from 1648 to 1830 and expressing themselves at first in pietism, then in sentimentality and cringing servility to princes and nobles, were not without economic effect. That was one of the greatest obstacles to recovery and was not shaken until the revolutionary and Napoleonic wars made the chronic misery an acute one. The economic situation therefore does not produce an automatic effect as people try here and there conveniently to imagine, but men make their history themselves, they do so however in a given environment, which conditions them, and on the basis of actual, already existing relations, among which the economic relations—however much they may be influenced by other, political and ideological, relations—are still ultimately the decisive ones, forming the keynote which alone leads to understanding.

(b) Men make their history themselves, but not as yet with a collective will according to a collective plan or even in a clearly defined given society. Their aspirations clash, and for that very reason all such societies are governed by *necessity,* whose complement and manifestation is *accident.* The necessity which here asserts itself through all accident is again ultimately economic necessity. In this connection one has to deal with the so-called great men. That such and such a man and precisely that man arises at a particular time in a particular country is, of course, pure chance. But if one eliminates him there is a demand for a substitute, and this substitute will be found, good or bad, but in the long run he will be found. That Napoleon, just that particular Corsican, should have been the military dictator whom the French Republic, exhausted by its own warfare, had rendered necessary, was chance; but that, if a Napoleon had been lacking, another would have filled the place, is proved by the fact that a man was always found as soon as he became necessary: Caesar, Augustus, Cromwell, etc. While Marx discovered the materialist conception of history,

Thierry, Mignet, Guizot and all the English historians up to 1850 are evidence that it was being striven for, and the discovery of the same conception by Morgan proves that the time was ripe for it and that it simply *had* to be discovered.

So with all the other contingencies, and apparent contingencies, of history. The further the particular sphere which we are investigating is removed from the economic sphere and approaches that of pure abstract ideology, the more shall we find it exhibiting accidents in its development, the more will its curve run zigzag. But if you plot the average axis of the curve, you will find that this axis will run more and more nearly parallel to the axis of economic development the longer the period considered and the wider the field dealt with.

In Germany the greatest hindrance to correct understanding is the irresponsible neglect by literature of economic history. It is very difficult not only to rid oneself of the historical notions drilled into one at school but still more to take up the necessary material for doing so. Who, for instance, has read even old G. von Gülich, whose dry collection of material nevertheless contains so much stuff for the clarification of innumerable political facts! . . . .

Please do not weigh each word in the above too scrupulously, but keep the general connection in mind; I regret that I have not the time to word what I am writing to you as exactly as I should be obliged to do for publication. . . .

Translated by Dona Torr

Appendix to the American Edition of *The Condition of the Working Class in England*

The book which is herewith submitted to the English-speaking public in its own language, was written rather more than forty years ago. The author, at the time, was young, twenty-four years of age, and his production bears the stamp of his youth with its good and its faulty features, of neither of which he feels ashamed. That it is now translated into English, is not in any way due to his initiative. Still he may be allowed to say a few words, "to show cause" why this translation should not be prevented from seeing the light of day.

The state of things described in this book belongs today in many respects to the past, as far as England is concerned. Though not expressly stated in our recognized treatises, it is still a law of modern Political Economy that the larger the scale on which Capitalistic Production is carried on, the less can it support the petty devices of swindling and pilfering which characterize its early stages. The pettifogging business-tricks of the Polish Jew, the representative in Europe of commerce in its lowest stage, those tricks that serve him so well in his own country, and are generally practiced there, he finds to be out of date and out of place when he comes to Hamburg or Berlin; and again the Commission Agent, who hails from Berlin or Hamburg, Jew or Christian, after frequenting the Manchester Exchange for a few months, finds out that in order to buy cotton-yarn or cloth cheap, he, too, had better drop those slightly more refined but still miserable wiles and subterfuges which are considered the acme of cleverness in his native country. The fact is, those tricks do not pay any longer in a large market, where time is money, and where a certain standard of commercial morality is unavoidably developed, purely as a means of saving time and trouble. And it is the same with the relation between the manufacturer and his "hands." The repeal of the corn laws, the discovery of the Californian and Australian gold fields, the almost complete crushing-out of domestic handweaving in India, the increasing access to the Chinese market, the rapid multiplication of railways and steamships all over the world, and other minor causes have given to English manufacturing industry such a colossal development, that the status of 1844 now appears to us as comparatively primitive and insignificant. And in proportion as this increase took place, in the same proportion did manufacturing industry become apparently moralized. The competition of manufacturer against manufacturer by means of petty thefts upon the workpeople did no longer pay. Trade had outgrown such low means of making money; they were not worth while practicing for the manufacturing millionaire, and served merely to keep alive the competition of smaller traders, thankful to pick up a penny wherever they could. Thus the truck system was suppressed; the Ten Hours' Bill was enacted, and a number of other secondary reforms introduced—much against the spirit of Free Trade and unbridled competition, but quite as much in favor of the giant-capitalist in his competition with his less favored brother. Moreover, the larger the concern, and with it the number of hands, the greater the loss and inconvenience caused by every conflict between master and men; and thus a new spirit came over the masters, especially the large ones, which taught them to avoid unnecessary squabbles, to acquiesce in the existence and power of Trades Unions, and finally even to discover in strikes— at opportune times—a powerful means to serve their own ends. The largest manufacturers, formerly the leaders of the war against the working class, were now the foremost to preach peace and harmony. And for a very good reason. The fact is, that all these concessions to justice and philanthropy were nothing else but means to accelerate the concentration of capital in the hands of the few, for whom the niggardly extra extortions of former years had lost all importance and had become actual nuisances; and to crush all the quicker and all the safer their smaller competitors who could not make both ends meet without such perquisites. Thus the development of production on the basis of the capitalistic system has of itself sufficed—at least in the leading industries, for in the more unimportant branches this is far from being the case— to do away with all those minor grievances that aggravated the workman's fate during its earlier stages. And thus it renders more and more evident the great central fact, that the cause of the miserable condition of the working class is to be sought, not in these minor grievances, but in the Capitalistic System itself. The wage worker sells to the capitalist his labor-force for a certain daily sum. After a few hours' work he has reproduced the value of that sum; but the substance of his contract is, that he has to work another series of hours to complete his working day; and the value he produces during these additional hours of surplus labor is surplus value which costs the capitalist nothing but yet goes into his pocket. That is the basis of the system which tends more and more to split up civilized society into a few Vanderbilts, the owners of all the means of production and subsistence, on the one hand, and an immense number of wage workers, the owners of nothing but their labor-force, on the other. And that this result is caused, not by this or that secondary grievance, but by the system itself—this fact has been brought out in bold relief by the development of Capitalism in England since 1847.

Again, the repeated visitations of cholera, typhus, small-pox and other epidemics have shown the British bourgeois the urgent necessity of sanitation in his towns and cities, if he wishes to save himself and family from falling victims to such diseases. Accordingly, the most crying abuses described in this book have either disappeared or have been made less conspicuous. Drainage has been introduced or improved, wide avenues have been opened out athwart many of the worst "slums" I had to describe. "Little Ireland" has disappeared and the "Seven Dials" are next on the list for sweeping away. But what of that? Whole districts which in 1844 I could describe as almost idyllic have now, with the growth of the towns, fallen into the same state of dilapidation, discomfort and misery. Only the pigs and the heaps of refuse are no longer tolerated. The bourgeoisie have made further progress in the art of hiding the distress of the working class. But that, in regard to their dwellings, no substantial improvement has taken place is amply proved by the Report of the Royal Commission "on the Housing of the Poor," 1885. And this is the case, too, in other respects. Police regulations have been plentiful as blackberries; but they can only hedge in the distress of the workers, they cannot remove it.

But while England has thus outgrown the juvenile state of capitalist exploitation described by me, other countries have only just attained it. France, Germany, and especially America, are the formidable competitors who at this moment—as foreseen by me in 1844—are more and more breaking up England's industrial monopoly. Their manufactures are young as compared with those of England, but increasing at a far more rapid rate than the latter; but curious enough, they have at this moment arrived at about the same phase of development as English manufacture in 1844. With regard to America, the parallel is indeed most striking. True, the external surroundings in which the working class is placed in America are very different, but the same economical laws are at work, and the results, if not identical in every respect, must still be of the same order. Hence was find in America the same struggles for a shorter working-day, for a legal limitation of the working time, especially of women and children in factories; we find the truck system in full blossom, and the cottage system, in rural districts, made use of by the "bosses" as a means of domination over the workers. At this very moment I am receiving the American papers with accounts of the great strike of twelve-thousand Pennsylvanian coal miners in the Connellsville district, and I seem but to read my own description of the North of England colliers' strike of 1844. The same cheating of the work-people by false measure; the same truck system; the same attempt to break the miners' resistance by the Capitalists' last, but crushing, resource, the eviction of the men out of their dwellings, the cottages owned by the companies.

There were two circumstances which for a long time prevented the unavoidable consequences of the Capitalist system from showing themselves in the full glare of day in America. These were the easy access to the ownership of cheap land, and the influx of immigration. They allowed, for many years, the great mass of the native American population to "retire" in early manhood from wage-labor and to become farmers, dealers, or employers of labor, while the hard work for wages, the position of a proletarian for life, mostly fell to the lot of immigrants. But America has outgrown this early stage. The boundless backwoods have disappeared, and the still more boundless prairies are fast and faster passing from the hands of the Nation and the States into those of private owners.

The great safety-valve against the formation of a permanent proletarian class has practically ceased to act. A class of lifelong and even hereditary proletarians exists at this hour in America. A nation of sixty millions striving hard to become—and with every chance of success, too—the leading manufacturing nation of the world—such a nation cannot permanently import its own wage-working class; not even if immigrants pour in at the rate of half a million a year. The tendency of the Capitalist system towards the ultimate splitting-up of society into two classes, a few millionaires on the one hand, and a great mass of mere wage-workers on the other, this tendency, though constantly crossed and counteracted by other social agencies, works nowhere with greater force than in America; and the result has been the production of a class of native American wage-workers, who form, indeed, the aristocracy of the wage-working class as compared with the immigrants, but who become conscious more and more every day of their solidarity with the latter and who feel all the more acutely their present condemnation to life-long wage-toil, because they still remember the bygone days, when it was comparatively easy to rise to a higher social level. Accordingly the working class movement, in America, has started with truly American vigor, and as on that side of the Atlantic things march with at least double the European speed, we may yet live to see America take the lead in this respect too.

I have not attempted, in this translation, to bring the book up to date, to point out in detail all the changes that have taken place since 1844. And for two reasons: Firstly, to do this properly, the size of the book must be about doubled, and the translation came upon me too suddenly to admit of my undertaking such a work. And secondly, the first volume of *Das Kapital,* by Karl Marx, an English translation of which is about to appear, contains a very ample description of the state of the British working class, as it was about 1865, that is to say, at the time when British industrial prosperity reached its culminating point. I should, then, have been obliged again to go over the ground already covered by Marx's celebrated work.

It will be hardly necessary to point out that the general theoretical standpoint of this book—philosophical, economical, political— does not exactly coincide with my standpoint of today. Modern international Socialism, since fully developed as a science, chiefly and almost exclusively through the efforts of Marx, did not as yet exist in 1844. My book represents one of the phases of its embryonic development; and as the human embryo, in its early stages, still reproduces the gill-arches of our fish ancestors, so this book exhibits everywhere the traces of the descent of Modern Socialism from one of its ancestors, German philosophy. Thus great stress is laid on the dictum that Communism is not a mere party doctrine of the working class, but a theory compassing the emancipation of society at large, including the Capitalist class, from its present narrow conditions. This is true enough in the abstract, but absolutely useless, and worse, in practice. So long as the wealthy classes not only do not feel the want of any emancipation, but strenuously oppose the self-emancipation of the working class, so long the social revolution will have to be prepared and fought out by the working class alone. The French bourgeois of 1789, too, declared the emancipation of the bourgeoisie to be the emancipation of the whole human race; but the nobility and clergy would not see it; the proposition—though for the time being, with respect to feudalism, an abstract historical truth—soon became a mere sentimentalism, and disappeared from view altogether in the fire of the revolutionary struggle. And today, the very people who, from the impartiality of their "superior standpoint" preach to the workers a Socialism soaring high above their class interests and class struggles, and tending to reconcile in a higher humanity the interests of both the contending classes—these people are either neophytes, who have still to learn a great deal, or they are the worst enemies of the workers—wolves in sheeps' clothing.

The recurring period of the great industrial crises is stated in the text as five years. This was the period apparently indicated by the course of events from 1825 to 1842. But the industrial history from 1842 to 1868 has shown that the real period is one of ten years; that the intermediate revolutions were secondary and tended more and more to disappear. Since 1868, the state of things has changed again, of which more anon.

I have taken care not to strike out of the text the many prophecies, among others that of an imminent social revolution in England, which my youthful ardor induced me to venture upon. The wonder is, not that a good many of them proved wrong, but that so many of them have proved right, and that the critical state of English trade, to be brought on by German and especially American competition, which I then foresaw—though in too short a period—has now actually come to pass. In this respect I can, and am bound to, bring the book up to date, by placing here an article which I published in the London "Commonweal" of March 1, 1885, under the heading: "England in 1845 and in 1885." It gives at the same time a short outline of the history of the English working class during these forty years.

London, February 25, 1886

Translator unknown

Introduction to *Socialism: Utopian and Scientific*

I am perfectly aware that the contents of this work will meet with objection from a considerable portion of the British public. But if we Continentals had taken the slightest notice of the prejudices of British "respectability"; we should be even worse off than we are. This book defends what we call "historical materialism," and the word materialism grates upon the ears of the immense majority of British readers. "Agnosticism" might be tolerated, but materialism is utterly inadmissible.

And yet the original home of all modern materialism, from the seventeenth century onwards, is England.

"Materialism is the natural-born son of Great Britain. Already the British schoolman, Duns Scotus, asked, 'whether it was impossible for matter to think?'

"In order to effect this miracle, he took refuge in God's omnipotence, i.e., he made theology preach materialism. Moreover, he was a nominalist. Nominalism, the first form of materialism, is chiefly found among the English schoolmen.

"The real progenitor of English materialism is Bacon. To him natural philosophy is the only true philosophy, and physics based upon the experience of the senses is the chiefest part of natural philosophy. Anaxagoras and his homoiomeriae, Democritus and his atoms, he often quotes as his authorities. According to him the senses are infallible and the source of all knowledge. All science is based on experience, and consists in subjecting the data furnished by the senses to a rational method of investigation. Induction, analysis, comparison, observation, experiment, are the principal forms of such a rational method. Among the qualities inherent in matter, motion is the first and foremost, not only in the form of mechanical and mathematical motion, but chiefly in the form of an impulse, a vital spirit, a tension—or a *qual,* to use a term of Jakob Böhme's*—of matter.

"In Bacon, its first creator, materialism still occludes within itself the germs of a many-sided development. On the one hand, matter, surrounded by a sensuous, poetic glamour, seems to attract man's whole entity by winning smiles. On the other, the aphoristically formulated doctrine pulluates with inconsistencies imported from theology.

"In its further evolution, materialism becomes one-sided. Hobbes is the man who systematizes Baconian materialism. Knowledge based upon the senses loses its poetic blossom, it passes into the abstract experience of the mathematician; geometry is proclaimed as the queen of sciences. Materialism takes to misanthropy. If it is to overcome its opponent, misanthropic, fleshless spiritualism, and that on the latter's own ground, materialism has to chastise its own flesh and turn ascetic. Thus, from a sensual, it passes into an intellectual entity; but thus, too, it evolves all the consistency, regardless of consequences, characteristic of the intellect.

"Hobbes, as Bacon's continuator, argues thus: if all human knowledge is furnished by the senses, then our concepts and ideas are but the phantoms, divested of their sensual forms, of the real world. Philosophy can but give names to these phantoms. One name may be applied to more than one of them. There may even be names of names. It would imply a contradiction if, on the one hand, we maintained that all ideas had their origin in the world of sensation, and, on the other, that a word was more than a word; that besides the beings known to us by our senses, beings which are one and all individuals, there existed also beings of a general, not individual, nature. An unbodily substance is the same absurdity as an unbodily body. Body, being, substance, are but different terms for the same reality. *It is impossible to separate thought from matter that thinks.* This matter is the substratum of all changes going

---

*"Qual" is a philosophical play upon words. Qual literally means torture, a pain which drives to action of some kind; at the same time the mystic Böhme puts into the German word something of the meaning of the Latin *qualitas;* his "qual" was the activating principle arising from, and promoting in its turn, the spontaneous development of the thing, relation, or person subject to it, in contradistinction to a pain inflicted from without.

on in the world. The word *infinite* is meaningless, unless it states that our mind is capable of performing an endless process of addition. Only material things being perceptible to us, we cannot know anything about the existence of God. My own existence alone is certain. Every human passion is a mechanical movement which has a beginning and an end. The objects of impulse are what we call good. Man is subject to the same laws as nature. Power and freedom are identical.

"Hobbes had systematized Bacon without, however, furnishing a proof for Bacon's fundamental principle, the origin of all human knowledge from the world of sensation. It was Locke who, in his Essay on the Human Understanding," supplied this proof.*

"Hobbes had shattered the theistic prejudices of Baconian materialism; Collins, Dodwell, Coward, Hartley, Priestley similarly shattered the last theological bars that still hemmed in Locke's sensationalism. At all events, for practical materialists, Theism is but an easygoing way of getting rid of religion."†

Thus Karl Marx wrote about the British origin of modern materialism. If Englishmen nowadays do not exactly relish the compliment he paid their ancestors, more's the pity. It is none the less undeniable that Bacon, Hobbes, and Locke are the fathers of that brilliant school of French materialists which made the eighteenth century, in spite of all battles on land and sea won over Frenchmen by Germans and Englishmen, a preeminently French century, even before that crowning French Revolution, the results of which we outsiders, in England as well as in Germany, are still trying to acclimatize.

There is no denying it. About the middle of this century, what struck every cultivated foreigner who set up his residence in England, was, what he was then bound to consider the religious bigotry and stupidity of the English respectable middle class. We, at that time, were all materialists, or, at least, very advanced freethinkers, and to us it appeared inconceivable that almost all educated people in England should believe in all sorts of impossible miracles, and that even geologists like Buckland and Mantell should contort the facts of their science so as not to clash too much with the myths of the book of Genesis; while, in order to find people who dared to use their own intellectual faculties with regard

---

*J. Locke, *An Essay Concerning Human Understanding*.
†Marx and Engels, *Die heilige Familie*, Frankfurt a. M., 1845, pp. 201–4.

to religious matters, you had to go amongst the uneducated, the "great unwashed," as they were then called, the working people, especially the Owenite Socialists.

But England has been "civilized" since then. The exhibition of 1851 sounded the knell of English insular exclusiveness. England became gradually internationalized—in diet, in manners, in ideas; so much so that I begin to wish that some English manners and customs had made as much headway on the Continent as other continental habits have made here. Anyhow, the introduction and spread of salad oil (before 1851 known only to the aristocracy) has been accompanied by a fatal spread of continental skepticism in matters religious, and it has come to this, that agnosticism, though not yet considered "the thing" quite as much as the Church of England, is yet very nearly on a par, as far as respectability goes, with Baptism, and decidedly ranks above the Salvation Army. And I cannot help believing that under these circumstances it will be consoling to many who sincerely regret and condemn this progress of infidelity to learn that these "new-fangled notions" are not of foreign origin, are not "made in Germany," like so many other articles of daily use, but are undoubtedly Old English, and that their British originators two hundred years ago went a good deal further than their descendants now dare to venture.

What, indeed, is agnosticism, but, to use an expressive Lancashire term, "shamefaced" materialism? The agnostic's conception of Nature is materialistic throughout. The entire natural world is governed by law, and absolutely excludes the intervention of action from without. But, he adds, we have no means either of ascertaining or of disproving the existence of some Supreme Being beyond the known universe. Now, this might hold good at the time when Laplace, to Napoleon's question, why in the great astronomer's *Mécanique céleste* the Creator was not even mentioned, proudly replied: *"Je n'avais pas besoin de cette hypothèse."** But nowadays, in our evolutionary conception of the universe, there is absolutely no room for either a Creator or a Ruler; and to talk of a Supreme Being shut out from the whole existing world, implies a contradiction in terms, and, as it seems to me, a gratuitous insult to the feelings of religious people.

Again, our agnostic admits that all our knowledge is based upon the information imparted to us by our senses. But, he adds, how

---

*"I had no need of this hypothesis."

do we know that our senses give us correct representations of the objects we perceive through them? And he proceeds to inform us that, whenever he speaks of objects or their qualities, he does in reality not mean these objects and qualities, of which he cannot know anything for certain, but merely the impressions which they have produced on his senses. Now, this line of reasoning seems undoubtedly hard to beat by mere argumentation. But before there was argumentation, there was action. *Im Anfang war die That.** And human action had solved the difficulty long before human ingenuity invented it. The proof of the pudding is in the eating. From the moment we turn to our own use these objects, according to the qualities we perceive in them, we put to an infallible test the correctness or otherwise of our sense-perceptions. If these perceptions have been wrong, then our estimate of the use to which an object can be turned must also be wrong, and our attempt must fail. But if we succeed in accomplishing our aim, if we find that the object does agree with our idea of it, and does answer the purpose we intended it for, then that is positive proof that our perceptions of it and of its qualities, *so far,* agree with reality outside ourselves. And whenever we find ourselves face to face with a failure, then we generally are not long in making out the cause that made us fail; we find that the perception upon which we acted was either incomplete and superficial, or combined with the results of other perceptions in a way not warranted by them—what we call defective reasoning. So long as we take care to train and to use our senses properly, and to keep our action within the limits prescribed by perceptions properly made and properly used, so long we shall find that the result of our action proves the conformity of our perceptions with the objective nature of the things perceived. Not in one single instance, so far, have we been led to the conclusion that our sense-perceptions, scientifically controlled, induce in our minds ideas respecting the outer world that are, by their very nature, at variance with reality, or that there is an inherent incompatibility between the outer world and our sense-perceptions of it.

But then come the neo-Kantian agnostics and say: We may correctly perceive the qualities of a thing, but we cannot by any sensible or mental process grasp the thing-in-itself. This "thing-in-itself" is beyond our ken. To this Hegel, long since, has replied: if

---

*"In the beginning was the deed" (see Goethe, *Faust,* part 1, scene 3, "Faust's Study").

you know all the qualities of a thing, you know the thing itself; nothing remains but the fact that the said thing exists without us; and when your senses have taught you that fact, you have grasped the last remnant of the thing-in-itself, Kant's celebrated unknowable *Ding an sich*. To which it may be added that in Kant's time our knowledge of natural objects was indeed so fragmentary that he might well suspect, behind the little we knew about each of them, a mysterious "thing-in-itself." But one after another these ungraspable things have been grasped, analyzed and, what is more, *reproduced* by the giant progress of science; and what we can produce, we certainly cannot consider as unknowable. To the chemistry of the first half of this century, organic substances were such mysterious objects; now we learn to build them up one after another from their chemical elements without the aid of organic processes. Modern chemists declare that as soon as the chemical constitution of no matter what body is known, it can be built up from its elements. We are still far from knowing the constitution of the highest organic substances, the albuminous bodies; but there is no reason why we should not, if only after centuries, arrive at that knowledge and, armed with it, produce artificial albumen. But if we arrive at that, we shall at the same time have produced organic life, for life, from its lowest to its highest forms, is but the normal mode of existence of albuminous bodies.

As soon, however, as our agnostic has made these formal mental reservations, he talks and acts as the rank materialist he at bottom is. He may say that, as far as *we* know, matter and motion, or as it is now called, energy, can neither be created nor destroyed, but that we have no proof of their not having been created at some time or other. But if you try to use this admission against him in any particular case, he will quickly put you out of court. If he admits the possibility of spiritualism *in abstracto,* he will have none of it *in concreto*. As far as we know and can know, he will tell you there is no Creator and no Ruler of the universe; as far as we are concerned, matter and energy can neither be created nor annihilated; for us, mind is a mode of energy, a function of the brain; all we know is that the material world is governed by immutable laws, and so forth. Thus, as far as he is a scientific man, as far as he *knows* anything, he is a materialist; outside his science, in spheres about which he knows nothing, he translates his ignorance into Greek and calls it agnosticism.

At all events, one thing seems clear: even if I was an agnostic, it is evident that I could not describe the conception of history sketched out in this little book as "historical agnosticism." Religious people would laugh at me, agnostics would indignantly ask, was I going to make fun of them? And thus I hope even British respectability will not be overshocked if I use, in English as well as in so many other languages, the term "historical materialism," to designate that view of the course of history which seeks the ultimate cause and the great moving power of all important historic events in the economic development of society, in the changes in the modes of production and exchange, in the consequent division of society into distinct classes, and in the struggles of these classes against one another.

This indulgence will perhaps be accorded to me all the sooner if I show that historical materialism may be of advantage even to British respectability. I have mentioned the fact that about forty or fifty years ago, any cultivated foreigner settling in England was struck by what he was then bound to consider the religious bigotry and stupidity of the English respectable middle class. I am now going to prove that the respectable English middle class of that time was not quite as stupid as it looked to the intelligent foreigner. Its religious leanings can be explained.

When Europe emerged from the Middle Ages, the rising middle class of the towns constituted its revolutionary element. It had conquered a recognised position within medieval feudal organization, but this position, also, had become too narrow for its expansive power. The development of the middle class, the *bourgeoisie,* became incompatible with the maintenance of the feudal system; the feudal system, therefore, had to fall.

But the great international centre of feudalism was the Roman Catholic Church. It united the whole of feudalized Western Europe, in spite of all internal wars, into one grand political system, opposed as much to the schismatic Greeks as to the Mohammedan countries. It surrounded feudal institutions with the halo of divine consecration. It had organized its own hierarchy on the feudal model, and, lastly, it was itself by far the most powerful feudal lord, holding, as it did, full one-third of the soil of the Catholic world. Before profane feudalism could be successfully attacked in each country and in detail, this, its sacred central organization, had to be destroyed.

Moreover, parallel with the rise of the middle class went the great revival of science; astronomy, mechanics, physics, anatomy, physiology, were again cultivated. And the bourgeoisie, for the development of its industrial production, required a science which ascertained the physical properties of natural objects and the modes of action of the forces of Nature. Now up to then science had but been the humble handmaid of the Church, had not been allowed to overstep the limits set by faith, and for that reason had been no science at all. Science rebelled against the Church; the bourgeoisie could not do without science, and, therefore, had to join in the rebellion.

The above, though touching but two of the points where the rising middle class was bound to come into collision with the established religion, will be sufficient to show, first, that the class most directly interested in the struggle against the pretensions of the Roman Church was the bourgeoisie; and second, that every struggle against feudalism, at that time, had to take on a religious disguise, had to be directed against the Church in the first instance. But if the universities and the traders of the cities started the cry, it was sure to find, and did find, a strong echo in the masses of the country people, the peasants, who everywhere had to struggle for their very existence with their feudal lords, spiritual and temporal.

The long fight of the bourgeoisie against feudalism culminated in three great, decisive battles.

The first was what is called the Protestant Reformation in Germany. The war cry raised against the Church by Luther was responded to by two insurrections of a political nature: first, that of the lower nobility under Franz von Sickingen (1523), then the great Peasants' War, 1525. Both were defeated, chiefly in consequence of the indecision of the parties most interested, the burghers of the towns—an indecision into the causes of which we cannot here enter. From that moment the struggle degenerated into a fight between the local princes and the central power, and ended by blotting out Germany, for two hundred years, from the politically active nations of Europe. The Lutheran Reformation produced a new creed indeed, a religion adapted to absolute monarchy. No sooner were the peasants of Northeast Germany converted to Lutheranism than they were reduced from freemen to serfs.

But where Luther failed, Calvin won the day. Calvin's creed was one fit for the boldest of the bourgeoisie of his time. His predestination doctrine was the religious expression of the fact that in the commercial world of competition success or failure does not depend upon a man's activity or cleverness, but upon circumstances uncontrollable by him. It is not of him that willeth or of him that runneth, but of the mercy of unknown superior economic powers; and this was especially true at a period of economic revolution, when all old commercial routes and centers were replaced by new ones, when India and America were opened to the world, and when even the most sacred economic articles of faith—the value of gold and silver—began to totter and to break down. Calvin's church constitution was thoroughly democratic and republican; and where the kingdom of God was republicanised, could the kingdoms of this world remain subject to monarchs, bishops and lords? While German Lutheranism became a willing tool in the hands of princes, Calvinism founded a republic in Holland, and active republican parties in England, and, above all, Scotland.

In Calvinism, the second great bourgeois upheaval found its doctrine ready cut and dried. This upheaval took place in England. The middle class of the towns brought it on, and the yeomanry of the country districts fought it out. Curiously enough, in all the three great bourgeois risings, the peasantry furnishes the army that has to do the fighting; and the peasantry is just the class that, the victory once gained, is most surely ruined by the economic consequences of that victory. A hundred years after Cromwell, the yeomanry of England had almost disappeared. Anyhow, had it not been for that yeomantry and for the *plebeian* element in the towns, the bourgeoisie alone would never have fought the matter out to the bitter end, and would never have brought Charles I to the scaffold. In order to secure even those conquests of the bourgeoisie that were ripe for gathering at the time, the revolution had to be carried considerably further—exactly as in 1793 in France and in 1848 in Germany. This seems, in fact, to be one of the laws of evolution of bourgeois society.

Well, upon this excess of revolutionary activity there necessarily followed the inevitable reaction which in its turn went beyond the point where it might have maintained itself. After a series of oscillations, the new center of gravity was at last attained and became a new starting-point. The grand period of English history, known to respectability under the name of "the Great Rebellion," and the struggles succeeding it, were brought to a close by the comparatively puny event entitled by Liberal historians, "the Glorious Revolution."

The new starting point was a compromise between the rising middle class and ex-feudal landowners. The latter, though called, as now, the aristocracy, had been long since on the way which led them to become what Louis Philippe in France became at a much later period, "the first bourgeois of the kingdom." Fortunately for England the old feudal barons had killed one another during the Wars of the Roses. Their successors, though mostly scions of the old families, had been so much out of the direct line of descent that they constituted quite a new body, with habits and tendencies far more bourgeois than feudal. They fully understood the value of money, and at once began to increase their rents by turning hundreds of small farmers out and replacing them by sheep. Henry VIII, while squandering the Church lands, created fresh bourgeois landlords by wholesale; the innumerable confiscations of estates, regranted to absolute or relative upstarts, and continued during the whole of the seventeenth century, had the same result. Consequently, ever since Henry VII, the English "aristocracy," far from counteracting the development of industrial production, had, on the contrary, sought to indirectly profit thereby; and there had always been a section of the great landowners willing, from economical or political reasons, to cooperate with the leading men of the financial and industrial bourgeoisie. The compromise of 1689 was, therefore, easily accomplished. The political spoils of "pelf and place" were left to the great landowning families, provided the economic interests of the financial, manufacturing, and commercial middle class were sufficiently attended to. And these economic interests were at that time powerful enough to determine the general policy of the nation. There might be squabbles about matters of detail, but, on the whole, the aristocratic oligarchy knew too well that its own economic prosperity was irretrievably bound up with that of the industrial and commercial middle class.

From that time, the bourgeoisie was a humble, but still a recognized component of the ruling classes of England. With the rest of them, it had a common interest in keeping in subjection the great working mass of the nation. The merchant or manufacturer himself stood in the position of master, or, as it was until lately called, of "natural superior" to his clerks, his workpeople, his domestic servants. His interest was to get as much and as good work out of them as he could; for this end they had to be trained to proper submission. He was himself religious, his religion had supplied the standard under which he had fought the king and the lords; he was not long in discovering the opportunities this same religion offered him for working upon the minds of his natural inferiors, and making them submissive to the behests of the masters it had pleased God to place over them. In short, the English bourgeoisie now had to take a part in keeping down the "lower orders," the great producing mass of the nation, and one of the means employed for that purpose was the influence of religion.

There was another fact that contributed to strengthen the religious leanings of the bourgeoisie. That was the rise of materialism in England. This new doctrine not only shocked the pious feelings of the middle class; it announced itself as a philosophy only fit for scholars and cultivated men of the world, in contrast to religion which was good enough for the uneducated masses, including the bourgeoisie. With Hobbes it stepped on the stage as a defender of royal prerogative and omnipotence; it called upon absolute monarchy to keep down that *puer robustus sed malitiosus,* to wit, the people. Similarly, with the successors of Hobbes, with Bolingbroke, Shaftesbury and so forth, the new deistic form of materialism remained an aristocratic, esoteric doctrine, and, therefore, hateful to the middle class both for its religious heresy and for its antibourgeois political connections. Accordingly, in opposition to the materialism and deism of the aristocracy, those Protestant sects which had furnished the flag and the fighting contingent against the Stuarts, continued to furnish the main strength of the progressive middle class, and form even today the backbone of "the Great Liberal Party."

In the meantime materialism passed from England to France, where it met and coalesced with another materialistic school of philosophers, a branch of Cartesianism. In France, too, it remained at first an exclusively aristocratic doctrine. But soon its revolutionary character asserted itself. The French materialists did not limit their criticism to matters of religious belief; they extended it to whatever scientific tradition or political institution they met with; and to prove the claim of their doctrine to universal application, they took the shortest cut, and boldly applied it to all subjects of knowledge in the giant work after which they were named—the *Encyclopédie.* Thus, in one or the other of its two forms—avowed materialism or deism—it became the creed of the whole cultured youth of France; so much so that, when the great Revolution broke out, the doctrine hatched by English Royalists gave a theoretical flag to French Republicans and Terrorists, and furnished the text for the Declaration of the Rights of Man.

The great French Revolution was the third uprising of the bourgeoisie, but the first that had entirely cast off the religious cloak, and was fought out on undisguised political lines; it was the first, too, that was really fought out up to the destruction of one of the combatants, the aristocracy, and the complete triumph of the other, the bourgeoisie. In England the continuity of pre-revolutionary and post-revolutionary institutions, and the compromise between landlords and capitalists, found its expression in the continuity of judicial precedents and in the religious preservation of the feudal forms of the law. In France the Revolution constituted a complete breach with the traditions of the past; it cleared out the very last vestiges of feudalism, and created in the *Code Civil* a masterly adaptation of the old Roman law—that almost perfect expression of the juridical relations corresponding to the economic stage called by Marx the production of commodities—to modern capitalistic conditions; so masterly that this French revolutionary code still serves as a model for reforms of the law of property in all other countries, not excepting England. Let us, however, not forget that if English law continues to express the economic relations of capitalistic society in that barbarous feudal language which corresponds to the thing expressed, just as English spelling corresponds to English pronunciation—*vous écrivez Londres et vous prononcez Constantinople,** said a Frenchman—that same English law is the only one which has preserved through ages, and transmitted to America and the Colonies, the best part of that old Germanic personal freedom, local self-government and independence from all interference but that of the law courts, which on the Continent has been lost during the period of absolute monarchy, and has nowhere been as yet fully recovered.

To return to our British bourgeois. The French Revolution gave him a splendid opportunity, with the help of the continental monarchies, to destroy French maritime commerce, to annex French colonies, and to crush the last French pretensions to maritime rivalry. That was one reason why he fought it. Another was that the ways of this revolution went very much against his grain. Not only its "execrable" terrorism, but the very attempt to carry bourgeois rule to extremes. What should the British bourgeois do without his

---

* "You write London, but pronounce Constantinople."

aristocracy, that taught him manners, such as they were, and invented fashions for him—that furnished officers for the army, which kept order at home, and the navy, which conquered colonial possessions and new markets abroad? There was indeed a progressive minority of the bourgeoisie, that minority whose interests were not so well attended to under the compromise; this section, composed chiefly of the less wealthy middle class, did sympathize with the Revolution, but it was powerless in Parliament.

Thus, if materialism became the creed of the French Revolution, the God-fearing English bourgeois held all the faster to his religion. Had not the reign of terror in Paris proved what was the upshot, if the religious instincts of the masses were lost? The more materialism spread from France to neighbouring countries, and was reinforced by similar doctrinal currents, notably by German philosophy, the more, in fact, materialism and free thought generally became, on the Continent, the necessary qualifications of a cultivated man, the more stubbornly the English middle class stuck to its manifold religious creeds. These creeds might differ from one another, but they were, all of them, distinctly religious, Christian creeds.

While the Revolution insured the political triumph of the bourgeoisie in France, in England Watt, Arkwright, Cartwright, and others initiated an industrial revolution, which completely shifted the center of gravity of economic power. The wealth of the bourgeoisie increased considerably faster than that of the landed aristocracy. Within the bourgeoisie itself, the financial aristocracy, the bankers, and so on, were more and more pushed into the background by the manufacturers. The compromise of 1689, even after the gradual changes it had undergone in favor of the bourgeoisie, no longer corresponded to the relative position of the parties to it. The character of these parties, too, had changed; the bourgeoisie of 1830 was very different from that of the preceding century. The political power still left to the aristocracy, and used by them to resist the pretensions of the new industrial bourgeoisie, became incompatible with the new economic interests. A fresh struggle with the aristocracy was necessary; it could end only in a victory of the new economic power. First, the Reform Act was pushed through, in spite of all resistance, under the impulse of the French Revolution of 1830. It gave to the bourgeoisie a recognized and powerful place in Parliament. Then the Repeal of the Corn Laws, which settled, once for all, the supremacy of the bourgeoisie, and especially of its most active portion, the manufacturers, over the landed aristocracy. This was the greatest victory of the bourgeoisie; it was, however, also the last it gained in its own exclusive interest. Whatever triumphs it obtained later on, it had to share with a new social power, first its ally, but soon its rival.

The industrial revolution had created a class of large manufacturing capitalists, but also a class—and a far more numerous one—of manufacturing workpeople. This class gradually increased in numbers, in proportion as the industrial revolution seized upon one branch of manufacture after another, and in the same proportion it increased in power. This power it proved as early as 1824, by forcing a reluctant Parliament to repeal the acts forbidding combinations of workmen. During the Reform agitation, the working men constituted the Radical wing of the Reform party; the Act of 1832 having excluded them from the suffrage, they formulated their demands in the People's Charter, and constituted themselves, in opposition to the great bourgeois Anti-Corn Law party, into an independent party, the Chartists, the first working men's party of modern times.

Then came the continental revolutions of February and March, 1848, in which the working people played such a prominent part, and, at least in Paris, put forward demands which were certainly inadmissible from the point of view of capitalist society. And then came the general reaction. First the defeat of the Chartists on April 10, 1848, then the crushing of the Paris working men's insurrection in June of the same year, then the disasters of 1849 in Italy, Hungary, South Germany, and at last the victory of Louis Bonaparte over Paris, December 2, 1851. For a time, at least, the bugbear of working-class pretensions was put down, but at what cost! If the British bourgeois had been convinced before of the necessity of maintaining the common people in a religious mood, how much more must he feel that necessity after all these experiences? Regardless of the sneers of his continental compeers, he continued to spend thousands and tens of thousands, year after year, upon the evangelization of the lower orders; not content with his own native religious machinery, he appealed to Brother Jonathan, the greatest organizer in existence of religion as a trade, and imported from America revivalism, Moody and Sankey, and the like; and, finally, he accepted the dangerous aid of the Salvation Army, which revives the propaganda of early Christianity, appeals to the poor as the elect, fights capitalism in a religious way, and thus fosters an element of early Christian class antagonism, which one day may become troublesome to the well-to-do people who now find the ready money for it.

It seems a law of historical development that the bourgeoisie can in no European country get hold of political power—at least for any length of time—in the same exclusive way in which the feudal aristocracy kept hold of it during the Middle Ages. Even in France, where feudalism was completely extinguished, the bourgeoisie, as a whole, has held full possession of the Government for very short periods only. During Louis Philippe's reign, 1830–48, a very small portion of the bourgeoisie ruled the kingdom; by far the larger part were excluded from the suffrage by the high qualification. Under the Second Republic, 1848–51, the whole bourgeoisie ruled, but for three years only; their incapacity brought on the Second Empire. It is only now, in the Third Republic, that the bourgeoisie as a whole have kept possession of the helm for more than twenty years; and they are already showing lively signs of decadence. A durable reign of the bourgeoisie has been possible only in countries like America, where feudalism was unknown, and society at the very beginning started from a bourgeois basis. And even in France and America, the successors of the bourgeoisie, the working people, are already knocking at the door.

In England, the bourgeoisie never held undivided sway. Even the victory of 1832 left the landed aristocracy in almost exclusive possession of all the leading Government offices. The meekness with which the wealthy middle class submitted to this, remained inconceivable to me until the great Liberal manufacturer, Mr. W. A. Forster, in a public speech implored the young men of Bradford to learn French, as a means to get on in the world, and quoted from his own experience how sheepish he looked when, as a Cabinet Minister, he had to move in society where French was, at least, as necessary as English! The fact was, the English middle class of that time were, as a rule, quite uneducated upstarts, and could not help leaving to the aristocracy those superior Government places where other qualifications were required than mere insular narrowness and insular conceit, seasoned by business sharpness.* Even now

---

*And even in business matters, the conceit of national chauvinism is but a sorry adviser. Up to quite recently, the average English manufacturer considered it derogatory from an Englishman to speak any language but his own, and felt rather proud than otherwise of the fact that "poor devils" of foreigners settled in England and

the endless newspaper debates about middle-class education show that the English middle class does not yet consider itself good enough for the best education, and looks to something more modest. Thus, even after the Repeal of the Corn Laws, it appeared a matter of course that the men who had carried the day, the Cobdens, Brights, Forsters, etc., should remain excluded from a share in the official government of the country, until twenty years afterward, a new Reform Act opened to them the door of the Cabinet. The English bourgeoisie are, up to the present day, so deeply penetrated by a sense of their social inferiority that they keep up, at their own expense and that of the nation, an ornamental caste of drones to represent the nation worthily at all state functions; and they consider themselves highly honored whenever one of themselves is found worthy of admission into this select and privileged body, manufactured, after all, by themselves.

The industrial and commercial middle class had, therefore, not yet succeeded in driving the landed aristocracy completely from political power when another competitor, the working class, appeared on the stage. The reaction after the Chartist movement and the continental revolutions, as well as the unparalleled extension of English trade from 1848 to 1866 (ascribed vulgarly to Free Trade alone, but due far more to the colossal development of railways, ocean steamers and means of intercourse generally), had again driven the working class into the dependency of the Liberal party, of which they formed, as in pre-Chartist times, the Radical wing. Their claims to the franchise, however, gradually became irresistible; while the Whig leaders of the Liberals "funked," Disraeli showed his superiority by making the Tories seize the favorable moment and introduce household suffrage in the boroughs, along with a redistribution of seats. Then followed the ballot; then in

---

took off his hands the trouble of disposing of his products abroad. He never noticed that these foreigners, mostly Germans, thus got command of a very large part of British foreign trade, imports and exports, and that the direct foreign trade of Englishmen became limited, almost entirely, to the colonies, China, the United States, and South America. Nor did he notice that these Germans traded with other Germans abroad, who gradually organised a complete network of commercial colonies all over the world. But when Germany, about forty years ago, seriously began manufacturing for export, this network served her admirably in her transformation in so short a time, from a corn-exporting into a first-rate manufacturing country. Then, about ten years ago, the British manufacturer got frightened, and asked his ambassadors and consuls how it was that he could no longer keep his customers together. The unanimous answer was: (1) You don't learn your cus-

1884 the extension of household suffrage to the counties and a fresh redistribution of seats, by which electoral districts were to some extent equalized. All these measures considerably increased the electoral-power of the working class, so much so that in at least one hundred fifty to two hundred constituencies that class now furnishes the majority of voters. But parliamentary government is a capital school for teaching respect for tradition; if the middle class look with awe and veneration upon what Lord John Manners playfully called "our old nobility," the mass of the working people then looked up with respect and deference to what used to be designated as "their betters," the middle class. Indeed, the British workman, some fifteen years ago, was the model workman, whose respectful regard for the position of his master, and whose self-restraining modesty in claiming rights for himself, consoled our German economists of the Katheder-Socialist school for the incurable communistic and revolutionary tendencies of their own working men at home.

But the English middle class—good men of business as they are—saw farther than the German professors. They had shared their power but reluctantly with the working class. They had learned, during the Chartist years, what that *puer robustus sed malitiosus,* the people, is capable of. And since that time, they had been compelled to incorporate the better part of the People's Charter in the Statutes of the United Kingdom. Now, if ever, the people must be kept in order by moral means, and the first and foremost of all moral means of action upon the masses is and remains— religion. Hence the parsons' majorities on the school boards, hence the increasing self-taxation of the bourgeoisie for the support of all sorts of revivalism, from ritualism to the Salvation Army.

And now came the triumph of British respectability over the free thought and religious laxity of the continental bourgeois. The workmen of France and Germany had become rebellious. They were thoroughly infected with socialism, and, for very good reasons, were not at all particular as to the legality of the means by which to secure their own ascendancy. The *puer robustus,* here, turned from day to day more *malitiosus.* Nothing remained to the French and German bourgeoisie as a last resource but to silently

---

tomer's language but expect him to speak your own; (2) You don't even try to suit your customer's wants, habits, and tastes, but expect him to conform to your English ones.

drop their free thought as a youngster, when sea-sickness creeps upon him, quietly drops the burning cigar he brought swaggeringly on board; one by one, the scoffers turned pious in outward behavior, spoke with respect of the Church, its dogmas and rites, and even conformed with the latter as far as could not be helped. French bourgeois dined *maigre** on Fridays, and German ones sat out long Protestant sermons in their pews on Sundays. They had come to grief with materialism. *"Die Religion muss dem Volk erhalten werden"*—religion must be kept alive for the people—that was the only and the last means to save society from utter ruin. Unfortunately for themselves, they did not find this out until they had done their level best to break up religion for ever. And now it was the turn of the British bourgeois to sneer and to say: "Why, you fools, I could have told you that two hundred years ago!"

However, I am afraid neither the religious stolidity of the British, nor the *post festum* conversion of the continental bourgeois will stem the rising proletarian tide. Tradition is a great retarding force, is the *vis inertiae* of history, but, being merely passive, is sure to be broken down; and thus religion will be no lasting safeguard to capitalist society. If our juridical, philosophical, and religious ideas are the more or less remote offshoots of the economical relations prevailing in a given society, such ideas cannot, in the long run, withstand the effects of a complete change in these relations. And, unless we believe in supernatural revelation, we must admit that no religious tenets will ever suffice to prop up a tottering society.

In fact, in England too, the working people have begun to move again. They are, no doubt, shackled by traditions of various kinds. Bourgeois traditions, such as the widespread belief that there can be but two parties, Conservatives and Liberals, and that the working class must work out its salvation by and through the great Liberal Party. Working men's traditions, inherited from their first tentative efforts at independent action, such as the exclusion, from ever so many old Trade Unions, of all applicants who have not gone through a regular apprenticeship; which means the breeding by every such union, of its own blacklegs. But for all that the English working class is moving, as even Professor Brentano has sorrowfully had to report to his brother Katheder-Socialists. It moves, like all things in England, with a slow and measured step, with hesitation here, with more or less unfruitful, tentative at-

---

*Without meat or milk.

tempts there; it moves now and then with an over-cautious mistrust of the name of Socialism, while it gradually absorbs the substance; and the movement spreads and seizes one layer of the workers after another. It has now shaken out of their torpor the unskilled laborers of the East End of London, and we all know what a splendid impulse these fresh forces have given it in return. And if the pace of the movement is not up to the impatience of some people, let them not forget that it is the working class which keeps alive the finest qualities of the English character, and that, if a step in advance is once gained in England, it is, as a rule, never lost afterward. If the sons of the old Chartists, for reasons explained above, were not quite up to the mark, the grandsons bid fair to be worthy of their forefathers.

But the triumph of the European working class does not depend upon England alone. It can only be secured by the cooperation of, at least, England, France, and Germany. In both the latter countries the working-class movement is well ahead of England. In Germany it is even within measurable distance of success. The progress it has there made during the last twenty-five years is unparalleled. It advances with ever-increasing velocity. If the German middle class have shown themselves lamentably deficient in political capacity, discipline, courage, energy, and perseverance, the German working class have given ample proof of all these qualities. Four hundred years ago, Germany was the starting point of the first upheaval of the European middle class; as things are now, is it outside the limits of possibility that Germany will be the scene, too, of the first great victory of the European proletariat?

April 20, 1892

KARL MARX

FRIEDRICH ENGELS

Selections from *The Manifesto of the Communist Party*

A specter is haunting Europe—the specter of Communism. All the Powers of old Europe have entered into a holy alliance to exorcise this specter: Pope and Czar, Metternich and Guizot, French Radicals and German police-spies.

Where is the party in opposition that has not been decried as Communistic by its opponents in power? Where the Opposition that has not hurled back the branding reproach of Communism, against the more advanced opposition parties, as well as against its reactionary adversaries?

Two things result from this fact:

I. Communism is already acknowledged by all European Powers to be itself a Power.

II. It is high time that Communists should openly, in the face of the whole world, publish their views, their aims, their tendencies, and meet this nursery tale of the Specter of Communism with a Manifesto of the party itself.

To this end, Communists of various nationalities have assembled in London, and sketched the following Manifesto, to be published in the English, French, German, Italian, Flemish and Danish languages.

* * *

"Undoubtedly," it will be said, "religious, moral, philosophical and juridical ideas have been modified in the course of historical development. But religion, morality, philosophy, political science, and law, constantly survived this change.

"There are, besides, eternal truths, such as Freedom, Justice, and so on, which are common to all states of society. But Communism abolishes eternal truths, it abolishes all religion and all morality, instead of constituting them on a new basis; it therefore acts in contradiction to all past historical experience."

What does this accusation reduce itself to? The history of all past society has consisted in the development of class antagonisms, antagonisms that assumed different forms at different epochs.

But whatever form they may have taken, one fact is common to all past ages, namely, the exploitation of one part of society by the other. No wonder, then, that the social consciousness of past ages, despite all the multiplicity and variety it displays, moves within certain common forms, or general ideas, which cannot completely vanish except with the total disappearance of class antagonisms.

The Communist revolution is the most radical rupture with traditional property relations; no wonder that its development involves the most radical rupture with traditional ideas.

But let us have done with the bourgeois objections to Communism.

We have seen above, that the first step in the revolution by the working class is to raise the proletariat to the position of ruling class, to win the battle of democracy.

The proletariat will use its political supremacy to wrest, by degrees, all capital from the bourgeoisie, to centralize all instruments of production in the hands of the State, i.e., of the proletariat organized as the ruling class; and to increase the total of productive forces as rapidly as possible.

Of course, in the beginning, this cannot be effected except by means of despotic inroads on the rights of property, and on the conditions of bourgeois production; by means of measures, therefore, which appear economically insufficient and untenable, but which, in the course of the movement, outstrip themselves, necessitate further inroads upon the old social order, and are unavoidable as a means of entirely revolutionizing the mode of production.

These measures will of course be different in different countries.

Nevertheless in the most advanced countries, the following will be pretty generally applicable:

(1) Abolition of property in land and application of all rents of land to public purposes.

(2) A heavy progressive or graduated income tax.

(3) Abolition of all right of inheritance.

(4) Confiscation of the property of all emigrants and rebels.

(5) Centralization of credit in the hands of the State, by means of a national bank with State capital and an exclusive monopoly.

(6) Centralization of the means of communication and transport in the hands of the State

(7) Extension of factories and instruments of production owned by the State; the bringing into cultivation of waste-lands, and the improvement of the soil generally in accordance with a common plan.

(8) Equal liability of all to labor. Establishment of industrial armies, especially for agriculture.

(9) Combination of agriculture with manufacturing industries; gradual abolition of the distinction between town and country, by more equable distribution of the population over the country.

(10) Free education for all children in public schools. Abolition of children's factory labor in its present form. Combination of education with industrial production, and so forth.

When, in the course of development, class distinctions have disappeared, and all production has been concentrated in the hands of a vast association of the whole nation, the public power will lose its political character. Political power, properly so called, is merely the organized power of one class for oppressing another. If the proletariat during its contest with the bourgeoisie is compelled, by the force of circumstances, to organize itself as a class, if, by means of a revolution, it makes itself the ruling class, and, as such, sweeps away by force the old conditions of production, then it will, along with these conditions, have swept away the conditions for the existence of class antagonisms and of classes generally, and will thereby have abolished its own supremacy as a class.

In place of the old bourgeois society, with its classes and class antagonisms, we shall have an association, in which the free development of each is the condition for the free development of all.

Translated by Samuel Moore

Bibliography

Arnold, N. S. *Marx's Radical Critique of Capitalist Society*. New York: Oxford University Press, 1990.

Carver, Terrell. *Marx and Engels: The Intellectual Relationship*. Brighton: Harvester Press, 1983.

Eubanks, Cecil L. *Karl Marx and Friedrich Engels: An Analytic Bibliography*. New York: Garland, 1984.

Geras, Norman. *Marx and Human Nature*. London: Verso, 1983.

Henry, Michel. *Marx: A Philosophy of Human Reality*. Bloomington: Indiana University Press, 1983.

Hunley, J. D. *The Life and Thought of Friedrich Engels*. New Haven: Yale University Press, 1991.

Jessop, R., ed. *Karl Marx's Social and Political Thought: Critical Assessments*. London: Routledge, 1990.

Kain, Philip J. *Marx and Modern Political Theory*. Lanham: Rowman and Littlefield, 1993.

Kitching, Gavin N. *Karl Marx and the Philosophy of Praxis*. London: Routledge, 1988.

Levin, Michael. *Marx, Engels, and Liberal Democracy*. Basingstoke: Macmillan, 1989.

Little, Daniel. *The Scientific Marx*. Minneapolis: University of Minnesota Press, 1986.

MacLellan, David. *Karl Marx: His Life and Thought*. London: Macmillan, 1973.

Mongar, Thomas M. *The Death of Communism and the Rebirth of Original Marxism*. Lewiston: Mellen, 1994.

Rigby, Stephen H. *Engels and the Formation of Marxism*. Manchester: Manchester University Press, 1992.

Sayers, Janet, ed., *Engels Revisited: New Feminist Essays*. London: Travistock, 1987.

Schmitt, Richard. *Introduction to Marx and Engels*. Boulder: Westview Press, 1987.

Wartofsky, Marx W. *Ludwig Feuerbach*. Cambridge: Cambridge University Press, 1977.

Wilson, Charles A. *Feuerbach and the Search for Otherness*. New York: Lang, 1989.

Acknowledgments

Every reasonable effort has been made to locate the owners of rights to previously published works and the translations printed here. We gratefully acknowledge permission to reprint the following material:

PREFACE AND INTRODUCTION from THE ESSENCE OF CHRISTIANITY by LUDWIG FEUERBACH. Copyright © 1957 by Harper & Row, Publishers, Inc. Reprinted by permission of HarperCollins Publishers, Inc.

The texts of Karl Marx and Friedrich Engels have been reprinted by permission of International Publishers Co., New York.